Successful
CLASSROOM
MANAGEMENT *and*
DISCIPLINE

3rd
edition

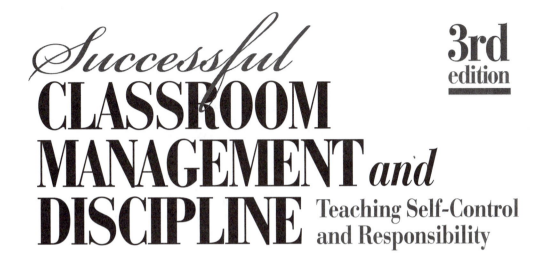

Successful CLASSROOM MANAGEMENT and DISCIPLINE

Teaching Self-Control and Responsibility

3rd edition

TOM V. SAVAGE

Santa Clara University

MARSHA K. SAVAGE

Santa Clara University

Los Angeles • London • New Delhi • Singapore • Washington DC

Previously published by Pearson Education, Inc.

For information:

SAGE Publications, Inc.
2455 Teller Road
Thousand Oaks, California 91320
E-mail: order@sagepub.com

SAGE Publications Ltd.
1 Oliver's Yard
55 City Road
London EC1Y 1SP
United Kingdom

SAGE Publications India Pvt. Ltd.
B 1/I 1 Mohan Cooperative Industrial Area
Mathura Road, New Delhi 110 044
India

SAGE Publications Asia-Pacific Pte. Ltd.
33 Pekin Street #02-01
Far East Square
Singapore 048763

Printed in the United States of America

Library of Congress Cataloging-in-Publication Data

Savage, Tom V.
Successful classroom management and discipline: teaching self-control and responsibility / Tom V. Savage, Marsha K. Savage. — 3rd ed.
    p. cm.
Rev. ed. of: Teaching self-control through management and discipline.
2nd ed. c1999.
Includes bibliographical references and index.
ISBN 978-1-4129-6678-8 (pbk. : alk. paper)

  1. Classroom management—United States. 2. School discipline—United States. 3. Self-control—United States. I. Savage, Marsha Kay, 1952- II. Savage, Tom V. Teaching self-control through management and discipline. III. Title.

LB3012.2.S28 2009
371.102'4—dc22   2008036878

This book is printed on acid-free paper.

09   10   11   12   13   10   9   8   7   6   5   4   3   2   1

Acquisitions Editor:	Steve Wainwright
Editorial Assistant:	Ashley Conlon
Production Editor:	Carla Freeman
Copy Editor:	Brenda Weight
Typesetter:	C&M Digitals (P) Ltd.
Proofreader:	Theresa Kay
Indexer:	Molly Hall
Cover Designer:	Glenn Vogel
Marketing Manager:	Christy Guilbaut

CONTENTS

PREFACE

We are living in a historic time in education. There is widespread concern about the quality of education, and there is no shortage of proposals for change. However, these proposals often neglect some of the most important educational variables. The first variable is the students. Students are humans with real needs and aspirations. If their needs are not taken into account, significant improvement is unlikely. A second variable is the purpose of education. Many proposals for educational improvement focus on how to get more content into the heads of students so they will do better on standardized tests of achievement. This focus ignores the historic thrust of American education to prepare individuals for productive roles in society. It has long been recognized that knowledge alone does not produce productive citizens.

This edition of *Successful Classroom Management and Discipline* focuses on two perspectives. First, we believe that there is an educational goal for classroom management and discipline that goes beyond facilitating content learning. That goal is the development of self-control. We believe that development of self-control is one of the most important educational objectives. If members of society do not have self-control, society is in grave trouble. Understanding that management and discipline has a goal of self-control assists educators in making decisions about how to manage classrooms and respond to problems. If students are not developing self-control as the school year unfolds, then the management and discipline plan is not working.

Helping individuals develop self-control as well as achieving educational objectives requires that the needs of students be taken into account. No two students are the same, so a single approach to all problems simply will not work. In this edition, we have provided some basic principles as well as a number of options that can be chosen in managing the classroom and responding to problems. The effectiveness of these options is related to the needs of the students and the values and beliefs of the teacher.

We believe that the two dimensions of management and discipline are related. Management is defined as developing an environment that takes into account individual needs in a way that facilitates their learning and the development of self-control. This dimension is the preventive dimension. Many problems are prevented through the implementation of effective management principles. Discipline is the response to behavioral problems. Because students are human, they will misbehave. Effective discipline respects the dignity of students and helps them learn from their mistakes.

In this edition, we have included some additional content. Bullying has become a major international concern. Clearly, bullying can have adverse consequences for both those who are bullied and for those who bully. It is time that educators recognize that bullying is not just harmless acts that are a part of growing up. We all need to take action to prevent bullying and create an environment where bullying is neither reinforced nor tolerated.

Another new chapter focuses on the legal issues relating to management and discipline. Unfortunately, many teachers are unaware of the legal principles that guide decisions about teacher and student rights. Ignorance of these principles can be personally and professionally devastating for teachers. Therefore, we believe that it is important for teachers to understand this important dimension of being a professional educator.

Together, we have several decades of experience in both elementary and secondary schools. We have observed the tragedy that occurs when teachers do not understand how to manage the classroom and respond to misbehavior. On the other hand, we have observed the pleasure that can accompany positive and well-managed classrooms. We believe that this ability can be learned, and that there are some principles and skills that can be used to achieve success. We have attempted to present those principles and perspectives in this edition with the hope that more educators can experience the joy and excitement that accompanies a successful classroom.

ACKNOWLEDGMENTS

We thank the many people who have assisted us in the completion of this project. First, we thank those friends and students who shared their stories with us. In particular, Marsha would like to thank the following teachers who opened their classrooms to her: Rani Bandermann, Michael Cummins, Theresa Diola, Jean Galvin, Mary MacLellan, Audrey Makris, and Kari Nygaard. We also want to thank the following reviewers for their insightful comments:

Kelli Beard
California State University, Dominguez Hills

Jim Black
Nazareth College

Steffanie N. Bowles
Marygrove College

Barbara Brock
Creighton University

Jamin Carson
East Carolina University

Frank Kohler
University of Northern Iowa

Denise G. Meister
Penn State University, Harrisburg

Finally, a special thank you to Steve Wainwright at SAGE, who initiated this project with us and assisted us throughout its development.

Chapter 1

MANAGING THE CONTEMPORARY CLASSROOM

CLASSROOM SCENARIO

It was the first day of teaching for Merrill. He had completed student teaching and had been employed to teach middle school social studies. He was eager to start even though his head was swimming with all the information that had been given at the new teacher orientation sessions. He didn't know there was so much that a teacher had to think about. Last week, he had met the faculty of the school at the beginning-of-the-year faculty meeting. The principal distributed another set of procedures that needed to be followed for everything from ordering materials to contacting parents. These were certainly not things he had learned in student teaching.

He had not slept very well last night, worrying about whether he had all the material he needed to begin and whether he remembered all the things that had to be done the first day. What was he supposed to do if someone was not on his class roster? He had arrived at the school in what he thought was plenty of time. However, distractions started the minute he went to the faculty mailboxes. The school secretary reminded him that he had some forms to complete and another teacher asked him about serving on a committee.

He made his way to the classroom and made sure he had a class roster for each of the classes he was teaching. He quickly checked to make sure he had enough books. He organized the material he needed for the first lesson, and suddenly, the bell rang! Students immediately started entering the classroom. Some were boisterous, some were quiet. A couple of the girls smiled at him. Others were shy and avoided his eyes. He noticed one boy with a sullen look on his face who sank into a desk at the back of the room. A couple of students were shoving each other and joking around. Then, they were all sitting at their desks and 35 sets of eyes were looking at him expectantly. He knew he needed to do something to get the first day started. However, his mind was blank. He could feel his pulse quicken and his anxiety start to rise. There was no one else to help him or get things started. With a growing sense of panic, he started talking about the first things that came to mind. "I'm Mr. Johnson and I have a dog."

CHAPTER OBJECTIVES

After completing this chapter you should be able to:

- State the importance of good management and discipline
- Define management and discipline
- Identify the primary goal of management and discipline
- Define teacher attitudes that are important in establishing a successful classroom
- State the elements of classrooms that make them complex environments
- Define basic principles or recurring themes that should be applied to establishing successful management and discipline in the classroom

Teaching can be an exciting and rewarding profession. There is no greater feeling than the satisfaction of helping students grow and learn. It is rewarding to see their eyes light up when a concept is understood and the door of comprehension opens. Teaching is also exciting because every day is different. Each student is unique, and each class of students is different. Because of this, every lesson is a new experience. Those who like variety and the challenge of working with impressionable and excitable young people find teaching exciting and rewarding. As one teacher stated, "I can't believe I'm paid to do this!"

However, teaching can also be frustrating and discouraging. Every year, thousands of new teachers enter teaching only to become discouraged and stressed. They soon leave for other occupations. For them, teaching did not meet their expectations, and they felt unfulfilled and even threatened. Some of these teachers find students who are unmotivated, apathetic, and maybe downright hostile. One teacher wrote a letter to the editor of a local newspaper in response to an article on the teacher shortage. She indicated that she had found students bored and apathetic. Some acted as if they hated her and were hostile. There simply was not enough time to deal with 30 students five periods a day. Teaching was not the noble profession she was expecting, so she chose to "leave the battle of teaching." Indeed, for some, the classroom is a battlefield where it seems there is constant conflict and teachers suffer emotional disturbances close to what has been labeled "battle fatigue."

What makes the difference? Are there actions teachers can take to create successful classrooms where both students and teachers want to be? While there are individual challenges resulting from the wide range of education settings across the nation, we believe there are actions teachers can take to help them move toward the goal of a successful and rewarding teaching experience.

As we reflect on Merrill in the opening scenario, we wonder which path his career will take. Will it be rewarding and personally satisfying or will it be threatening and unfulfilling? Is there anything he can do to influence the direction of his career? We believe there is.

Years of experience, as well as summaries of research, indicate that one of the key components in achieving a successful and productive classroom is management and discipline. Experienced teachers identify the establishment of good management and discipline as one of the major goals that needs to be accomplished in the first weeks of the year. Beginning teachers cite management and discipline as one of their most serious challenges. School administrators indicate poor management and discipline is a major reason for low evaluations as well as a primary reason why teachers are not rehired (Good & Brophy, 2003). They note that if teachers cannot manage the classroom and exercise control, learning cannot take place. Surveys of public attitudes toward education indicate that the public views student discipline as one of the most serious problems facing education.

Effective management and discipline are crucial to teachers' sense of satisfaction and well-being. Management and discipline problems lead to increased teacher reports of stress and anxiety (Good & Brophy, 2003). The inability to resolve the challenges posed by these anxieties is a major cause of job dissatisfaction and teacher burnout (Evertson & Weinstein, 2006). Many of these teachers eventually leave teaching. However, the more tragic story might be those who stay on in the classroom because they feel trapped. Their continued presence does harm to themselves and to the students they teach.

Given the importance of management and discipline, one might expect that the management and discipline domain would receive considerable attention in teacher preparation programs and in research. However, this is not the case.

Classroom management and discipline tends to receive minor emphasis in teacher preparation programs. For example, one survey found that only 37% of education professors thought that it was absolutely essential to prepare teachers to handle management and discipline problems in the classroom (Farkas & Johnson, 1997). What explains this neglect?

One major reason is that management and discipline has been poorly defined. Although there are numerous books and articles that contain tips and insights, few have attempted to clearly define the management and discipline domain in a systematic way. As a result, many higher education professors view management and discipline as little more than the passing on of "conventional wisdom and myths." Lacking a clearly defined field of study, and with an absence of solid evidence, many professors have little to say other than "This is what I did" (Good & Brophy, 2003).

Some examples of the simplistic conventional wisdom and myths include advice to "love and trust" the students and the problems will disappear. Others urge students of teaching to be "tough," "show the students you are the boss," and "don't smile until Christmas." These myths have great appeal to many because they have an element of reality and appear to be believable. For example, teachers who do enjoy and respect students have fewer problems than those who do not, and it is important to establish teacher authority in the classroom. However, these well-intentioned bits of advice certainly do not address the complexity of the classroom environment or provide guidance for identifying why things go wrong and what can be done about it. Even those who really like students discover that students still may not respond in desired ways. Those who attempt to be tough discover that they are engaged in constant power struggles with students. Table 1.1 lists some conventional wisdom that is often provided to new teachers.

Although some of the conventional wisdom contains excellent advice, it needs to be submitted to critical appraisal. It is only then that these bits of advice can be

Table 1.1   Conventional Wisdom About Management and Discipline

- Just communicate to the students that you care about them. That will prevent problems.
- Keep the students busy so that they do not have time to misbehave.
- Start the first day by showing them that you are the boss and you will not tolerate inappropriate behavior.
- Don't smile until Christmas.
- Remember that you are the teacher, not a friend.
- Overplan and overprepare. Avoid times when students have nothing to do.
- Begin the first day by establishing the rules and regulations. Keep your rules simple and focus on what they should be doing rather than what they should not be doing.
- Be consistent and follow through. Do what you say you will do.
- Be assertive from the first day and let them know you expect to be treated with respect.

put into a proper perspective and become useful in actually managing a classroom. The sobering fact is that there is no "quick fix" to management and discipline problems. If there were, this would not be such a source of frustration for beginning and seasoned educators alike.

Another contributing factor in the lack of emphasis on management and discipline has been the view that success in management and discipline is basically related to the personality of the teacher and therefore cannot be taught. Again, there is an element of reality to this perception. For, example, Hoover and Kindsvetter (1997) claim that teacher personality is probably the most important factor in determining success in classroom management and discipline. Some individuals do have personality variables that predispose them to work with students in ways that facilitate success. However, although certain personality traits may be useful, they are not the whole story. A number of variables help all teachers achieve success, even those who possess undesirable personality traits.

A third perception that has hindered the development of a systematic and realistic approach to management and discipline is the view that learning to control the classroom can be learned only through experience and the school of "hard knocks." Although experience is important and does make a difference, this view condemns many teachers to failure while the lessons of "experience" are learned. In addition, experience is much more effective when there is a framework within which that experience can be placed and interpreted.

This text will provide a framework for the management and discipline domain. This framework can help teachers identify the relationship between different dimensions that can be addressed in creating a successful and rewarding classroom.

This framework includes two major components: (a) the prevention of problems and (b) responses when problems do occur. Research indicates that one of the key variables in successful classrooms is an emphasis on preventive, rather than reactive, management techniques (Emmer & Stough, 2001). Many new teachers want to know what they should do when faced with a problem, but they would be better served to consider what to do to prevent the problem in the first place. However, even with the best prevention, problems will occur in the classroom because students (and teachers) are simply imperfect human beings who sometimes make poor choices.

DEFINING MANAGEMENT AND DISCIPLINE

Over the years, teachers have attached different definitions to the terms *management* and *discipline*. What you view as appropriate practice is related to how you define

Schools are complex and diverse environments.

© Digital Vision

these two terms. To give us some common ground for discussion throughout the book, we offer the following definitions. These can assist us in our recommendations for professional practice.

Management

Management refers to your role as a teacher in creating a classroom environment where success is possible. It refers to how order is established and maintained in the classroom. Bringing order to complex classrooms includes arranging the physical environment, organizing lessons that have a logical flow, making productive use of time, motivating students to strive toward educational goals, and establishing teacher leadership and authority.

Classroom management is the prevention dimension. Attending to good principles of classroom management helps prevent many problems. Some teachers, when asked about discipline problems in their classroom, respond that they have few discipline problems. This is generally an indication that the teacher has applied good classroom management techniques.

Some educators have been troubled by the term *management* because they define it as an autocratic power relationship between teacher and students in which the teacher is the "boss" and the students are to follow with unquestioned obedience. This is certainly not the definition of management we hold. In fact, this concept of management has even been rejected by much of the business community as ineffective. They now focus more on collaborative, humane, and democratic models of management.

Glasser (1990) defines the type of management we support as that of *lead management*, a management style where the teacher is the leader rather than the "boss" in the classroom. In lead management, power among classroom participants is shared and teacher power is used in service to others rather than as something to enhance one's status. Glasser (1990) identifies the following characteristics of lead management:

- The teacher involves the students and gets their input in discussions of what needs to be done and under what conditions.
- The teacher communicates expectations clearly and models successful performance. Student input is continuously solicited.
- Students evaluate their own work and the teacher is willing to listen to students and accept that they do know a good deal about how to produce high-quality work.
- The teacher facilitates student work and provides students with assistance that is noncoercive and nonadversarial (pp. 31–32).

This idea of lead management has some important implications in the way power is defined and used in the classroom. In more traditional management styles, where the teacher is portrayed as "the boss," there is a constant struggle for power and status in the classroom. These teachers perceive power as a fixed-sum commodity. Therefore, if one person gains power, then someone else must lose power. If the teacher gives power to the students, the teacher's power and authority will be diminished.

However, teachers who understand the teacher as leader and "lead" management ideas have a different perspective on the nature and use of power in the classroom. They understand that power is not a fixed sum but is more like an expandable pie. The more everyone in the classroom feels a sense of power and influence, the greater their investment in the classroom, the greater their commitment to success, and the stronger their attachment to the teacher. This means that by sharing power with the students, the teacher actually gains power and influence. This concept was expressed by a business executive in the corporate world. He stated, "I had to give up power to gain power" (Kouzes & Posner, 1987, p. 164).

Discipline

Some individuals define *discipline* as a synonym for punishment. However, we define discipline differently. Discipline is defined as actions that facilitate the development of self-control, responsibility, and character. This definition indicates that discipline is more than a response to misbehavior in order to efficiently deliver the curriculum. This definition recognizes that the development of self-control is a major goal of education and one that is achieved through democratic and humane management and discipline. This definition provides clear guidance when responding to student behavior. When choosing a response, the teacher should ask, "What action will be the best choice in helping the student move toward self-control?" The outcomes of discipline are not fear of authority and intimidation but, rather, productive and satisfying patterns of living in harmony with those around us.

This definition is consistent with the highest purposes of education. It is an essential component of living in a democratic society and recognizes that the goal of education is to develop good people as well as good students. If society becomes one where individuals do not exercise self-control or accept responsibility, then our entire way of life is threatened.

Although achievement of academic goals is important, it is instructive to note that citizenship outcomes have long been a major focus of education. Citizenship requires that individuals work cooperatively with others and have respect for laws and the dignity of others. However, it is not unquestioned obedience to the will of the authorities. In contemporary society, there is much emphasis on the importance of creativity and change in order for our nation to remain competitive with others. Creativity and change is certainly not facilitated by unquestioned conformity.

Development of self-control and the acceptance of responsibility are outcomes that are facilitated by caring teachers interacting with students in ways that help them understand the consequences of their choices. In this context, discipline is not an unfortunate by-product of the exercise of power, it is an opportunity to help individuals achieve one of the most important goals of education, the development of self-control and the acceptance of responsibility. Thus discipline is an essential component of everyone's education and absolutely critical to the development of healthy individuals. Table 1.2 compares the characteristics of management and discipline.

ACHIEVING THE GOAL OF IMPROVED SELF-CONTROL

Improving self-control means that individuals learn to choose and act in ways that are consistent with self-chosen beliefs and principles. They demonstrate

Table 1.2 Comparing Management and Discipline

Management *The Prevention Component*	Discipline *The Reaction Component*
Organizing the environment for success	Responding to misbehavior in order to teach self-control
Keeping the students engaged	Stopping misbehavior quickly
Eliciting the cooperation of students	Respecting the dignity of students
Sharing power and authority	Helping students learn to accept responsibility for their actions

responsibility and accept the consequences of their choices. Glasser (1965) defines responsibility as fulfilling our needs without interfering with the ability of others to fulfill their needs. Therefore, responsibility has a social component that also considers the needs and values of others.

How is self-control learned? Individuals learn self-control by being allowed to make choices and reflect on the consequences of their choices. Individuals who are constantly shielded from the consequences of their actions are deprived of the opportunity to reflect on their actions and consider their impact on others. They are hindered in their development of self-control. Individuals must learn to ask themselves, "What will happen if I make this choice? Is that what I want to happen?"

Helping students develop self-control requires teachers to do something more than implementing a method or a set of actions when misbehavior occurs. Rather, it is incorporating a set of teacher attitudes (Good & Brophy, 2003). Those attitudes include the following:

- Liking students and respecting them as individuals
- Holding high but realistic expectations
- Enjoying teaching
- Possessing a concern for the individual welfare of students
- Believing that students can be trusted with responsibility

Teachers who hold these attitudes develop classrooms where student input and choice is allowed, peer cooperation is emphasized, and classroom management and discipline is viewed as a process of creating and maintaining a healthy learning environment rather than as a means of asserting teacher authority and power.

The peer group is an important influence on behavior.

© Banana Stock

BASIC PRINCIPLES

We have organized this text around several basic themes or principles. These ideas will be applied in different ways throughout the chapters. Keeping these principles in mind will assist you in developing your individual philosophy and approach to classroom management and discipline.

The goal of management and discipline is growth in self-control and acceptance of responsibility. Education has goals beyond the acquisition of content knowledge. There are goals related to the social and moral dimensions. How we respond to students affects their social and moral growth. Specifically, the social and moral dimensions relate to the development of self-control and the acceptance of responsibility. Our contention is that these dimensions of learning are just as important as the knowledge outcomes.

Understanding that management and discipline has some specific goals other than covering the curriculum provides a framework for making decisions about your actions, for understanding the developmental level of the student, and for evaluating your discipline plan. What this means is that, as you make choices about how to organize your classroom, the rules and procedures you establish, and how to respond to behavioral incidents, you should be asking how your actions impact the growth of self-control and the acceptance of responsibility.

In addition, when you are making decisions relating to specific students, you should consider the developmental level of the student. How much self-control has the student demonstrated? What would be an appropriate response given the developmental level of the student?

Finally, teachers need to be reflective. We all grow professionally when we reflect on our actions and grow from our mistakes. The focus of reflection on the management and discipline dimension should be the growth of students in the area of self-control. As the year progresses, are students demonstrating more self-control? Are they accepting responsibility for their own actions? If they are not, there is reason to reflect on one's management and discipline style.

Positive relationships are essential for good classroom management and discipline. Teachers cannot expect to be successful in creating a rewarding learning environment if they are constantly engaged in power struggles and adversarial relationships with students. Successful classrooms are those where the teacher and the students are working together rather than working against each other. This means that a primary task of the teacher is that of establishing positive relationships with students. This involves gaining the respect of the students, treating students with dignity and respect, and demonstrating an interest in the welfare of the students. Surveys of students consistently indicate that good teachers care about the students.

Establishing positive relationships with students is far more important than establishing a set of procedures to follow or actions to be taken when problems occur. There have been numerous approaches to discipline problems that prescribe specific steps to be followed. The promise is that these steps will solve all (or at least most) of your discipline problems. Time after time, these specific sets of steps have been found wanting. Specific actions will have little or no impact on the classroom behavior if there is not a positive relationship between the teacher and the students. Developing positive relationships and gaining the respect of the students is not something that just happens. It must be earned.

Establishing positive relationships in the classroom does not mean that there are no limits or demands. The difference is that the limits and demands are reasonable ones that are understood and accepted by the students. Teachers who arbitrarily establish classroom rules and who seem more interested in their power than the welfare of the students have difficulty establishing a positive classroom environment. The term *warm demander* is sometimes used to describe the role of the teacher in establishing a positive classroom environment. A warm demander is someone who is warm, responsive, and caring. However, he or she is also demanding and insists that students make responsible choices and holds them accountable for the choices they do make.

Your goal as a teacher should be to establish a warm yet businesslike classroom environment. You need to establish a classroom where students feel safe from both physical and psychological intimidation. They need to believe that the teacher cares about them but also holds high expectations.

Teaching is decision making. In an age of accountability with a search for "what works" in classrooms, there is a tendency to move toward highly prescribed classroom procedures. There are even some curriculum programs that provide a "script" for teachers to follow. However, the bottom line is that good teaching requires decision making. Thus, good teachers are good decision-makers. In the area of management and discipline, there are numerous decisions that must be made every day. The bracing truth is that there are no easy answers. If there were, the area of management and discipline would not be such a major area of concern.

You will need to make decisions based on the needs and attitudes of the students, their developmental level, your needs as a teacher, and the nature of the problem. These choices cannot be prescribed. You can learn some concepts and ideas that will help you prevent many problems, you can develop knowledge about what to consider when making a decision, and you can be given some alternatives to choose from when taking an action. However, in the final analysis, the decisions will be yours as you work with a unique group of students in a unique and rapidly changing environment. One of our purposes of this book is to assist you in becoming informed decision-makers who understand alternatives and the possible consequences of different alternatives.

Teachers must create predictable, consistent, and success-oriented environments. All of us need a high degree of predictability in our lives. For example, if we work or live in environments that are highly unpredictable, we develop high levels of anxiety. When students enter a classroom, they should have a high degree of certainty regarding the rules, procedures, and expectations. This does not mean that there is no creativity or change in the daily classroom routines. That would certainly lead to boredom and a lack of motivation. However, students need to be able to predict what will be happening in the classroom, how the teacher is likely to respond to situations, and what the expectations are for them.

One of the key elements of a successful classroom is teacher consistency. Teacher consistency comprises several elements. One of those elements is consistency in enforcing rules. If something is against the rules on Monday, it should be the same for the rest of the week. If students are unaware of the limits due to inconsistency, they will be constantly testing to try to establish what is acceptable.

Another element of teacher consistency is that of being consistent across all students. This is a major concern of secondary students. They lose respect for teachers and become upset if they believe that some students are being treated unfairly.

Because a student is a "good" student doesn't mean that he or she should not be held accountable if his or her behavior is inappropriate. Just because a student has a "bad" reputation doesn't mean that he or she should be the focus of attention every time there is a problem.

A third element of consistency in creating a constant and predictable classroom is teacher follow-through. Students need to know that if something is promised, it will be delivered. This means that you need to be careful what you promise. You should not promise an action that you cannot deliver.

The causes of behavior need to be identified and addressed. An important part of professional growth is becoming a reflective teacher. Reflective teachers are those who reflect on what is happening in the classroom and what might be the causes of their successes and failures. Reflection is important if a teacher is to engage in professional growth. Part of reflection is identifying the causes of behavior in the classroom.

Suggestions for dealing with discipline problems in the classroom often focus on how to stop a behavior. Although this might be effective for the short term, if long-term solutions are to be found, then the causes of the behavior need to be identified and addressed. Rather than just deciding whether the lesson was or was not a success or that students were or were not on task or that they misbehaved, the question needs to be asked, "Why was it successful or unsuccessful?" "Why were students on task or why did they misbehave?"

Asking these questions may lead to uncomfortable conclusions that the teaching methods might have been one of the causes of failure or misbehavior. However, it is necessary if teachers are to learn from their experiences and continue to move toward the goal of a rewarding and successful classroom. The KWL chart in Table 1.3 gives you an opportunity to reflect on your concerns. Consider those principles you already know and then add to the chart as you learn new ones.

Table 1.3 What Are Your Concerns?

Directions: When preparing to learn something new, it is useful to reflect on what you already know and what you think you need to learn. Take a piece of paper and divide it into four columns. Label the columns as shown below. Take the time to give each column some serious thought. Keep this chart in a convenient locale so that you can review it from time to time. Add concerns as they occur to you and add information to the "What do I already know?" column as you learn new ideas and concepts.

What do I already know?	What are my concerns and what do I want to learn?	Where can I learn what I need to know?	How can I evaluate the value of what I learn?

TEACHERS AND STRESS

Stress is a normal part of being a teacher. Teaching is especially stressful because classrooms are complex environments with interaction between an educated adult and a number of young individuals who are in need of knowledge and socialization. Teachers do not have the luxury of working with students on an individual basis as might be true of other helping professions. In addition, the students are generally in the classroom because they have to be there rather than because they want to be there. Teaching is a very personal activity. When individuals teach, they put their knowledge, their personality, their skill, and their values on display for everyone to observe. Each lesson is a reflection and an extension of the teacher. When teaching is not successful, it is taken as a personal failure. As one teacher stated, "When you have an unsuccessful lesson, it is like someone telling you that you have an ugly baby!"

Not only is teaching personal, it is very public. Numerous individuals, including students, administrators, and parents, observe every statement and every action of the teacher. Every failure is open for all to see. Being on stage all the time and knowing that numerous individuals are evaluating every move and every statement is extremely stressful. Teaching is one of the few professions where success and satisfaction every day are dependent on the cooperation and the good will of others. Students can be a pleasure and are one of the primary reasons why individuals enjoy teaching. However, students are immature, are trying to satisfy their own needs, are seeking their own identity, and are often insensitive to the feelings of others. Teachers need to have a healthy self-concept and sufficient confidence to help them weather the ups and downs of students.

Individuals who choose teaching generally have high aspirations. Many consider teaching a personal calling that is of critical importance in the preservation of society (Sarason, 1999). As a part of the role of teaching, they desire to be an important figure who has an impact on students and who is a role model. They want respect and gratitude, and they desire to be viewed by students, parents, and administrators as a respected professional. However, if these aspirations are not realized, individuals become stressed and may experience burnout (Friedman, 2006).

The consensus among researchers is that the most common sources of stress among teachers stem from relationships with students. The most important issue in the teacher–student relationship relates to classroom management and discipline (Friedman, 2006). Students have keen observational skills and are aware of behaviors that stress teachers. They generally identify three main types of behavior that teachers find stressful. Those are (a) not listening to the teacher, (b) demonstrating a lack of motivation, and (c) displaying misbehavior. These behaviors all interfere with teaching success and contribute toward the labeling of the teacher as a failure.

The fact that students are very aware of what causes teacher stress means that students have the ability to influence teachers and their feelings of stress, frustration, and failure. In addition, students perceive that their academic failure is actually teacher failure (Friedman, 2006). Therefore, students have the perspective that they can stress the teacher and give the teacher feelings of failure by simply failing to learn!

The implication of students' awareness of how to cause the teacher stress and frustration is that a major ingredient to success in teaching is in establishing constructive relationships with students. This means that teachers must earn the respect of the students and must have effective classroom and management skills. There simply is no other choice. The intent of this book is to assist teachers in obtaining the knowledge and skills necessary for successful management and discipline so that they can reduce stress and achieve the great satisfactions that can be obtained from teaching.

REVIEW OF MAIN IDEAS

1. Success in managing the classroom and establishing control is key in achieving success in teaching.

2. There are two major components to this important domain of teaching. These two components are prevention and response.

3. Management refers to the prevention dimension. It is defined as how order is established and maintained in the classroom.

4. The style of management that is needed is warm, collaborative, humane, and democratic. In this management style, the teacher is the leader in the classroom, not the "boss." Teacher power is used for the benefit of others rather than just for self.

5. Discipline refers to the response dimension. The purpose of discipline is not just the development of unquestioned obedience. Rather, the goals of discipline are advancing the social and moral goals of education. Specifically, discipline refers to the actions that are taken to promote the goals of increased self-control and acceptance of responsibility.

6. Self-control is learned when individuals make choices, experience the consequences of their choices, and reflect on the link between their actions and the consequences.

7. Helping students develop self-control requires more than a set of actions applied routinely across all students. It requires teacher attitudes that include respecting and caring about students, trusting students, enjoying teaching, and holding high expectations.

8. There are several basic principles or recurring themes that will be encountered throughout this text. Those include the following:
   - Self-control and acceptance of responsibility are the major goals of management and discipline.
   - Positive relationships between the teacher and students are essential.
   - Teaching is decision making, and teachers need to accept the challenge of making informed decisions.
   - Classroom environments need to be developed that are predictable, consistent, and success oriented.
   - Causes of behavior need to be identified and addressed. Unless the causes of behavior are identified, problems will continue to disrupt the classroom.

9. Teaching is inherently stressful, and students are keenly aware of what causes teacher stress. They will play an important role in either creating stress or helping to reduce stress. Therefore, teachers must implement management and discipline procedures that have the probability of capturing student support.

APPLICATION AND ENRICHMENT

1. Interview a teacher on the topic of classroom management and discipline. How serious is the problem in his or her school? What does he or she see as the most important challenges for teachers? What advice does he or she have for someone entering teaching? How does his or her perspective compare with those expressed in this chapter?

2. Interview students at the age level you expect to teach. How serious do they view the problem of discipline in their school? What do they think is the cause of behavioral problems? What are some things that good teachers do to manage the classroom? What are some things that poor teachers do that cause problems?

3. Think of teachers that you have had that you consider good teachers. What did they do that made them effective? Think of a teacher that you did not consider effective. What did they do that interfered with their effectiveness?

4. Based on the data you gathered from these interviews and from the content of the chapter, begin to develop your own personal philosophy of classroom management

and discipline. Begin to write down the questions and concerns that you have. Identify what you think you need to learn in this domain. Begin writing down some principles that you will follow as a teacher.

REFERENCES

Emmer, E., & Stough, L. (2001). Classroom management: A critical part of educational psychology, with implications for teacher education. *Educational Psychologist, 36,* 103–112.

Evertson, C. M., & Weinstein, C. S. (2006). Classroom management as a field of inquiry. In C. M. Evertson & C. S. Weinstein (Eds.), *Handbook of classroom management: Research, practice, and contemporary issues* (pp. 3–16). Mahwah, NJ: Lawrence Erlbaum.

Farkas, S., & Johnson, J. (1997). *Different drummers: How teachers of teachers view public education.* New York: Public Agenda.

Friedman, I. (2006). Classroom management and teacher stress and burnout. In C. M. Evertson & C. S. Weinstein (Eds.), *Handbook of classroom management: Research, practice, and contemporary issues* (pp. 925–944). Mahwah, NJ: Lawrence Erlbaum.

Glasser, W. (1965). *Reality therapy: A new approach to psychiatry.* New York: Harper & Row.

Glasser, W. (1990). *The quality school: Managing students without coercion.* New York: Harper & Row.

Good, T., & Brophy, J. (2003). *Looking in classrooms* (9th ed.). Boston: Allyn & Bacon.

Hoover, R. L., & Kindsvetter, R. (1997). *Democratic discipline: Foundation and practice.* Columbus, OH: Merrill.

Kouzes, J. L., & Posner, B. Z. (1987). *The leadership challenge: How to get extraordinary things done in organizations.* San Francisco: Jossey-Bass.

Sarason, S. (1999). *Teaching as a performing art.* New York: Teachers College Press.

Chapter 2

LEARNING TO BE AN EFFECTIVE CLASSROOM MANAGER

CLASSROOM SCENARIO

It was with a great deal of excitement and no small amount of fear that Kelly approached student teaching. This was it. This was the most important step in becoming a teacher. Although Kelly had a fair amount of confidence in her knowledge of the subject, she was concerned about her ability to maintain control in the classroom. After all, she was just a few years older than many of the students she would encounter in the high school classroom. As she thought back on her high school experience, she remembered how some of her classmates treated substitute teachers and student teachers. Would they do that to her? Would they respect her authority? What would she do if they simply refused to cooperate? Although she knew that she would have an experienced teacher in the room to assist her, she also knew that she would be expected to demonstrate that she could handle the classroom if she was to get a good student teaching evaluation.

One day, Kelly was discussing her upcoming student teaching with an older friend, someone who had taught for a number of years. The friend gave her the following advice:

"Remember to establish your authority in the classroom right away. Make sure they know you are in charge from the first hour you step into the classroom. Don't try to be friends with the students and don't worry about being viewed as mean. It will be to your advantage if they think you are tough. Remember, you are the teacher, not just another student. You should start off with the class by spelling out your rules and expectations. Tell them what they will be expected to do and how they will be expected to behave and that you will tolerate no nonsense. Then, when the first student steps out of line, come down hard. Make the student an example so that the rest of the class will know you mean business. This will establish your authority in the classroom and will prevent a lot of problems."

As Kelly reflected on this advice, she was somewhat troubled. Could she do this? It was not her style to be tough and unfriendly. Was she too idealistic?

CHAPTER OBJECTIVES

After completing this chapter, you should be able to:

- Define teacher leadership and explain why it is important
- Compare the advantages and disadvantages of authoritarian and democratic methods of management
- Define different types of teacher authority and power and explain how they apply to the classroom
- List a process for defining classroom rules and responsibilities

Teachers manage complex environments. In a single day, an elementary teacher may engage in over 1,000 interpersonal exchanges with students. In secondary classrooms, teachers frequently have interactions with over 150 students (Good & Brophy, 2003). This complexity requires good management skills, and managing the classroom is the responsibility of the teacher. Success or failure of a particular classroom begins and ends with the teacher. No one expects students to arrive in the typical classroom with the knowledge and self-control required to manage the classroom! The students look to the teacher as the classroom leader, and a good share of teacher credibility depends on how this leadership is handled. Teachers are expected to be organized, handle problems as they occur in the classroom, interact positively with different students, know the subject matter, and gain student cooperation. How can that be done? What are the elements of leadership? Can it be learned? These are some of the questions addressed in this chapter.

Leadership is an essential component of any successful group, and teachers must accept responsibility for classroom leadership. Although a particular group of students may influence a teacher's leadership style in a particular setting, studies have shown that patterns of leadership remain relatively stable over time. One might conclude, then, that teachers establish patterns of leadership behavior in the classroom rather than merely responding to students (Soar & Soar, 1987). How do you respond when you are given authority? What is your leadership style? How do you think that will work out in a classroom? In the classroom scenario at the beginning of the chapter, what was the leadership style being advocated by the experienced teacher?

Boles and Davenport (1975) emphasize that leadership exists only when the leader–follower relationship is such that the followers accept an individual as the leader. In other words, leadership is earned. In a classroom context, it is important that students accept the teacher as the leader. If they do not, the classroom will be an unproductive one filled with problems. In these situations, it can be predicted that a perpetual power struggle will exist between the teacher and the students. On the other hand, when students do accept the teacher as the leader, the classroom will function much more smoothly with fewer problems and less stress. Reflecting on the classroom scenario at the beginning of the chapter, do you think the suggestions given will lead to the acceptance of the teacher as a leader? Why or why not?

Being accepted as the classroom leader and learning how to be an effective manager requires more than just applying a set of procedures and techniques. Although there are some management skills that can be learned and applied, leadership is a somewhat elusive characteristic that involves attitudes and beliefs as well as actions.

Leadership in the classroom involves attitude and action.

WHAT IS LEADERSHIP?

Simply having a role or a title does not make a person a leader. A position and a title might confer authority; it does not grant leadership. Leadership is enhanced through attitudes, beliefs, and personality. A beginning step in developing leadership requires a self-evaluation of beliefs, attitudes, expectations, and interaction style. The recurring principles of this book focusing on establishing positive relationships with students and having respect for them as individuals undergird the attitudes that are required in order to establish productive classroom leadership. The development of leadership in the classroom is also related to the concept of *lead management* described in Chapter 1. Lead management focuses on power and authority. Effective leaders use their power and authority in substantially different ways than ineffective leaders. Lead managers do not use power to control; they use it to promote success for others. They know how to share power so that members of the group have a sense of shared ownership and commitment to success (Kouzes & Posner, 1987).

Studies of leadership in areas outside of education provide us with some insight into the essential ingredients of teacher leadership. Kouzes and Posner (1987) conducted a study of characteristics of successful leaders in business, and their findings can be effectively applied to education. One major characteristic they found was that leaders had a deep respect for the aspirations of others. In other words, leaders are not just focused on meeting their needs, they are aware of the needs and aspirations of others. If individuals believe that a leader is helping them achieve their goals, then it is in their self-interest to follow that leader. Consider how this characteristic relates to teacher leadership. The central focus of teaching should be on meeting the needs of the students and helping students achieve their goals and aspirations, not on demonstrating teacher authority.

Another important component of leadership is credibility. People must believe in their leaders. A major test of credibility is consistency between words and actions. If behavior is not consistent with stated beliefs, respect and credibility are lost. False promises, deceptions, and inconsistent behavior harm credibility. Once credibility is lost, it is difficult to regain.

Individuals who are honest, competent, and inspiring, and who have a clear sense of direction, are looked to for leadership. People are drawn to leaders who demonstrate genuine acts of caring. We respect leaders who inspire a commitment by breathing life into our hopes and dreams. It is a part of the job of the leader to help individuals believe they can achieve success.

Trust is another important dimension of leadership. Leaders are people who are trusted. Trust, however, is a two-way street. It seems that the leader must be the

Table 2.1   Teacher Leadership in the Classroom

Directions: Look at the following chart on characteristics of leadership and identify specific actions that a teacher can take to apply each characteristic to the classroom.

Leadership Characteristic	How Can It Be Applied to the Classroom?
Credible	
Trustworthy	
Honest	
Competent	
Respectful of the aspirations of others	
Inspirational	
A learner	
Good model	
One who recognizes good ideas	
Fun	

first to demonstrate trust. When followers believe they are trusted, they return that trust to the leader.

Additional findings on the characteristics of leadership indicate that an effective leader is perceived as a competent person, a good model, one who recognizes and supports good ideas, and one who is also fun to be around. Leaders are also learners; they learn from mistakes as well as successes. Importantly, Kouzes and Posner (1987) contend that leadership can be learned. Table 2.1 lists characteristics of leadership for you to consider. Think about how each of these characteristics might be applied in the classroom.

In addition to these dimensions of leadership, surveys of students indicate that they rank enthusiasm as an important teacher quality. Enthusiasm is contagious. When the teacher is enthusiastic, the students catch that enthusiasm. If the teacher appears bored and lacks enthusiasm, students will also be bored and lack enthusiasm.

ESTABLISHING LEADERSHIP IN THE CLASSROOM

How does a teacher learn to apply leadership in the classroom? Establishing and developing leadership in the classroom requires an understanding of different types of power and authority. Once again, a framework developed outside of education can be useful. This framework is based on the differences between assigned authority and ascribed authority (French & Raven, 1959). The French and Raven framework defines five different types of power and authority:

- Legitimate power and authority
- Reward power and authority
- Coercive power and authority
- Expert power and authority
- Referent, or "attractive," power and authority

Each of these has an application to the classroom, so understanding them can be useful in helping you establish yourself as a leader in the classroom.

Legitimate Power and Authority

Some positions and roles carry with them a certain amount of power or authority regardless of the person filling that role. This type of authority is sometimes called "positional authority." It is authority that comes with a position and is therefore ascribed. The person who fills the position is given the "legitimate" power or authority to make certain decisions. For example, the position of president of the United States always carries with it the authority or right to make certain decisions and exercise certain powers, regardless of who occupies that position.

The position of "teacher" also has a certain amount of legitimate authority. There are decisions to make about the exercise of authority that is expected of any person who assumes the role of teacher. This is expected by the public, the administration, and, to some extent, the students.

There are, however, some limitations to legitimate authority in teaching. First, unquestioned obedience is not something that is taught or valued in our society. Even the legitimate authority of those in the highest offices is frequently challenged. The public does not hesitate to call into question the legitimate authority of the president, elected representatives, or law enforcement officers. In fact, citizenship education focusing on teaching students to question authority and resist blindly following the leadership of others has been a fundamental purpose of education since the founding of the nation.

Second, although authority is conferred on the teacher by state and local school officials, the students have no input in the decision. They have not voluntarily given authority to the teacher.

In fact, many of them seem bent on challenging teacher authority! In addition, although legitimate authority accompanies the role of teacher, it is very limited. Parents and administrators frequently question the decision of teachers. The media often portray teachers as ineffective, incompetent, poorly educated, and weak.

Students who come to school having been immersed in a culture where the authority of teachers is questioned are not likely to view them as having much legitimate authority. Why should we expect students to respect the authority of the teacher when teachers are denigrated and criticized openly and frequently throughout society? Perhaps there was a greater amount of legitimate authority assigned to the role of teacher in the past; however, there certainly is a limited amount now.

Gender issues have also influenced the legitimate authority of teachers. Teaching has long been regarded as a feminine profession. For many decades, it was one of the few professions women were allowed to enter. The teaching force is still largely female, and teaching is still regarded as acceptable for women but somewhat inappropriate for "strong" males. Because our society has been reluctant to grant females leadership roles, the authority ascribed to the role of teacher has traditionally been weak.

If you enter the classroom assuming that your position as teacher will carry with it immediate respect for your power and authority, you are likely to be extremely disappointed. The expectation that students will obey simply because they are told to do so by the teacher is a false one. We have often observed the impact of these erroneous expectations in new teachers who become frustrated when they enter the classroom and find students do not listen to them, do not obey their commands, and deliberately challenge their authority. Tauber (1985) makes the point very clearly that it can no longer be taken for granted that learners come to school with an automatic respect for teachers' legitimate power. This appears to be a major part of the problems underlying the frustrations of the teacher cited in Chapter 1, who left the "battle of teaching."

Another limitation associated with legitimate authority is that some teachers interpret it in ways that are harmful to the development of a successful classroom environment. Hoover and Kindsvetter (1997) point out that some people are drawn to teaching because it provides access to power and authority. These may well be individuals with inadequate self-concepts searching for social environments where they can feel significant and powerful. These individuals often become disenfranchised when they are unable to fulfill their needs.

Even though there are some limits associated with legitimate power, there are some useful applications in the classroom. For example, legitimate power can be most helpful at the beginning of the school year, when the majority of students enter the classroom with little or no knowledge of the teacher. They are temporarily willing to submit to the legitimate authority of the teacher and will usually follow reasonable rules and teacher requests. During this beginning phase, when students are often on their best behavior, legitimate power can be used to provide the beginning steps in developing teacher leadership built around earned authority and respect. If the teacher exercises legitimate authority in responsible and respectful ways, the teacher can begin to earn the respect of the students. Interestingly, as the teacher earns respect, legitimate authority also increases.

Reward Power and Authority

Another type of power and authority that is somewhat related to legitimate authority is *reward power and authority*. Reward power is based on the ability to give rewards or incentives that accompany a given position. Individuals in positions of authority can give rewards and incentives to others, and this usually provides incentives for others to follow their leadership.

The position of teacher carries with it the authority to provide rewards and benefits to students. There are many ways that teachers give rewards. There are the tangible awards, such as grades, special responsibilities, and privileges, and there are social rewards, such as attention, praise, status, and prestige. Teachers are constantly giving out rewards in one form or another. This gives them a certain amount of power. However, like legitimate authority, there are some limits to the reward authority of teachers.

One of the serious limitations is that reward authority is not earned. If the class does not respect the person giving the rewards, the rewards may even become a disincentive to cooperation. For example, teacher praise from an unpopular teacher is something that may be embarrassing rather than reinforcing to a student. Additionally, if students believe that the teacher is showing favoritism in giving rewards, the credibility of the teacher is undermined. Therefore, reward authority and power must be used wisely, applied fairly, and given for legitimate efforts.

If reward power is abused and rewards are given only to a select few (perhaps only to the teacher's favorites), or are given arbitrarily, and are not perceived as linked to legitimate accomplishments, then the authority to give rewards is relatively meaningless. For example, if grades are viewed as arbitrary rewards not linked to genuine achievement, then the credibility of the teacher is undermined and reward authority is lost. Good and Brophy (2003) provide excellent guidelines for making teacher praise effective, and those guidelines can be extended to cover other types of rewards. The following is a selection of some of the guidelines:

A reward . . .

Is given in recognition of noteworthy efforts

Provides information to the students about their competence and the value of their accomplishments

Rewards attainment of specific performance criteria

Shows spontaneity, variety, and other signs of credibility

Attributes success to effort and ability

Another limitation associated with reward authority is that teachers do not have the power to administer some of the most powerful rewards that are desired by students. For example, one of the most common rewards given in the classroom is grades. However, many students in school do not place high value on grades. In fact, some students ridicule those who work for grades. If grades are not valued, they are worthless as rewards and, therefore, the reward power of the teacher is severely diminished. This can be a problem for some individuals who enter teaching. They valued good grades and would obey teacher and school directives in order to obtain them. They become frustrated and do not know what to do when informed that students don't care about the grade.

Coercive Power and Authority

Another type of authority that flows from legitimate authority is the power and authority to give punishments, the opposite of reward authority. Some positions, such as teaching, carry with them the authority to administer punishment, and there are some individuals who enter teaching believing that the only way they can obtain respect and power is through intimidation or coercion. They are quick to remind students that failure to follow their demands will result in swift and sure punishment. Some teachers argue that, given the nature of contemporary society, this is the only type of power and authority respected by students.

Coercive authority can have some short-term benefits. It may be useful in immediately stopping an undesirable behavior. Because of this immediate impact, one might conclude that coercion is the best method for establishing teacher authority. However, power based on coercion has some undesirable side effects and limitations.

One such side effect is that coercion power creates power struggles between the teacher and students. Students often feel intimidated and angry and resort to demonstrating their own power by refusing to cooperate. This challenge to teacher authority can seldom be won by the teacher. Some students may express their power using passive resistance by simply refusing to do any work or professing ignorance or pretending a disability. Others will respond more aggressively by disrupting the classroom or overtly challenging the teacher. Other more serious side effects of students who feel powerless are anger, bullying, truancy, and vandalism.

Another problem with heavy use of coercion in the classroom is that coercion and fear are not foundations for building positive relationships. Teachers soon learn that unless they have the cooperation and good will of the students, they will have difficulty surviving. The normal school year is around 180 school days, a long time to try to survive constant power struggles. It certainly does not create a satisfying and pleasant working environment.

In summary, there are times when an inappropriate behavior needs to be quickly stopped in the classroom. However, relying on coercion as the main plank in a discipline plan is likely to have some counterproductive and harmful side effects. Coercion in the classroom goes against the principles of respecting students and creating positive relationships between teacher and students.

Expert Power and Authority

Some types of authority are earned rather than positional. One of these is *expert power and authority*. When an individual is perceived to be an expert or to have superior knowledge about a subject, that person has considerable power and authority. For example, a person who has demonstrated superior economic understanding and ability can influence the stock market just by making some recommendations. Similarly, a well-respected scientist can influence public policies on issues such as global warming by making recommendations.

Expert authority is extremely important in the classroom. One of the most important ingredients in teacher leadership is being perceived as an expert. Teacher expertise includes but is not limited to being knowledgeable about the subject being taught, demonstrating good teaching skills by making lessons understandable and meaningful, and handling unanticipated events skillfully.

Think back to those teachers in your life that you would identify as outstanding. The probabilities are great that one of the major characteristics of those teachers is that they were regarded as experts in content knowledge and teaching skill. Surveys of student attitudes toward teachers highlight the importance of expert power. For example, the ability to explain and clarify content is high on the list of attributes that learners identify about teachers they like and respect (Tanner, 1978).

Experts often demonstrate several recognizable characteristics. They have confidence and poise when confronting an issue or problem, and their confidence gives confidence to others. In addition, the expert usually has enthusiasm for the topic or task. Because of their enthusiasm and confidence, experts demonstrate a high degree of task persistence and do not give up easily.

New teachers often have difficulty developing expert authority because they are uncertain about their skills and thus do not exhibit confidence and poise. They may have an initial enthusiasm, but it quickly diminishes if things do not go well. Their lack of confidence is also revealed by their hesitant behavior when confronting an unexpected event. If these actions persist, students begin to question the competence of the teacher and an important source of authority and power is lost.

How does one obtain expert power? A beginning point is prior knowledge and skill. Teachers need to be well grounded in their subject matter knowledge. This requires more than just completing a given number of hours in the subject at the university. It involves understanding the key concepts, key ideas, and basic questions of the subject.

Teachers also need to have a solid foundation in understanding teaching and learning. Subject matter knowledge alone does not guarantee good teaching. Teachers need to know how to make the subject matter meaningful and understandable to students. To do this requires an understanding of student development and learning theory, because students are not just miniature adults. They think quite differently than adults.

Being prepared for class is also very important in developing student respect for teacher expertise. Planning gives new teachers immediate psychological rewards in terms of the reduction of uncertainty and an increase in self-confidence (Clark & Peterson, 1986). These feelings are communicated to learners through the confidence and the certainty of the teacher. It is not surprising that there is a relationship between the quality of teacher planning and student achievement.

Referent Power and Authority

Another type of authority and power that is earned is that of *referent,* or "attractive," *power and authority.* This refers to individuals who have desirable values and personal qualities. When certain individuals are perceived as trustworthy, ethical, caring, and interested in our welfare, we are willing to give them some authority. We listen to their point of view and are willing to follow their lead because we do trust them. Those who aspire to leadership roles must develop referent authority. Even the leadership attempts of experts will be ignored if the expert is perceived to be unethical or untrustworthy. However, the combination of expert and referent authority is very powerful and is characteristic of the most effective leaders.

Applying referent power to the classroom emphasizes the importance of teachers who like students and demonstrate a sincere interest in their welfare (Glasser, 1986).

Teachers who have negative feelings about students or who enter the classroom with low expectations are not likely to demonstrate behaviors that increase referent authority. Students as a group are generally keen observers and quickly identify teachers who are not genuine in their concern about students. A lack of trust and respect is communicated in many subtle ways that build the "history" of a classroom.

Prospective teachers need to engage in self-reflection. What are your views of the nature of students? Do you believe they are inherently good or inherently bad? Do you believe that students are worthy of respect? What about a certain groups of students; do you think they are motivated and capable of learning? Is your motivation to teach based on an interest in helping students achieve their potential or is your motivation something else? Honest answers to these questions will help define your potential for developing referent authority in the classroom.

Referent authority is especially important at the secondary level. At the elementary level, the majority of the students begin the school year with respect for the teachers. The elementary teacher usually just needs to maintain and build on that foundation of respect.

However, many secondary students, because of their level of social development, begin the school year with a healthy dose of skepticism. Students who have experienced limited success in school may well start with the belief that teachers do not care about their welfare. Therefore, secondary teachers must start at the beginning of the year demonstrating behaviors and taking actions that build respect from the students.

On the other hand, those teachers who do not attempt to build their referent authority are creating conditions that are likely to increase problems. For example, high school students cite that a major reason for their misbehavior in the classroom is the teacher's lack of respect for them. They did not perceive the teacher as respectful or caring, and their behavior is their way of retaliating and demonstrating lack of respect for the teacher.

How is referent authority increased? There are several actions that can be taken to increase referent authority. However, you must keep in mind that as a teacher you must demonstrate genuine interest in students and respect their dignity. If you are not genuine, mere actions will not work.

A simple beginning is learning the names of the students, providing genuine encouragement and praise, and avoiding sarcasm. Closely connected is creating a warm and personal classroom where students feel safe and respected. They need to believe their presence is recognized and they are free from psychological intimidation. For example, one negative example we encountered was a high school teacher who claimed that he did not try to learn student names or engage them in any personal way because this would interfere with his objectivity when he had to grade students. We doubt that students in his classroom gave him any referent authority.

Another factor that contributes to the development of referent authority is that of fairness in testing and grading. When teachers create tests designed to "trick" students rather than to measure important learning outcomes, they conclude that the teacher is not really concerned about their learning and is more concerned with finding ways to spread students out on the grading curve. Students are especially concerned about fair grading. If grades seem to be somewhat arbitrary, then students again perceive this as a sign that the teacher is unfair and does not care about

Teachers must earn power and authority.

© Photodisc

the welfare of students. This does not mean that all students should be given good grades. It means that the basis for grading needs to be fair and clear.

In summary, developing productive leadership in the classroom is based on the establishment of expert and referent authority. Going to class well prepared, demonstrating good teaching skills, being sensitive to student needs, and treating students with respect are the ingredients in building expert and referent authority.

TEACHER CONSISTENCY

Consistency is an important element in developing teacher credibility and leadership. What is teacher consistency and why is it important? Teacher consistency is related to fairness and predictability.

Individuals need some predictability in any environment. Environments that present some sense of predictability provide a sense of security. Predictability in the classroom is typically related to three factors: consistent or predictable application of the rules, follow-through, and fairness. Predictability occurs when students know what to expect. If a behavior is identified as unacceptable, it is always unacceptable. The definition of what is acceptable remains the same regardless of other variables such as the mood of the teacher. If students are unclear about what constitutes acceptable behavior and when consequences for unacceptable behavior will be applied, they are left with a great deal of uncertainty. The result is often constant "testing" to determine what is acceptable and what is unacceptable. In addition, interpersonal relationships may be strained when they are reprimanded for a behavior they did not realize was unacceptable. This whole cycle often leads to anxiety, anger, and even hostility.

Teachers demonstrate the second factor, follow-through, when they ensure that consequences follow misbehavior. Students need to know that if they act in acceptable ways, certain positive consequences will follow, and if they act in unacceptable ways, certain negative consequences will follow. Therefore, you need to make sure that you follow through in applying both positive and negative consequences in the classroom. Do not make promises that you cannot deliver.

Finally, fairness is demonstrated by teachers who apply rules and consequences to all students no matter who they are. Do not allow students to avoid following the rules or avoid consequences because they are usually well behaved or because they are favorites! On the other hand, do not reprimand or punish "problem students" for the least infraction while allowing high achievers or usually well-behaved students more freedom. This selective enforcement creates hostility not only between teacher and student but also among students. Students resent those who seem to be accorded special favors. Selective enforcement of rules interferes with teacher credibility and undermines teacher leadership.

In summary, when teachers create an environment where acceptable and unacceptable behavior is clearly defined and the consequences are consistently applied, there is a reduction of anxiety and problems are prevented. When students feel that all students in the classroom, regardless of ability and reputation, are being treated fairly and held to the same set of rules, respect for the teacher increases and teacher leadership is increased.

SHARING POWER AND RESPONSIBILITY

Another dimension of developing teacher leadership is a willingness to share responsibility and power with the students. Research findings have consistently indicated that a characteristic of effective schools is that they provide opportunities for students to assume responsibility and to participate in making decisions. Increased student participation has been associated with higher levels of academic achievement and less disruptive behavior (Rutter, 1983).

Involving Students in Classroom Management

As indicated earlier, classrooms are complex environments. An important task for teachers in achieving success is learning how to reduce the complexity of the classroom so that they can focus on important decisions and actions. Many routines and predictable tasks can be delegated to the students. Not only does this reduce management complexity but it also creates an environment in which students enjoy being involved. For example, one art teacher had created something of a mess in the classroom. A couple of students stayed beyond the dismissal bell to help clean up. She said, "You don't need to do this. It is not your responsibility." One of the students replied, "Maybe we like to help."

Younger children enjoy doing many routine tasks that that might not be appealing to older students. However, older students can assist in operating computers and equipment, or work as assistants to the teacher. These jobs make them feel important and give them some ownership and authority. Take some time to think about all the recurring tasks that occur on a regular basis. Identify those that can be done by the students and decide on a process you can use to assign those tasks to students.

One bit of caution: Take care to ensure fairness in assigning the responsibilities. Don't always assign the tasks to the same few students. Try to find a way of involving as many students as possible. For example, you might accomplish this by changing responsibilities every few weeks so that different students have the opportunity to have some responsibility and authority.

Sharing responsibility with students has the added advantage of providing them with a sense of ownership and belonging in the classroom. They feel that they are important and that they are a part of the school. If students have some responsibility for the classroom computers, they have an investment in making sure they are not abused. This provides students with the opportunity to exercise power in constructive ways. They are then less inclined to try to show their power and importance by challenging the authority of the teacher.

Sharing Power in the Establishment of Classroom Rules

Reasonable rules are an important part of any social situation. Rules permeate all of life and are important in helping individuals construct meaning and relate productively to others (Carter & Doyle, 2006). This is especially true in diverse classrooms where individuals with different understandings and prior experiences come together. Classrooms are busy and complex places, so basic understandings of rules and procedures are necessary if anything is to be accomplished.

The importance of good rules in promoting productive classroom life was underscored in a study by Marzano (2003). He found that in classes where rules and procedures were implemented effectively, the number of disruptions was about 28 percentile points less than in classrooms where rules and procedures were not implemented effectively.

Some individuals argue that rules stifle creativity and curiosity. However, others argue that creativity takes place within the context of overcoming limits. The task is that of establishing fair rules that help direct creativity and curiosity in productive ways.

Rules might take the form of unwritten expectations assumed by both parties, or they may be more explicit. Some teachers rely on vague or unwritten rules. One teacher reports that the only rule in his class is the "golden rule." This might work for a few teachers, but it is not generally a good idea to try to manage anything on the basis of vague or unclear rules. The golden rule leaves room for wide interpretation of specific behaviors. Some students may not understand the specific behaviors related to this broad statement. For example, is it acceptable to be out of the desk wandering around the room as long as it is not disrespectful to others?

Unwritten expectations often lead to disagreement and conflict. If individuals do not have clear guidelines for choosing a behavior, they may do something that conflicts with the expectations of others. For example, anyone who has had to live with a roommate can relate to the disagreements that can arise unless there is a clarification of expectations by the roommates. This is especially true in classrooms populated by individuals with different expectations and understandings. Therefore, teachers must spend time at the beginning of any new class establishing and clarifying classroom rules and expectations.

One approach to the establishment of rules is the assertive, authoritarian approach (Canter & Canter, 1976). This approach is based on legitimate, reward, and coercive types of authority. The teacher establishes the rules, informs the students of the rules, and identifies the consequences for violating them. This approach communicates to the students that the teacher is in charge and means business, an important step in developing teacher leadership. The students need to know that the teacher is serious about being the classroom leader and in making sure a climate is established where learning can occur. This approach also has the advantage of providing the teachers with a sense of security and control. You can take time before students even arrive in the classroom to define the rules and consequences. Inexperienced teachers often find it comforting to know what the rules will be and to have some clear consequences to apply when rules are violated.

Some research also indicates that there is a benefit to this approach. Teachers who successfully communicate to students in a firm but positive manner that they mean business and will not tolerate disturbances increase student on-task behavior. A potential problem, however, is that the authoritarian approach also seems to prompt student aggression toward the teacher (Mendler & Curwin, 1983).

Another option for establishing classroom rules is the democratic approach. This method involves shared decision making and gives the student a voice in establishing rules. It communicates that student participation is desired and that their views are important. The authors have observed that students in democratically oriented classrooms usually exhibit higher academic output and have more positive attitudes toward the teacher. In addition, the democratic approach is consistent with important goals of education in preparing students to become participating citizens in society and for helping them accept responsibility for their behavior. The basis of the democratic approach is referent and expert authority.

Some potential issues must be addressed when using the democratic approach. The approach is more time-consuming than the authoritarian approach of just telling the students what the rules will be. In addition, the process is a messy one and is less predictable than the authoritarian approach. Teachers often ask, "What if the students do not establish appropriate rules?" Using the democratic approach requires some confidence in the judgments of the students. Most students do want a positive and productive classroom. If they believe that they are trusted and their views are important, they will take the task seriously. If there are a couple of rules that the teacher must have, those should be shared at the beginning. Being honest and open by informing students of your needs is usually accepted by the students and increases their respect for the teacher.

Inexperienced teachers sometimes lack confidence and are hesitant about using the democratic approach. They need to remember that the democratic approach does not communicate uncertainty or an abdication of teacher responsibility. Although it does add a little unpredictability for the teacher, it also has some potential benefits in increasing student acceptance of the teacher as a trusted leader and in increasing, rather than diminishing, teacher authority. Table 2.2 identifies some tasks that teachers should consider as they plan their management strategies.

Regardless of the management style you choose, consider the following basic steps: rule specification, rule clarification, rule practice, and rule monitoring. Including these four steps can help ensure that behavioral expectations are clear and understood by all students, that problems are prevented, and that you have communicated your need for students to take rules seriously.

Rule Specification

Rule specification is the process of deciding on classroom rules. For the authoritarian teacher, rule specification is his or her responsibility. Rules are determined by the teacher and then shared with the students. In contrast, the democratic teacher shares the rule specification task with students. Mendler and Curwin (1983) recommend the social contract approach as a democratic rule specification method. A social contract is an agreement on a set of rules reached by group consensus. Three

Table 2.2 Developing Teacher Leadership

Directions: Consider how you will establish your leadership while performing the following tasks.

Task	How It Will Be Accomplished
Earning authority by Demonstrating knowledge of content Demonstrating knowledge of teaching Planning Organizing the classroom effectively Developing a warm yet businesslike classroom Giving rewards	
Positive relationship with students through Developing trust Sharing power in establishing rules Demonstrating respect for students Knowing student needs and interests Developing a positive atmosphere Creating fun Providing encouragement	
Demonstrating consistency when Establishing classroom rules and routines Grading procedures Monitoring student behavior Following through on promises Being fair in enforcing rules Following predictable routines	

types of rules are included in the development of the social contract. The first type are the rules the teacher must have, the second type are the rules the students have for each other, and the third type are rules for the teacher. The social contract method of rule specification includes the following steps:

- The teacher states the rules that are nonnegotiable.
- Small groups of class members discuss and propose rules they think are needed in order for them to work together productively.
- All proposed rules are discussed and voted on by the entire class. Group consensus is preferred but if that is not possible, at least two thirds of the class should agree on the rule before it is adopted.
- Small groups discuss and propose rules for the teacher.
- Rules for the teacher are discussed. If a rule is inappropriate or interferes with the authority of the teacher to conduct the classroom in an appropriate manner, the teacher can exercise veto power.
- Possible consequences for all rules are then discussed. Either the teacher or the students may propose consequences for rule violation. The teacher must

approve the consequences and has the right to veto any consequences that are dangerous or illegal.

Some teachers are uncomfortable with the idea of allowing students to propose rules for the teacher. They worry that students will establish unreasonable rules that will limit teacher authority. However, experience with the procedure indicates that students usually take the process seriously and propose reasonable rules for the teacher. This procedure demonstrates that rules are for everyone and everyone needs to follow reasonable rules, even the teacher.

One advantage of the social contract approach is that it can provide useful diagnostic information to the teacher. Through this discussion, the teacher gains insight into student views of fairness and justice. Some of the behaviors students consider offensive may not have occurred to the teacher. For example, secondary students may establish rules relating to teacher's respecting their privacy, letting the class out on time so that they have time to go to their lockers or get to the next class on time, avoiding the use of "put-downs" or sarcasm, or giving sufficient time to allow students to plan for the completion of time-consuming projects. Identifying these concerns at the beginning of the school year helps the teacher avoid actions that anger students. In addition, allowing students to specify rules for the teacher communicates to them that the teacher recognizes the value of rules and allows the teacher an opportunity to model the process of exercising self-control and accepting consequences when rules are violated.

Rule Clarification

The purpose of rule clarification is to make sure that all learners understand what a rule means and what constitutes appropriate and inappropriate behavior. An important component of rule clarification is that of stating each rule clearly and concisely. When possible, a rule should state what learners should do rather than what they should not do. For example, it is more productive to state that "we raise our hand before talking," rather than "we do not talk out of turn." Each rule should then be discussed and ambiguous terms removed or defined. Students should then identify acceptable and unacceptable examples of behavior for each rule. Taking time for rule clarification helps eliminate a common excuse for misbehavior, "I didn't understand."

Rule Practice

Learning rules, like anything else, requires practice. Time needs to be allocated to practice the rules. Rule practice is generally more important for young students and for rules that might be vague or unfamiliar. For example, secondary students probably do not need to practice how to raise their hand if they want to make a contribution to the class discussion. However, they will need to practice safe behavior in physical education, science, and some vocational classes.

A concluding step in rule practice could be for the students to take a short test on the rules. One junior high science teacher identifies, clarifies, and practices rules on the first day of school and gives a quiz on the rules on the second day. The quiz is kept short and simple so that all students pass. The teacher keeps these tests on file. This serves two purposes: (a) If there is ever a legal challenge regarding whether students were informed of the rules, the test provides evidence, and (b) if students profess ignorance of the rules, the test can be used to remind the students that they were informed.

Rule Monitoring

Rules will have little impact if compliance is not monitored. Some teachers have difficulty with classroom management because they do no not monitor rules very closely or do not follow rule violations with consequences. As a result, students choose to violate classroom rules because the probability of the teacher taking action is slight. The rules then become meaningless, and respect for the teacher and the rules are lost. Teacher monitoring of the rules is especially critical during the first few weeks of the school year (Emmer, Evertson, Sanford, Clements, & Worsham, 1982). It is important that positive reinforcements and rewards be administered when rules are followed, as well as appropriate consequences when they are not.

What Would You Do?

Read the following incident and suggest what you would do.

At the beginning of the school year, Ms. Wagner's third-grade students appeared to be cooperative and well behaved. Ms. Wagner, in her first year of teaching, was pleased that the students already demonstrated good self-control. However, as the year has developed, they seem to have regressed. During lessons, students seldom appear to be paying attention and many of the students are engaged in socializing. Sometimes Ms. Wagner has to terminate the lesson before the conclusion in order to try to gain control.

In one observation, while Ms. Wagner was working with a group of students, others wandered around the room and bothered others. A couple of students made several trips to the drinking fountain and a few spent time at the pencil sharpener.

Ms. Wagner is clearly getting frustrated and her demeanor is turning from smiling and friendly to angry.

- What do you think could account for the change in the behavior of the students?

- What are specific steps you would take to regain control of this classroom?

REVIEW OF MAIN IDEAS

1. A role or a given position might confer authority; however, it does not establish leadership. Leadership must be earned. To be productive classroom leaders, teachers must earn the right to be the leader.

2. There are several types of authority and power. Legitimate power and authority is the type of power that accompanies a given role. The role of teacher has some legitimate authority.

3. Reward power is the power that accompanies the ability to give rewards. Teachers have the power to give rewards such as praise, recognition, and grades. Many discipline programs emphasize this type of power.

4. Coercive power is the power a person possesses when in a role that enables the person to give punishments. Some teachers rely on coercive power as a means of controlling the classroom.

5. Expert power is the type of authority that comes from being perceived as an expert. This type of power and authority is earned. Teachers who are perceived to be expert teachers have this type of power and authority.

6. Referent or attractive power and authority is the type of authority that comes from being perceived to be an honest, trustworthy, and caring person. This type of power must also be earned and is an important component of establishing teacher leadership and authority.

7. The most powerful type of power and authority is the combination of expert power and referent power. When teachers are perceived by students as being experts as well as individuals who are trustworthy and caring, they have a tremendous amount of authority and power.

8. Another part of earning teacher leadership is in acting consistently. Consistency in the classroom means following through on promises, enforcing the rules, and fairly applying rules to all students.

9. When teachers share power and responsibility with students, they do not lose power and authority, they gain power and authority. Involving students in classroom decisions gives them some ownership.

10. Establishing rules and routines involves rule specification, rule clarification, rule practice, and rule monitoring.

APPLICATION AND ENRICHMENT

1. Your values and beliefs are important components in developing teacher leadership. Performing a self-analysis can help you move toward success. Take a few minutes to perform a self-analysis by responding honestly to the following questions:

- Why do you want to be a teacher?
- What rewards or benefits do you expect to gain from teaching?
- What are your attitudes toward students? Do you believe they are trustworthy?
- How do you view the role of the teacher in establishing authority in the classroom?
- How do you demonstrate self-control?
- What worries you most about managing the classroom?

2. Think back to your days as a student. Identify a teacher you considered to be effective and one that you considered ineffective. Compare the two and identify the differences. How do their characteristics relate to the content of the chapter?

3. Brainstorm the types of tasks and responsibilities that students might be able to perform in your classroom. Develop a list of tasks and consider how you will involve students in the management of your classroom.

REFERENCES

Boles, H. W., & Davenport, J. A. (1975). *Introduction of educational leadership.* New York: Harper & Row.

Canter, L., & Canter, M. (1976). *Assertive discipline: A take charge approach for today's educator.* Santa Monica, CA: Canter.

Carter, K., & Doyle, W. (2006). Classroom management in early childhood and elementary classrooms. In C. M. Evertson & C. S. Weinstein (Eds.), *Handbook of classroom management* (pp. 373–406). Mahwah, NJ: Lawrence Erlbaum.

Clark, C. M., & Peterson, P. L. (1986). Teacher's thought processes. In M. Wittrock (Ed.), *Handbook of research and teaching* (3rd ed., pp. 225–296). New York: Macmillan.

Emmer, E., Evertson, C., Sanford, J., Clements, B., & Worsham, W. (1982). *Organizing and managing the junior high classroom.* Austin, TX: Research and Development Center for Teacher Education, University of Texas.

French, J. R. P., & Raven, B. H. (1959). The bases of social power. In D. Cartwright (Ed.), *Studies in social power* (pp. 150–167). Ann Arbor: University of Michigan Press.

Glasser, W. (1986). *Control theory in the classroom*. New York: Harper & Row.

Good, T. L., & Brophy, J. E. (2003). *Looking in classrooms* (9th ed.). New York: Longman.

Hoover, R. L., & Kindsvetter, R. (1997). *Democratic discipline: Foundations for practice.* Columbus, OH: Merrill.

Kouzes, J. L., & Posner, B. Z. (1987). *The leadership challenge: How to get extraordinary things done in organizations.* San Francisco: Jossey-Bass.

Marzano, R. J. (2003). *Classroom management that works: Research based strategies for every teacher.* Alexandria, VA: Association for Supervision and Curriculum Development.

Mendler, A. N., & Curwin, R. L. (1983). *Taking charge in the classroom: A practical guide to effective discipline.* Reston, VA: Association for Supervision and Curriculum Development.

Rutter, M. (1983). School effects on pupil progress: Research findings and policy implications. In L. Shulman & G. Sykes (Eds.), *Handbook of teaching and policy* (pp. 3–41). New York: Longman.

Soar, R. S., & Soar, R. M. (1987). Classroom climate. In M. Biddle (Ed.), *The international encyclopedia of teaching and teacher education* (pp. 336–342). New York: Pergamon.

Tanner, L. (1978). *Classroom discipline for effective teaching and learning.* New York: Holt, Rinehart & Winston.

Tauber, R. T. (1985). Power bases: Their application to classroom and school management. *Journal of Education for Teaching, 11*(20), 133–144.

Chapter 3

CLASSROOM BEHAVIOR AND MOTIVATION

The Essential Link

CLASSROOM SCENARIO

Joan settled down for another night of grading the work of her fifth-grade students. About halfway through the papers, she came across Richard's paper. Her frustration grew as she saw that once again he had submitted a paper that was blank except for his name.

Richard was not an especially troublesome student; he just would not do any work. The school year was about a month old, and every day it was the same pattern. When she gave the work assignments, Richard would sit with his head down and look at the floor. Joan knew that academically he was behind where he ought to be. She also realized that letting this continue would be a disaster when it came time for the state competency tests. However, she simply did not know what to do to get Richard to do his work.

The next day, when Joan made the work assignment, she walked around the classroom until she was next to Richard. She could see that he had not started the assignment. She commented to him that he needed to get to work. She helped a few others get started and made it back to Richard. Still no progress. Out of frustration she said to him, "Richard, what are you going to do when you get done with school and you have to get a job?"

Richard looked up and said, "I'm going to paint fences."

Joan was surprised that he had such a ready answer, but the answer mystified her. "Paint fences? Why do you want to paint fences?"

"Well," said Richard, "when you paint fences, all you need is a can of paint and a paint brush. Then you just go up and down, up and down. You don't need to know how to read, spell, or do math!"

CHAPTER OBJECTIVES

After completing this chapter you should be able to:

- State the importance of motivation in teaching
- Define the relationship between motivation and behavior
- Identify basic motivation principles
- Define the role of the teacher in establishing a motivational climate
- Apply a model of motivation to the classroom

An essential element of a successful classroom is motivated students. Motivation and behavior are closely linked. You might consider how Richard's failure to complete assignments might be related to his motivation. What could Joan do to motivate him to complete the work that was assigned?

Although most teachers state the importance of motivation, research indicates that they spend a relatively small amount of classroom time focusing on student motivation (Good & Brophy, 2003). Teachers who want to achieve the dream of an eager class of cooperative students must focus considerable attention on engaging the students in learning. Motivation is not something that just happens in the classroom. It requires considerable thought and effort, and teachers play an important role in establishing a motivating learning climate. The beliefs that teachers have about teaching and learning and their expectations exert a powerful influence on the motivational climate in the classroom. Teachers who hold high but reasonable expectations for student learning will usually have students who are learning. One of the most important challenges in teaching is identifying reasonable goals for students, getting students to accept the goals as important, and keeping the students engaged.

Some individuals expressing an interest in the improvement of education seek to do so by implementing strong programs of social control aimed at stopping inappropriate behavior. It is assumed that if students are not misbehaving, they will be learning. However, this is a questionable assumption. Those authoritarian-based methods of social control often ignore principles of human motivation. Therefore, they have limited success and soon fall out of favor. Instead, we need to direct attention to approaches that have the likelihood of engaging students in learning (Mental Health in Schools Center, 2002).

A common complaint of contemporary teachers is that students lack motivation. The problem is not that students lack motivation; they are highly motivated in certain areas. They are just not motivated by academic goals and school. The task of the teacher is to establish a learning environment where students' needs are being met in the classroom and where they see that it is in their best interest to

Motivation is an essential element of problem prevention.

© Photos.com

cooperate and learn. In this chapter, we discuss a few principles of motivation that can help teachers move toward the goal of a motivated and successful classroom.

THE LINK BETWEEN MOTIVATION AND STUDENT BEHAVIOR

What energizes and directs student activity on school tasks? Why do some students quickly comply with school expectations and others resist? Why do some individuals appear to be curious about new information and others do not? Why do some students respond to criticism and failure by working harder and others by just giving up? Why do some students seem to respond positively in one classroom and negatively in another? These are questions that often trouble teachers.

Most teachers understand that the key to answering these questions is an understanding of motivation. However, they are often unsure of the link between motivation and student behavior.

One psychologist, Slavin (2005), stated that it is not the task of the teacher to increase student motivation. Motivation already exists. It is the role of the teacher to discover, direct, and sustain student motivation to learn and behave appropriately. This means that teachers apply the link between motivation and behavior by diagnosing student motivation, relating student motivation to educational tasks, and helping students persist until they achieve success. Thus motivation occurs at the beginning of a learning sequence to direct student attention, during a learning sequence to sustain student attention, and at the end of a learning sequence to reinforce success.

Understanding the link between student motivation and classroom behavior may lead to the uncomfortable discovery that some inappropriate student behaviors are related to poor teaching practices, the failure to make the curriculum meaningful to students, or a threatening classroom environment. In other words, teachers do have a responsibility to apply principles of motivation to the classroom. They should not expect that everyone who enters their classroom will have an intrinsic interest in the subject or will have the persistence to complete the task.

One way to begin is by conducting some self-discovery. Respond to the questions in Table 3.1 and consider how what you discover might help you approach motivation in your classroom.

SOME BASIC PRINCIPLES OF MOTIVATION

A beginning point in understanding motivation is the understanding that there are two basic types of motivation. One type, *extrinsic motivation,* is motivation that is directed by forces external to the individual. These might be in the form of

Table 3.1   What Do You Find Motivating?

Directions: Take a few minutes to think about your motivations. How might this understanding relate to your teaching?

- When you were a student, what made the difference between a class that was interesting to you and one that was not?
- What do you think accounted for the difference between those classes where you were successful and those where you had difficulty? How did you respond when you had difficulty or were not interested in a particular class?
- Think of a favorite teacher. What did this teacher do that inspired you to behave well and achieve success in that classroom?
- Think of a teacher who was unsuccessful in motivating you to learn. What was the difference between this teacher and one who motivated you?
- What is your motivation for being a teacher?
- As you consider your experience as a student, what are two or three statements that you could make about motivation and teaching?

---

reinforcers such as awards, prizes, praise, candy, or money. One theory holds that behaviors that achieve desirable results are likely to be repeated. In other words, when a behavior is reinforced, it is likely to continue. Certainly, all of us can identify that there are certain things we do because they achieve desirable results. Extrinsic motivation is frequently applied in education. One does not need to spend much time in classrooms to note the use of external reinforcers such as praise, grades, and privileges. If you applied extrinsic motivation to Richard in the scenario mentioned at the beginning of the chapter, what might you try?

One reason why extrinsic reinforcement is common in school settings is that it is easy to use. However, the effects of extrinsic reinforcement are usually short lived and they vary from individual to individual. Extrinsic motivation may be useful in getting the initial attention of some students. However, this needs to be followed with attention to motivational variables beyond just getting a reward.

The second type of motivation is *intrinsic motivation.* Intrinsic motivation is directed by factors or reinforcement that come from within the individual. Intrinsic motivation is related to the values, needs, interests, curiosities, and feelings of achievement or competence that come from within an individual. Intrinsic motivation is clearly the more powerful type, and our goal as teachers should be to increase the intrinsic motivation of students. If you were to apply intrinsic motivation to Richard in the scenario at the first of the chapter, what might you try?

To illustrate the limitations of extrinsic motivation and the importance of intrinsic motivation, we are reminded of a program that was directed toward getting middle school boys to increase their reading. Certain goals were established for the boys, and every time they completed the designated reading assignment, they were given external reinforcement. In this particular case, it was money. However, after a period of time, the funds for the program were exhausted. The boys were interviewed after the program was stopped and were asked if they were going to keep on reading. Several boys replied, "No, why should we? We don't get any more money." These boys still saw reading as just another school chore rather than as an activity that could bring adventure, excitement, and joy to their lives. Extrinsic reinforcement did not result in any long-term behavior change.

Intrinsic motivation varies from individual to individual. Because of our prior experience and background, we have different curiosities and interests. Therefore, it requires more effort and creativity in order to identify the interests and needs of students and in relating educational objectives to those curiosities and interests.

Applying motivation in the classroom requires an understanding that behavior is not random but purposeful. People have personal goals, and these goals help direct their attention and energy as they make choices between competing demands for their attention and energy. They engage in activities that they think have the potential to help them achieve their personal goals. A challenge of teaching and parenting is to help the young establish worthwhile goals and make wise choices.

Understanding that behavior is purposeful can also be applied to understanding inappropriate behavior. If student behavior persists, the question should be asked, "What goal might this behavior be fulfilling?"

Understanding that individuals are attempting to accomplish personal goals is only the start in applying motivation to the classroom. Even though an individual might have worthwhile goals, if the person believes that there is a low probability of success, or that success will require more effort than they are willing to spend, their motivation is likely to be low. For example, if an individual perceives that the effort required to complete a school task competently is too great, the person might then seek to meet achievement needs by being the most competent class clown.

What this implies is that motivation is a complex phenomenon that has a personal dimension. Productive motivation means that the teacher must understand the students they are teaching, their needs and wants and how they perceive themselves as students.

Applying motivation to the classroom is made even more difficult because there are several theories related to human motivation. Even those individuals who have completed a course on learning theory and human motivation can have difficulty understanding how to apply motivational theory to classrooms populated by 30 or more individuals coming from diverse backgrounds. Some of the motivation principles developed in laboratories where there is a one-to-one correspondence between experimenter and subject do not seem to be relevant. For example, in the laboratory the experimenter might be controlling the reinforcement. However, in a classroom, other students might be providing the reinforcement, and their reinforcement might be more valued than that of the teacher.

A characteristic of the classroom that might make motivation more difficult than the laboratory is the fact that classrooms are not just academic settings. They are also social settings, and individuals have social as well as academic goals. The classroom contains a variety of individuals, all of whom can influence the perceptions of a given student. Social goals involve the establishment of personal relationships, learning how to behave in ways that are relevant to the situation, gaining acceptance and approval, achieving positive outcomes for the individual, and satisfying personal needs and wants.

There are times when social and academic goals conflict. A teacher might have an academic goal for the students to master the subject and to engage in critical and creative thinking. However, students also have goals related to the establishment of personal relationships. If they believe that mastering the subject matter will interfere with the establishment of personal relationships, they may give priority to the development of personal relationships. This highlights the importance of peers and peer approval. Students often find themselves in conflict. They want the approval of both the teacher and of the other students. If they must make a choice, they are more likely to choose the approval of their peers. They are more likely to be motivated to achieve school tasks if they believe that they can achieve the academic goals of the classroom while also achieving their own personal goals (Wentzel, 2006).

In summary, motivation includes a number of variables, such as personality, goal orientation, curiosity, needs, wants, level of anxiety, past history of success and failure, attributions of success and failure, self-concept, and the nature of the social setting (Slavin, 2005). When approaching motivation in the school setting, a teacher needs to remember that motivation is related to student perceptions of the setting, not teacher perceptions.

A beginning point in organizing our thoughts about motivation so that we can apply motivation to the classroom is to consider a combination of the two forces outlined at the beginning of the chapter: student goals and their perceptions of the value of the academic goals and the perceived probability of achieving success.

Increase the Value of Learning Goals

A beginning point for addressing motivation in the classroom is to consider the value of what students are to learn and how to get them to accept these goals as important. Part of this task begins prior to stepping into the classroom. The questions need to be asked: "Why is this content important for students to know?" and "How can it be related to the goals of the students in the classroom?" Just because something is a state standard that is likely to be tested on a standardized examination is not sufficient to motivate many students. Similarly, threatening students that they need to learn the content in order to get a good grade may serve to motivate only those students who already view academic success as important.

What Would You Do?

Read the following and suggest what you would do.

Pat Taylor was a first-year teacher. Pat had chosen to take a teaching position in a school in a low socioeconomic part of the community. Pat knew about the "achievement gap" between low-SES (socioeconomic status) communities and high-SES communities and was motivated by social justice concerns.

However, Pat was frustrated. Things that had motivated Pat didn't seem to work with these students. Efforts to motivate the middle school students had been spectacularly unsuccessful. When Pat excitedly explained to them that what they were going to learn would help them get ready for college, they laughed. "We ain't going to no college," they replied. "Why would we do that?" Next, Pat pointed out in that the spring term they would all have to take a test and that if they failed, they might not graduate. "Who cares about some old test?" they responded. "That's a long time away and we don't do well on tests." "Don't you want to graduate from school?" asked Pat. "Well, that would be nice," one student responded. "However, it is just a piece of paper. My cousin graduated a couple of years ago and it didn't help him get a job. He's still just standing around all day. There aren't any jobs around here. Why should I spend my time doing things that aren't going to help me get along around here on Saturdays?"

- What do you think is the major issue in this situation?

- What would you recommend that Pat do to try to motivate the students?

- How might Pat's background have hindered his efforts to motivate these students?

- What can you take from this scenario that will be helpful for your teaching?

Link Learning to Student Needs and Interests

One component of helping students understand the importance of learning is to link learning to individuals' needs and interests. Individuals direct their time and energy toward activities that appear interesting to them or that have the potential for meeting their needs. Students who feel that their needs are met in the classroom seldom cause discipline problems because interfering with something that is meeting a need is contrary to their self-interest. Glaser (1986) defined a good school as a place where almost all the students believe that if they put forth some effort, some of their needs will be satisfied. He maintains that many school discipline problems are related to schools not taking into account whether or not the educational experience is meeting needs so that it is a satisfying place to be.

There are several ways that needs might be categorized. For our purposes, we have divided them into three groups: physiological needs, psychological needs, and social needs. Although we will discuss these needs separately, remember that there are many ways that they are interrelated.

Student Needs

Physiological Needs. Physiological needs are those fundamental needs that must be accommodated prior to addressing other needs. Unmet physiological needs make it almost impossible for individuals to be motivated toward any activity other than meeting the physiological needs. These needs include the need for nutrition, rest, comfort, movement, freedom from illness, and sensory stimulation. Although some of these needs might be beyond the control of the teacher, understanding that these factors can interfere with the achievement of educational goals can help teachers when they address discipline problems and the apparent lack of academic motivation.

It is unfortunate in a society of abundance that many children come to school every day with inadequate nutrition. Some come to school hungry while others have eaten little more than junk food that has scant nutritional value. Lack of adequate nutrition has been identified as a major contributor to behavior disorders and to violence (Schauss, 1985). Educators are limited in what they can do to address this physiological need. There have been recent efforts to replace junk foods that are sold on school campuses with healthier alternatives. Free or reduced-price breakfast and lunch programs have also attempted to address nutrition concerns. One of the most important roles for teachers is to be aware of nutrition as a source of behavior problems. If this is a problem identified, then efforts can be focused on finding ways of providing adequate nutrition. Trying to teach students who are hungry is ineffective and frustrating.

Another physiological need is that of mobility. Students, especially younger ones, need to be able to move. It is physically impossible for some students to sit still for extended periods of time. When teachers establish schedules that require extended periods of time without movement, they are establishing conditions that lead to behavior problems. For example, observations in one first-grade classroom revealed that the teacher was giving students worksheets and requiring that students sit in their seats quietly for up to 45 minutes. When the inevitable restlessness occurred, she became upset and reprimanded students for making noise and getting out of their seats. This led to student frustration and anger and even more discipline problems. Changing the schedule and changing activities to allow the students an opportunity to move is an easy solution that would increase the satisfaction of the students and the teacher.

All of us are aware that it is difficult to concentrate and stay on task when we are uncomfortable. However, we often forget to apply this to students in the classroom. Since many classrooms are climate controlled and lighting is standard, many teachers assume that the comfort dimension has been met. However, there is much more to comfort than temperature and lighting. One problem relates to seating. Many teachers forget how uncomfortable it can be to sit in typical school chairs for an extended period of time. This can be an especially acute problem at the secondary level, where students with varying body types are expected to sit in standardized workspaces, and where there is little opportunity to move about. For example, observe a typical middle school during a class break. The students are jumping and moving around at a rapid rate. Their developmental level requires this.

Another dimension of comfort in the classroom is related to the density of students—the number of students who inhabit a given space. All individuals have something that is called *personal space.* When we believe that our personal space is being invaded, we become tense and aggressive. This leads to a discomfort that, if not met, will result in disruptive behavior.

Personal space has something of a cultural dimension. Most of us raised in the United States have expectations of more personal space than individuals from some other cultures. As teachers plan the classroom environment, they should consider the spacing of student work areas so that they can reduce the density of students in a given space. Unfortunately, in many of our classrooms, large numbers of students prevent the effective spacing of work areas.

Another physiological need that must be addressed is the need for sensory stimulation. The brain needs something to process, and the lack of sensory stimulation can actually be painful. For example, when some of us have to wait in an area where there is an absence of sensory stimulation, such as an airport waiting room or a doctor's office, we get painful manifestations such as headaches. Sensory deprivation is related to boredom, and boredom is one of the primary causes of inappropriate behavior.

What this implies for teachers is that they need to consider how the sensory stimulation needs of the students can be met. Are there things in the classroom environment that can stimulate their senses? Are there a variety of presentation modes that require students to do more than just sit and listen?

In summary, when addressing student needs, a beginning point is to consider the physiological needs of the students. Do they have adequate nutrition and rest? How can their movement needs be satisfied? What is the density of students in the classroom? Is there adequate sensory stimulation?

Psychological Needs. All individuals have psychological needs. We all want to be accepted, loved, and respected; feel significant; and feel psychologically safe. School is one of the dominant features in the life of a student. Unfortunately, for many students, it is one of the few places where they have the opportunity to feel significant and worthwhile. Teachers and schools that work hard at helping students feel significant and important discover that even the most difficult students can develop an excitement about learning and a commitment to maintaining a productive school climate.

One of the most important psychological needs is that of security, a need to be in a safe place. If individuals do not feel safe, they will direct their attention and energies to those things that will increase their feelings of safety. Feeling safe includes psychological threat as well as physical threat. Fear of failure is a common fear in society that blocks much risk taking. In classrooms, students who fear failure are unwilling to try. Psychologically, it is more satisfying for them to rationalize that the activity was unimportant than to try and fail.

Much has been made of the need for physical safety in schools. Some of the major threats to physical safety relate to bullying and the fear of weapons in schools. In recent years, there has been a great deal of attention directed at the area of physical threat. Some schools have installed metal detectors in an effort to keep weapons out of the school environment. The problem of bullying and the creation of a hostile environment is increasingly being addressed. We will address the problem of bullying in Chapter 10.

In the concern for physical safety, psychological safety issues are often overlooked. Psychological threat may be the result of sarcasm, ridicule, verbal assaults, lack of respect, and fears of failure. There are some teachers who seem to believe that psychological intimidation is an important tool in maintaining order in the classroom. Indeed, there are numerous examples in society and in the media where psychological intimidation is glorified. Some teachers defend their actions by stating that the world is a difficult place, so they must prepare students for reality. However, the reality is that individuals are better prepared to deal with the harsh realities of the world through success and support rather than through fear and intimidation. The fact is that psychological intimidation interferes with learning and invites power struggles between individuals. Psychological intimidation creates excessive anxiety and triggers fight-or-flight responses. Neither of these is conducive to a successful classroom. Students need to be given opportunities to take risks and even to fail. They need to feel that they are entering a safe place where they will be accepted and respected. Surveys of secondary students indicate that one of the major reasons they misbehave is because they feel disrespect from the teacher.

Another dimension of psychological needs is that of self-esteem. Self-esteem is the self-portrait that individuals have in their mind, a set of subjective beliefs about their value. All individuals need to believe that they are worthy, adequate, and competent. In other words, they need a positive self-image. It is important to remember that the self-portrait that individuals have of themselves is largely learned in the "mirror of others." In other words, the feedback we receive from others helps us construct our beliefs about self. Individuals who are reared in an environment of constant criticism and intimidation will develop low self-esteem. This, in turn, will influence their feelings of security and their willingness to learn.

Because the teacher is a significant person for many students, the reactions of the teacher are especially important to students. If the teacher's reactions to students communicate low expectations or emphasize failure rather than success, they are likely to receive the message that they do not have value and are less able than others. This will, in turn, influence their motivation, task persistence, and their ultimate success. A lack of success then serves to validate their earlier beliefs that they are less able than others.

The self-esteem of individuals guides their behavior and their responses to different situations. A confident individual with positive self-esteem is likely to view a new task as a challenge. Those with low self-esteem are likely to view a new task as a threat, or something to be avoided. Individuals with a positive self-esteem have more confidence and a higher expectation of success. They are willing to persist when encountering obstacles. These are certainly attributes that we value in students.

Success is one of the most powerful motivators. It builds our self-esteem and makes us more willing to engage in an activity the next time we encounter it. Success builds our sense of adequacy and competence, a concept called "achievement motivation." Achievement motivation relates to the need we all have to feel that we are growing, learning, and improving. Unfortunately, some teachers and parents have the notion that failure is somehow good for students because it keeps them humble and motivates them to do better. However, strong doses of success are needed in order for individuals to overcome failure and learn from their mistakes. The best way to prepare for the frustrations of life is through numerous successful experiences. Remember that all individuals, especially those who have not been successful in the school environment, have self-esteem needs. If these needs are not met in productive ways, they may substitute other goals that can be detrimental to a productive classroom. For example, can you remember how some students may have satisfied their self-esteem needs by always challenging the authority of the teacher or being perceived as the "toughest" student in school? It would be much more productive to build a positive self-esteem for accomplishing worthwhile education goals so that students will not feel the need to engage in the pursuit of unproductive ones.

Social Needs. As stated earlier in the chapter, classrooms are social settings and students have social goals. A considerable amount of student behavior can be explained in relationship to social goals. One of the most important dimensions of the social setting is the peer group. Peer group norms and sanctions are powerful influences. Classrooms will run much smoother and have fewer problems if teachers attend to the social needs in the classroom. Social needs include the need to belong, the need for affection, the need for fun, and the need for social interaction.

Driekurs (1968) identified the need to belong as one of the most basic and powerful social needs. This is especially the case during the adolescent years. Fewer things are more important during this stage of development than belonging to a peer group. Students will go to great lengths in order to be accepted by a peer group. This need helps explain gang membership. Many adolescents join gangs because they want to belong. Often these are students who have had trouble being accepted in other groups. If individuals have trouble gaining acceptance in positive and constructive groups, they often seek membership in more dangerous and less socially acceptable groups.

Albert (1996) notes that understanding student behavior requires an understanding of their goals. Four goals are identified that help explain student behavior. Those goals are attention seeking, power seeking, revenge seeking, and failure avoidance. If students are unable to gain attention through acceptable and constructive means, they may seek attention through unacceptable behavior. Students with high attention needs find it more acceptable to be reprimanded than to be ignored.

Individuals who are unable to gain a feeling of power and control through acceptable channels may seek to meet their power needs through unacceptable actions. Challenging the authority of teachers and continually questioning the teachers, the value of assignments, and teacher motivations and abilities are often characteristics of power-seeking students. Others may attempt to demonstrate their power by being assertive and attempting to dominate other students. If this continues, it may lead to bullying.

When individuals become extremely frustrated in gaining attention and power, they begin to believe that everyone is against them and revenge becomes their goal. When this is their goal, they are reinforced when others are hurt or feel pain. Because they are convinced that everyone is against them, they behave in ways that provoke and frustrate others. They then take these reactions as confirmation that the world is against them. Fewer situations are more frustrating for teachers than having students in the classroom with revenge as their goal. Although the sources of the feelings of revenge are related to factors outside the classroom, teachers are good targets and often experience the consequences of the actions of revenge-seeking students. Revenge-seeking students are in psychological trouble and often need the assistance of someone other than the teacher.

Other students who become frustrated in meeting social goals might seek failure avoidance by withdrawing. These students feel defeated and hopeless. Their goal is to be left alone. Students who have failure avoidance as a goal are often not disruptive; they simply will not try. Although it is easier to ignore the failure-avoidance students, they are at great risk and need help. Teachers should not give up on these students. The challenge is to find some places where the student can have success and begin on these success experiences.

Another important social need is the need for love and affection. All of us need to feel that someone cares. Unfortunately, there are students who come to school feeling as if they are not loved and no one really cares. The mobility of society has broken the bonds of extended families that could communicate a sense of love and caring. Frequent moves from community to community make it more difficult to establish solid relationships with others. Many youngsters live in single-parent homes or homes where both parents must work. This means that there may be fewer opportunities to engage in those activities that make a youngster feel loved.

It can be difficult for teachers to meet the love and affection needs of students. Teachers cannot become surrogate parents, and concerns about sexual abuse have led some school districts to forbid teachers to even touch students. This means that teachers must find other ways of communicating to students that they care. There are many ways that this can be done. Taking time to talk with students, finding out what interests them, and being aware of their participation in extracurricular activities are just a few suggestions. Communicating a caring attitude is revealed in what one middle grade student wrote about her favorite teacher: "Mr. S. was just a great teacher. He always had faith and believed in me. I know other teachers did as well but they rarely expressed it. His class (math) was one of my most difficult subjects. I worked hard all year but still had trouble. Mr. S. always said, 'You'll get 'em next time!' Mr. S. believed in me all the way! So, I owe a lot to him."

Another social need that is often overlooked in the classroom is the need for fun and enjoyment. Many of us have encountered teachers who claim that education is a serious business and it is not the role of the teacher to "entertain" students. Although there is an element of truth in this assertion, it is also true that we all seek to have some fun and enjoyment in our lives. Few of us would persist in our jobs if we never had any fun or enjoyment. Learning can also be fun, and teachers can use this need to help motivate students. This does not mean that everything in the classroom needs to be fun. Rather, introducing fun and taking time to celebrate success at appropriate times goes a long way in making the classroom a place where students want to be. This is especially true in high school, where faculty members have done such things as dress up in period costumes in a history course. In a high school mathematics class, student achievement improved when the teacher taught mathematics principles and formulas using rap music. In these classrooms, attendance rates soar because the students don't know what the next class will bring.

Looking for the unusual, the novel, and the entertaining aspects of the subject can help make the subject fun and interesting. In addition, setting aside some time during the week to have some fun helps make the classroom a place where students want to be. Students are more likely to persist in the difficult parts of the subject if they know there will also be opportunities for enjoyment.

In summary, keep in mind that the classroom is a social setting. However, it is also a forced social setting. The students did not choose to be in this particular group; they were assigned. Some of them may be reluctant to be in this group and some might even be fearful. It is the responsibility of the teacher to begin building a supportive social climate so that the classroom is viewed by students as a place where they want to be.

Student Interests

In addition to meeting needs, we must also explore ways to use student interests as a motivating variable. One of the rewarding parts of being a teacher is discovering the interests and talents of the students in the classroom. The interests students bring to school are unpredictable and almost always astounding. One of us once had a boy in a fourth-grade classroom who seemed unmotivated to read. Most of the students in this particular class were from low-income families who lived in a housing project. Finally, the boy was pulled aside and asked why he did not like to read. "Have you ever heard of the Greeks and the Romans?" he asked. "Well, I like to read about them but we never get to do that." This is a good example of the unpredictability of students.

Student interests can be identified by having students complete an interest survey at the beginning of the year. Taking time to talk with students and listening to their conversations can reveal a wealth of information that might be used in the classroom. One teacher made it a habit to have lunch with a few students at least once a week. This provided an opportunity to get to know the students on a personal level.

Keeping up with current trends and fads can also provide information that can be used to relate the subject to student interests. For example, a number of years ago, a social studies textbook included interviews of current rock stars and actors. Their experiences and how they had used things they learned in school in their careers was not only entertaining, but it also helped students think about the content of the curriculum in new ways.

APPLYING A BASIC MODEL OF MOTIVATION

Motivation is a complex phenomenon. New teachers are often overwhelmed as they try to sort out motivational principles and apply them to the classroom. To assist teachers in making sense of motivation in the classroom, we have developed a three-step model as a starting point. This model is based on seeking the answers to three basic questions: (a) How can I relate the content to the needs and interests of the students? (b) How can I structure the learning environment so that students are not overwhelmed by their perceptions of the effort required? and (c) How can I increase the probability of success?

Relate the Content to Student Needs and Interests

In the previous section of this chapter, we have discussed several categories of student needs and interests that can be used to motivate students. The fact that student needs and interests vary from student to student does make this dimension of the model complex. However, keep in mind that there are some general things that tend to interest students at a given age. For example, most elementary teachers can tell you that primary-grade students are frequently fascinated by prehistoric creatures such as dinosaurs, and many are often interested in sports and adventure. Many students enjoy certain video games and watch certain television programs. This can be a beginning point for relating content to student needs and interests. Ask yourself, "What is it that students at this age generally like to do?" This means that as a teacher you need to keep current on pop culture and trends even though this might not be your interest. For example, is there some way that you could relate the popularity of a program like *Survivor* to the subject? One high school has capitalized on the interest in the television program *CSI* and has developed a science class that has students exploring the scientific basis for some of the techniques used in crime scene investigations.

After beginning with these broader interests, you should then keep alert to specific interests and talents of students. Think about how individual projects of enrichment activities might be tailored to the interests of these individual students. You will be amazed at how much effort students will put into a project when it is something of interest to them.

Keep in mind that addressing the needs and interests of the students is only a beginning point. It does not guarantee that students will persist to completion and attain success. For example, every fall thousands of people who are interested in football and who need exercise sit in the stands and watch 22 individuals actively participate in the sport. Many of them would love to be on the field. Why are they content to be spectators? There are a couple of other variables that influence their decisions. First, they may perceive that it requires too much time and effort, and second, they estimate their probability of success in making the team and performing as extremely low. So, once you have considered student needs and interests, you need to consider how to present the material so that the amount of effort required is not overwhelming and all individuals believe that if they put forth effort they will attain success.

Alter Perceptions of Required Effort

You can alter perceptions of required effort by placing it in terms of cost and reward. What is the reward and is it worth the effort? Some students may perceive the reward (learning something important or getting a good grade) as worth the effort. However, even these students will look for the most efficient way of gaining the reward. If the reward is very important to them, but they think the cost is too high, they may try to change the amount of effort required by engaging in inappropriate behavior such as cheating. For some students, the goal of a good grade is not sufficiently important for them to expend their time on the task.

Altering perceptions of required effort requires attention to the rewards associated with the task. In other words, what is the payoff of task completion? However, even if the task is valued, individuals will not engage in the task if they believe the task requires a high expenditure of effort and energy. You have probably experienced this feeling the first day of a college course when you were presented with the course syllabus. When you saw the course requirements and assignments, you may have experienced panic! If it was too overwhelming, perhaps you dropped the course. However, because you had a history of school success, you probably persevered and completed the course. Think of students who have not had a history of success. Although physically dropping the course may not be an option for them, they may intellectually drop out and simply refuse to become engaged.

Perception of the effort required to complete a task is related to several variables: a clear understanding of what the task requires, the complexity of the task, and estimates of the length of the task. If the nature of the task is unclear, those students with a history of academic difficulty will usually assume that the task requires too much effort. Similarly, if individuals have a clear understanding of the task but believe that the task is very complex, they will be reluctant to commit to the task. This is also true for lengthy tasks. Most students need frequent feedback about their progress that is often missing in lengthy tasks.

Understanding these variables can help you construct a learning environment that helps alter perceptions of task difficulty. Let's think back to that college course where you were overwhelmed with the course requirements. What did you do? One of the first things you probably did was try to clarify the nature of the task. You probably asked questions of the instructor seeking clarification of the task and exactly what was expected. Then, if dropping the course was not an option, you probably tried to break the requirements into smaller steps. What would be the first thing that you would do? Where might you go for help? What resources would you need? Successful students may have established a schedule so that they would have guidance in helping decide how to allocate their time.

The same process can be applied in the classroom, except that the teacher needs to provide the guidance rather than relying on the perceptions and study skills of the students. For example, rather than presenting the requirements of a whole term to students on the first day, it makes sense to present them with a set of steps or goals. In other words, break lengthy and complex tasks into a series of smaller tasks. This is something that is referred to as *task analysis*. You analyze the task, break out smaller steps, sequence the steps in a logical order, identify the prerequisites, and then present each step with a great deal of clarity so that the students know exactly what is expected of them. This can be accomplished by providing the students with clear learning objectives that indicate how success can be measured. Taking time to help them see how this task relates to their previous knowledge can also help them perceive that they do possess the necessary knowledge and skill to be successful.

Modeling is another step in making sure that students have a clear perception of the effort required. When students see the task performed and have a model of a completed task, they are more likely to arrive at a realistic assessment of what is required of them. However, make sure that the model is not so complex that it discourages students.

Once the students engage in the task, they need to be presented with feedback and encouragement. The feedback needs to be concrete and specific, including an affirmation of what they are doing correctly as well as correction for those dimensions of the task that are not being done correctly. This helps inform the students that their efforts are paying off and they are making progress toward the goal.

Increase the Probability of Success

Success is highly motivating. We all have a need for a feeling of competence and growth. Individuals are drawn to activities where they believe there is a high probability of success. This meets their needs for competence, attention, and power. Motivating students in the classroom means that students need to believe that there is a high probability of success if they engage in the learning activities. This does not mean that everything must be easy. Challenges that require little or no effort do not meet achievement needs.

Remember that there is a difference between challenge and threats. Individuals are challenged when they are faced with a task where they believe they can be successful. They are threatened when faced with a task where they believe there is no opportunity for success. The difficulty is that challenges and threats exist within the student, not the teacher. Teachers may think they are challenging students, when in reality they are threatening them. Threat increases anxiety and promotes task avoidance rather than effort. Few of us will expend time and energy on something where we believe there is no opportunity for success.

The majority of students believe that achieving success in school is important. However, many have been so unsuccessful they have quit trying. For example, young students maintain high expectations for success even when they face repeated failure. However, older students do not (Ames, 1990). Older students have developed a negative self-image that leads to low estimates of the probability of success and therefore expend less effort than younger students, who are still positive about themselves and their ability to achieve success.

To consider how students might feel and respond to threat, consider for a moment how you would feel if you were being forced every morning to go to a place where you had no chance of success. You would soon be discouraged and angry. You might have a knot in your stomach every morning and even develop headaches or other physical symptoms. When actually in the threatening environment, you would probably either strike out at the cause of the feelings of failure or withdraw from the situation. You might even try to share your feelings of frustration and anger by making sure others, especially teachers, also experience failure. Unfortunately, this is exactly what can be observed in many classrooms. The important question is how can we begin to change a sense of hopelessness to a sense of hopefulness? An important component is changing the self-concept of the students so that they believe they are capable and, with some effort, they can achieve success.

Increasing the probability of success can be accomplished in several ways. The first step involves diagnosing current ability levels and presenting tasks to students that build on their prior knowledge. This may mean returning to content that was taught in a previous grade.

Another step is to break complex tasks down into small steps and then provide reinforcement when the student is successful at each step.

Overreliance on competition may also frustrate students and cause them to have a low estimate of the probability of success. If they believe they must compete against students with a history of success, they may perceive that it is a waste of

Table 3.2   Apply Motivation Throughout the Lesson

Motivation is not something that is best done at the beginning of a lesson and then forgotten. Rather, attention to motivation needs to occur at different points of a lesson or learning sequence.

Motivational Variables in Lesson or Learning Sequence		
Beginning	*During*	*At Completion*
To get students started learning:	**To enhance task persistence and keep students interested:**	**To develop students' sense of competence and success:**
• Appeal to the curiosity of students • Relate the new learning to previous achievement • Break longer learning tasks into segments so that the perceived effort required is reasonable • Allow students some freedom and choice in what they will do to meet objectives	• Provide models of successful performance • Reinforce student effort and progress • Diagnose difficulties and help students correct problems • Change activities and student involvement; use grouping and cooperative learning • Keep a relatively brisk pace but one where there is a high degree of success	• Celebrate success • Help students relate success to their efforts • Identify how the task relates to their interests and curiosities • Identify new questions or curiosities that arise as a result of completion of the task

time to even try. It is better to reduce the competition between students and help them establish realistic goals and benchmarks for success.

When teachers help students perceive that they can be successful if they put forth some effort, the rewards can be very satisfying. Students want to be successful, and if they believe that they can and that the teacher is interested in helping them achieve success, it is contrary to the best interests of the student to disrupt that classroom. Many behavior problems just seem to disappear. Table 3.2 provides suggestions for motivational activities throughout the learning sequence.

REVIEW OF MAIN IDEAS

1. Motivation is a key variable in establishing a successful classroom with attentive students and few discipline problems.

2. Student motivation does not just happen in the classroom. It requires the effort and attention of the teacher. The role of the teacher is that of discovering, directing, and sustaining student motivation.

3. There are two basic types of motivation: Extrinsic motivation comes from forces outside the student, and intrinsic motivation comes from within. Extrinsic motivation is often used in classrooms, and it does have value. However, there are limitations to extrinsic motivation and effort needs to be directed toward using intrinsic motivation.

4. Motivation is a complex phenomenon that has some personal dimensions such as the goal orientation, the needs, the wants, and the previous history of a given student.

5. An important step in school motivation is that of increasing the perceived value of learning goals. Students need to understand why achieving an academic goal is important and how it relates to their needs and interests.

6. Students are attempting to meet three basic needs: physiological needs, psychological needs, and social needs.

7. A model that can be useful for teachers as they plan for motivation in the classroom is to (a) relate course content to the needs and interests of the students, (b) alter student perceptions of the effort required of them, and (c) increase students' perceived probability of success.

APPLICATION AND ENRICHMENT

1. Visit a classroom and observe the students. What percentage of the students appear to be interested in the lesson? What do you think accounts for the interest or lack of interest?

2. Observe a teacher during a lesson. What does the teacher do to enhance student motivation at the beginning of a learning sequence? What does the teacher do during the learning sequence? What is done at the end of a learning sequence?

3. Survey students at an age that interests you. Ask the following questions:
   - What are the things in school and out of school that they find interesting and fun?
   - What do they do with their time when given a choice?
   - How do they view themselves as students?
   - What percentage of the time do they feel they can be successful in school?
   - Do they think the teacher expects them to be successful?
   - What do they think would make the classroom/school a better place to learn?

4. Identify a topic or subject of interest to you. Brainstorm some motivational variables that you might use to enhance student motivation. How might you appeal to student curiosity? What dimensions of your topic do you think students would find interesting? What might be some creative ideas for getting students more interested in the subject?

REFERENCES

Albert, L. (1996). *Cooperative discipline.* Circle Pines, MN: American Guidance Service.

Ames, C. A. (1990). Motivation: What teachers need to know. *Teachers College Record, 91*(3), 409–421.

Driekurs, R. (1968). *Psychology in the classroom* (2nd ed.). New York: Harper & Row.

Glaser, W. (1986). *Control theory in the classroom.* New York: Harper & Row.

Good, T., & Brophy, J. (2003). *Looking in classrooms.* New York: Longmans.

Mental Health in Schools Center. (2002, Winter). Addressing barriers to learning (University of California at Los Angeles, School Mental Health Project). *Newsletter, 7*(1).

Schauss, A. (1985, Winter). Research links nutrition to behavior disorders. *School Safety,* pp. 20–28.

Slavin, R. E. (2005). *Educational psychology: Theory and practice* (8th ed.). Boston: Allyn & Bacon.

Wentzel, K. R. (2006). A social motivation perspective for classroom management. In C. M. Evertson & C. S. Weinstein, *Handbook of classroom management: Research, practice and contemporary issues* (pp. 619–643). Mahwah, NJ: Lawrence Erlbaum.

Chapter 4

MANAGING THE LEARNING ENVIRONMENT

CLASSROOM SCENARIO

The final bell indicating the start of another school day had rung, and students were slowly filtering into the classroom. They stopped and talked with friends on their way to their desks. Meanwhile, the teacher, Ms. Johnson, was trying to get the attention of the students and take attendance. Finally all the students were in their seats, and she began to call the roll. The teacher then called for everyone to turn in his or her homework from yesterday. Amid much grumbling, students started digging papers out of their backpacks. Ms. Johnson collected the homework papers and instructed the students to take out their books. Again, there was considerable shuffling and several student complaints: "I forgot to bring my book." "I didn't have time to go get it before class."

Finally, all the students were in their seats with the needed material. The school day was only 15 minutes old, and already Ms. Johnson felt tired!

CHAPTER OBJECTIVES

After completing this chapter you should be able to:

- Identify the ways the physical environment impacts behavior
- Define behavioral settings

- List elements of the spatial environment that need to be considered in planning the learning environment
- Define the action zone and how it relates to management and discipline
- State dimensions of the classroom ambiance that need to be addressed
- Define different types of classroom time
- List predictable and recurring events where routines need to be created
- State a procedure for providing assistance to students

We define *management* as those actions taken to create an environment that makes it possible for teachers to teach and students to learn. This means creating a supportive, inclusive, and nonthreatening environment. Well-managed classrooms promote learning and prevent many disruptions. Poorly managed classrooms create uncertainty and conflict and reduce student opportunities to learn. Reviews of research have explored the connection between good management and academic learning (Brophy, 2006; Carter & Doyle, 2006; Gettinger & Kohler, 2006).

However, we must also remember that the goal is for students to develop self-control and the acceptance of responsibility. This means that the process of classroom management is one that engages and involves the students rather than one that reduces their opportunities for participation. The management style of the teacher is a key ingredient in building teaching authority and respect.

The management dimensions that will be discussed in this chapter begin with a focus on the physical environment. Every activity is shaped by the physical environment. Some influences are very obvious, whereas others are quite subtle. Even though teachers are limited by classroom assignment and number of students, they can take a variety of actions to create a positive learning environment regardless of the space that is assigned.

Another main focus in this chapter is on managing classroom events. Teachers can identify recurring events and activities that occur in any classroom. These events and activities vary by grade level. For example, early elementary teachers may use learning centers so that much of the learning involves students working individually or in groups. They then come together as a group, often on a rug, and spend a relatively brief time as a whole group. As the grade level increases, more and more of the activities involve whole-group work with students sitting at a desk for most if not all of the assigned time. These different activity structures must be handled with routines and procedures that allow students to quickly engage in the learning opportunities presented to them.

A major component of the chapter will be methods for establishing procedures and routines that will help simplify the environment and help students make choices and decisions.

DIMENSIONS OF THE PHYSICAL ENVIRONMENT

The Spatial Dimension

Several aspects of the physical environment need to be considered. One of the most important aspects is the spatial dimension—the size, shape, and organization of objects within the space.

The size and shape of the room, the location of doors and windows, and the movement of individuals within that space combine to form the spatial dimension of a classroom. This dimension creates the setting where activities will take place, and the setting influences the types of activities that are possible as well as the behavior of those engaged in them.

Behavioral Settings

A key concept in understanding the impact of the spatial dimension on behavior is that of *behavioral settings* (Carter & Doyle, 2006). The concept of a behavioral setting refers to environments that are designed to influence the behaviors or actions of those who occupy the setting. For example, places of worship use elements of the physical environment such as seating, lighting, symbols, and color to create a setting that communicates to all who enter the space certain behavioral expectations. Classrooms likewise need to be considered as behavioral settings. The arrangement of the space, including furniture and bulletin boards, should communicate to all who enter what will be expected of them while they occupy the space.

Think about your first impressions when you enter a classroom. What are the impressions that you form regarding what will be happening in the classroom and what the expectations will be for your behavior? Does the space indicate the types of activities that are likely to occur and what type of participation is expected? Does the space communicate a sense of excitement and interest or a sense of boredom?

Developing a behavioral setting consistent with your purposes requires attention to several elements of the physical environment. This involves teaching stations, learning stations, student desks, teacher's desk, location of instructional materials, and classroom displays and decorations. Because a classroom is a behavioral setting, it is important for teachers to ask, "What types of behaviors do I want the students to exhibit? Do I want to excite students or calm them down? Do I want to encourage or discourage social interaction?" Once teachers are clear about the answers to such questions, they can consider how the environment needs to be changed in order to create the setting that will elicit the desired behaviors. Teachers who design very informal classrooms should not be surprised when students behave informally. Similarly, teachers who design very stiff and formal classrooms should not be surprised when students lack spontaneity.

A beginning point in arranging the spatial environment is to consider how the physical elements need to be arranged in order to promote behavior consistent with your goals and purposes. This means that you need to reflect on your goals and purposes and the nature of the students. You may need to change the physical environment at different times of the year as you address different instructional and student needs. For example, at the beginning of a new school year, your basic goal might be to first establish order in the classroom and diagnose student learning. Therefore, the original environment might deemphasize group work and student interaction. As you establish procedures and understand the nature of the group of students, you may then change the environment to emphasize more student interaction and group work.

Teachers who wish to create behavioral settings where creativity is promoted can use bright colors, a variety of objects to provide sensory stimulation, and bulletin boards that pose questions rather than give information. Teachers concerned with decreasing student activity can use softer colors, plan bulletin boards that are calming rather than stimulating, soften the lighting, and create a very orderly classroom appearance.

Arranging Student Desks

The arrangement of the desks provides the major setting, or "frame," that shapes teacher–student interaction and the behavior of students (Rosenfield, Lambert, & Black, 1985). Because different arrangements influence behavior in different ways, there is no best way to arrange desks. Instead, consider the teaching approach you use, the type of interaction you desire, the student characteristics, and your ability to maintain classroom control.

Weinstein (1979) explored the impact of seating arrangements on student behavior. In a second-grade classroom, a teacher and a researcher worked together and identified a number of behavioral problems. In an attempt to solve the problems, the seating arrangements were then systematically changed. The result was a statistically significant decrease in the number of behavioral problems.

Other studies found that the participation of high school and college students in classroom discussions was influenced by seating arrangement (Becker, 1981). Weinstein (1979) also found that seating position influenced student attitudes toward the class and toward the teacher. In summary, it appears that attending to seating arrangements can have an important payoff by influencing student behavior, classroom participation, and student attitudes.

The three basic seating arrangements most commonly used in classrooms are rows, clusters, and circular or semicircular patterns. There are advantages and disadvantages to each. A typical arrangement of the physical environment of many classrooms is that of student desks arranged in rows facing the front of the classroom. This arrangement communicates that the major task of the students will be that of listening and working independently.

When desks are arranged in rows all facing in one direction, student interaction with each other is limited, listening is enhanced, and independent work is facilitated. Many teachers find that the row arrangement is easier for them to monitor and helps establish and maintain classroom control. Weinstein (1979) cites studies indicating that desk organization that limits student-to-student interaction leads to higher on-task behavior, less off-task movement, and less disruptive talk. However, when participation in a discussion was used as a criterion, those seated in rows had higher incidents of withdrawal and more off-task verbal comments. If your teaching approach will be primarily direct instruction, you want students to work independently, and you are concerned about your ability to promote on-task behavior, arrangement of desks in rows would be the best choice. This arrangement would require more movement and monitoring in order to keep students alert and focused.

Teacher movement keeps students on task.

© Photodisc

Rosenfield et al. (1985) cite the advantages of the circular arrangement. In fifth- and sixth-grade classrooms, they found that a circular pattern increased student comments related to the content and that students had increased attending behavior. They also found higher incidents of out-of-turn responses by students seated in a circle. This may indicate more student spontaneity when they are arranged in this format. If your primary mode of teaching will be class discussion, you are not concerned about students speaking out of turn, and you want to increase student attending and verbal participation, a circular pattern would be the best choice.

Students seated in cluster arrangements demonstrated more ordered turns while still maintaining a high percentage of on-task verbal behaviors. Clustered arrangements are most commonly used in cooperative learning. If your mode of instruction is cooperative learning, then clustering students into small groups would be the most appropriate arrangement.

Some authorities recommend that you begin the school year with desks in rows facing the major instructional areas and then move to other desk arrangements after you have established control of the classroom (Emmer, Evertson, Sanford, Clements, & Worsham, 2000). This prevents discipline problems during the critical beginning phases of the school year. This suggestion has a great deal of merit if you are insecure and are concerned about your ability to control the classroom. Once your confidence grows, you may use less traditional arrangements.

Student self-control is another factor to consider when arranging seating. Those students who have a high degree of self-control might be grouped into clusters for a large portion of the day. Such students are able to overcome the distractions of others seated near them and can resist the temptation to socialize at inappropriate times. However, those students who lack self-control should be arranged in rows so that the possibilities of social interaction are limited. As they develop self-control and learn to participate in discussions and cooperative learning groups, then the arrangement might be gradually changed to more of a circular or cluster arrangement.

In summary, the arrangement of the student desks needs to be related to your goals and objectives and the instructional modes that you use most frequently.

Student Density

One consideration when arranging student desks and workspaces relates to the issue of student density. Student density refers to the number of individuals who occupy a given space. Whereas many individuals worry about the teacher–student ratio, and that is important, another concern that is often overlooked is the issue of overcrowded classrooms, or classrooms that have a high density. Most teachers will indicate that it seems much more difficult and more tiring to teach in over-crowded classrooms. There have been some studies that support these conclusions. Students in crowded classrooms demonstrate more aggression and deviant behav-ior and are less attentive (Probansky & Fabian, 1987). This might be explained by the perception of students that their personal space is being invaded and they are being threatened.

Density does have a cultural dimension. Individuals from certain cultures and environments are able to tolerate more people in a space without feeling that it is overcrowded. However, other individuals seem to develop anxiety with moder-ately low levels of density. The important concern for the teacher is not to have some prescribed formula, but to watch for signs that students are becoming anxious and stressed because of the density of the classroom.

Several factors explain the impact of density on student and teacher behavior. High-density classrooms decrease the amount of privacy for students and increase opportunities for social interaction. These two factors may then result in anxiety and interpersonal conflict. High-density classrooms also create competition for the attention of the teacher. Students who have high attention needs may feel they have to misbehave in order to attract attention. The loss of opportunities to inter-act with the teacher may also be a factor influencing student achievement in high-density classrooms.

Lowering the density of individuals in a given space may not always be desir-able. Placing more individuals into a smaller space will increase the interaction among individuals. Therefore, higher densities are desirable when the task to be completed requires communication and cooperation among students. Activities such as cooperative learning and small-group work are then enhanced.

Although it may be difficult for you to change the density of students in your classroom, you need to realize that too many students in a given space will lead to problems. Increased aggression and anxiety are a couple of indicators that students may feel crowded and that someone is invading their personal space. These prob-lems may not be related to your skill as a teacher but are simply artifacts of the sit-uation. If you find yourself in this situation, you may want to consider if there are ways you can create feelings of decreased density. Perhaps you can move some objects, such as file cabinets or your desk, from the room in order to reduce the feeling of crowdedness. You may need to sacrifice small-group work areas in order to spread out student desks so they do not feel crowded.

Overcrowded classrooms with little sensory stimulation create off-task behavior.

© Photodisc

Action Zone

Researchers have defined the action zone as that spot in the classroom where students are most attentive and involved in classroom interactions (Adams & Biddle, 1970). The action zone usually consists of those seats nearest the basic teaching position. If the primary teaching position of the teacher is at the front of the classroom, the action zone is those seats that form a "T" across the front of the classroom and down the center. Those students sitting in this area tend to participate in the class more, stay on task longer, have higher achievement, and develop more positive attitudes toward the class. What could explain these findings? One possible explanation is that better students tend to choose these locations. There is some validity to this contention. Dykman and Reis (1979) found that the students who choose to sit on the periphery of the classroom generally feel more threatened and exhibit lower self-esteem than those who sit in the action zone. They suggest that students who choose to sit on the periphery want to distance themselves from the threat posed by the teacher.

However, there is some evidence that positive outcomes occur when students are assigned seats in the action zone. Dykman and Reis (1979) offer a partial explanation for this finding. Because students with lower self-esteem often find the teacher threatening, they tend to choose seats most distant from the teacher. The result is they are called upon less frequently, their progress receives less teacher monitoring, and they are generally less involved in the classroom. This condition leads to less success. However, when they are assigned seats in the action zone, they are monitored more closely, they are called upon more frequently, and they have opportunities to interact more with the teacher. These conditions contribute to increased success.

Knowledge of the action zone is useful in constructing the physical environment. One application is to arrange the seating so those students with academic and behavioral difficulties are placed in the action zone. Moving students into this area will increase the amount of time they spend on task, allow them to receive more constructive feedback, and result in their higher feelings of academic competence.

Because the action zone is defined in reference to the location of the teacher, the location of the action zone depends on your location when instructing the class. The action zone can be changed by changing the teaching station. Therefore, teaching from different spots in the classroom expands the number of students that are included in the action zone.

Some teachers prefer to allow students the opportunity, at least at the beginning of the year, to choose their own seats. This practice does have merit. Smith (1987) found in a study of student achievement that gains were greater in classes where students were allowed to choose their own seats. The security and comfort of choosing one's location in the classroom may well create a more positive climate where students feel more comfortable and are more open to instruction. A variation of this approach would be to allow students to initially choose their own seats. Those few students who experience difficulty might then be gradually and unobtrusively moved into the action zone.

Teacher Proximity

The idea of an action zone emphasizes the importance of teacher proximity to students. Other studies also indicate the importance of the teacher remaining as close to students as possible. For example, Weinstein (1979) found that grades decrease as a student is seated farther away from the teacher. In addition, student participation and positive student attitudes decline as the distance between the teacher and students increases (Smith, 1987). What could explain these findings? It may be that teachers have more difficulty monitoring the work of students who are seated farther away from them. This lack of monitoring does not provide students with the immediate feedback they might need to increase their understanding and therefore improve their grades. The distance factor may also contribute to a lack of teacher–student contact that could contribute to positive interpersonal interactions and feelings. Students do tend to stay on task when the teacher is physically closer, and this increased learning time could also translate into higher achievement and grades and therefore more positive feelings.

These findings emphasize that it is important for you to be as close as possible to the largest number of students for the greatest amount of time. How can this be accomplished? One technique would be to increase the number of students who are seated in the front of the class. Look at the physical dimensions of the classroom. If the space is rectangular, choose a primary teaching station on one of the long sides so that you will have more rows with fewer students. This will allow you closer contact with those students across the front and will reduce the space between you and those seated in the back row. Another technique would be to place your desk in a location that is near the largest number of students. Do not isolate the desk in some far corner of the classroom. One suggestion is to have a primary teaching station on one side of the classroom and the teacher's desk on the opposite side. This maximizes teacher proximity to the greatest number of students by increasing teacher presence in two different areas of the classroom.

Teacher proximity can also be increased by attending to the traffic patterns and movement around the classroom. Regardless of the seating arrangement, the traffic patterns should make it easy for the teacher to get to any part of the classroom quickly and easily. If movement is restricted, it is likely that the teacher will not get to all the students.

Traffic Patterns

Traffic patterns in the classroom are very important. Students need to be able to enter and exit the classroom quickly, they need to have easy access to materials, and they need to be able to move about without disturbing others. High traffic areas need to have plenty of space and be kept free of obstructions. Teacher movement is important in order to monitor student work and behavior. Therefore, the room arrangement should allow the teacher easy access to all learners. The best designs allow for easy access to all students.

The Teacher's Desk

Although the placement of the teacher's desk is often given little thought, it is an important consideration in the arrangement of physical space. It often impacts teacher behavior in some subtle ways and influences the traffic pattern. It is often a spot of high-frequency use. A traditional location for the teacher's desk has been in the front of the classroom. Most classrooms still have the desk front and center. The teacher often teaches from the desk and sits at the desk while students are working, and students go to this location when they need assistance. However, the traditional front-and-center location may not be the best arrangement. A better spot for the teacher's desk is in a less dominant and obtrusive spot, preferably in a corner or near the rear of the room (Weinstein, 1979).

There are several reasons for this recommendation. As stated above, the desk often becomes a focal point for many classroom activities. If the desk is at the front of the room, any activity at the desk is easily observable and can be distracting to everyone in the classroom. Therefore, rather than staying on task, students are watching what is happening around the teacher's desk. In addition, they can easily watch the teacher and determine when it is "safe" to go off task or engage in other activities. When placed near the rear of the classroom, students must turn around to observe what the teacher is doing. A teacher that is a keen observer can easily note those students who are going off task and take corrective action.

Placing the desk at the front of the room also makes it convenient as a teaching station. This prompts the bad habit of directing all activities from the desk and cuts down on the amount of movement of the teacher around the room. Some well-meaning teachers even succumb to the temptation to teach while sitting at the desk. This communicates a lack of enthusiasm for the subject as well as limits the ability of the teacher to monitor student progress and adjust in order to keep all students engaged. There is evidence that teaching from behind the teacher's desk results in more off-task behavior and lower positive student attitudes toward the teacher (Smith, 1987).

Placing the teacher's desk in an unobtrusive spot also allows the teacher the opportunity to conduct conferences with students with a little more privacy. The conference does not become a central focus of the class, and any potential embarrassment related to being in the front of the entire class is reduced. If the conference is related to discipline matters, the need for the student to save face in front of the rest of the class is reduced.

Teacher Movement

When designing the physical environment, it is important to consider how the teacher will move throughout the space. Unfortunately, some teachers develop poor habits of moving only to certain parts of the classroom and interacting with only a few of the students. Poorly designed classroom environments will hinder teacher movement and can interfere with the learning of all students.

When designing the physical space, it is useful to design the space so that the teacher can be next to any desk in the classroom in a matter of seconds. This is important for a couple of reasons. The first reason is that when there is a problem, it is important for the teacher to get to the area immediately and deal with the problem before it spreads or becomes a major incident. Second, it is better to keep the students in their desks and go to them to provide assistance than to have them leave their desks and crowd around the teacher's desk. Ease of access to all students helps the teacher provide assistance quickly and unobtrusively.

Activity Boundaries

Another important aspect of the arrangement of physical space is the identification of space and boundaries for different types of activities. Identifying activity boundaries is more important in an elementary classroom, where students inhabit the same space for many different types of activities. However, secondary teachers should also consider arranging space to allow for different activities such as independent study, group work, small-group discussion, and the use of technology.

Identifying boundaries for different activities helps provide students with a sense of security and assists them in maintaining self-control. Clearly delineated boundaries serve as reminders of the types of behavior appropriate in different areas of the room and for different activities. Bookcases and file cabinets are especially useful for this purpose and can be used to change the shape of the physical environment, for example, to separate small-group work areas, learning centers, and independent work areas from large-group instruction.

In addition, changing the shape of the classroom serves to promote sensory stimulation by making the room different from others. Students tend to get bored when every classroom is the same size, the same shape, and organized in rows facing in the same direction. Care should be taken, however, that boundaries do not interfere with the ability of the teacher to monitor quickly all areas of the classroom. The placement of visual barriers so that student behavior cannot be quickly and quietly observed creates a condition that invites misbehavior.

In summary, the physical environment of a classroom does influence student and teacher behavior. The design of the space makes some activities possible and eliminates others. The basic principle to organizing space is that the organization should be related to the purposes of the teacher (Carter & Doyle, 2006).

THE CLASSROOM AMBIANCE

Ambiance refers to the feelings that an individual gets when entering a place. An environment might communicate a feeling of excitement, a sense of quiet and peace, or chaos and threat. The ambiance of a place is created through light, sound, texture, color, temperature, and order. The ambiance of classrooms and classroom decor has been the subject of considerable debate. Some teachers argue that the environment is of minor importance and it is not their role to be a decorator. Other teachers believe that the room environment does impact student attitudes and that it is important to have a pleasant environment. The basic issue, however, is not the creation of beautiful environments but, rather, how the environment impacts the behavior and learning of those who must occupy the space.

I'm a Teacher, Not a Decorator!

Some teachers complain that it is not their role to decorate the classroom. They see this as wasted time that is better spent preparing lessons. Secondary teachers often view decorating the classroom as something more suitable for elementary classrooms. In addition, these teachers point out that attractiveness is in the eye of the beholder and what might be termed as attractive or creative by one person may be unattractive to others.

What do you think?

- What is the proper role of a teacher in decorating a classroom?

- What basic principles should apply to decorating a classroom?

- Does the physical arrangement of a classroom and its attractiveness influence your behavior?

Studies have indicated that well-ordered environments do influence behavior in positive ways. For example, Weinstein and Mignano (1993) found that pleasant and comfortable environments increase task persistence and have a positive effect on group cohesion, class participation, and attendance. On the other hand, individuals in "ugly" environments report increased headaches, fatigue, discomfort, and conflict among students. The environment also appears to impact teacher attitudes and behaviors. The number of teacher control statements increases as the quality of the classroom environment decreases (Weinstein & Mignano, 1993).

These findings support the idea that time spent creating a pleasant classroom ambiance does have payoffs. A pleasant environment will help develop positive attitudes on the part of both students and teachers, and will increase on-task behavior and learning.

Softening the Environment

One way to create a more positive ambiance in the classroom is to soften the environment. Many classrooms are quite "hard" environments, with hard walls and floors, harsh lighting, and a lack of color. Hard environments tend to be very "cold" and informal. They do not create a feeling of comfort or a place where individuals want to be. Some of us learned this when we first attended college and found ourselves assigned a dormitory room that seemed to prompt us to spend as much time as possible outside the room. We learned that there were some things we could do to make the space more comfortable. Studies of high school and college students indicate better attendance, more student participation, and higher student evaluations of the teacher in rooms where the environment was classified as soft rather than hard. In recent years, the impact of the environment on learning has been recognized and more classrooms are being built that do include carpeting and flexible lighting.

Several relatively simple things can be done to soften an environment. For example, simply adding a few plants to an environment can have an immediate impact. Other actions include adding decorations to the walls, adding some pieces of carpet to the floor, and creating more flexible lighting.

If you find yourself in a classroom that is cold and hard, consider adding some live plants at visible locations. Look at the walls and consider if you could hang some wall decorations such as a tapestry or some colorful posters related to the content the students will be studying. If the room allows for a corner where students can retreat to read, consider placing a floor lamp in the corner where you can turn off the harsh overhead light and use the warmer light of the floor lamp. If possible, a couple of small rugs might be placed at strategic locations to break up the effect of hard flooring. (Note: Take care to ensure that these are safely anchored to hard floors!)

All of these little touches will serve to make the room softer and more appealing to students. You may be surprised at the impact such changes have on student behavior. Elementary teachers often find it is easier than secondary teachers to soften the environment. However, secondary teachers who spend a little effort on softening the environment will find that it is time well spent.

Background Music

Another feature of classroom ambiance is sound. Sound has long been used in business and industry to influence behavior. Stores often play music designed to lift spirits and increase buying, and elevators have soft music designed to comfort and lower anxiety. The impact of sound also applies to classroom settings, and the use of background music can be helpful in creating a positive ambiance that increases student task persistence and productivity. For example, soft background music used when students are working independently helps mask intruding sounds and lower student anxiety.

A problem with music is that not everyone enjoys the same type of music. Music that might be stimulating to one individual might be irritating to another. Therefore, a teacher needs to understand the students in the classroom and their likes and dislikes.

In summary, you need to create a classroom ambiance that is businesslike yet warm and inviting. Students should enter the room with a clear understanding that they will be expected to learn. However, they also need to feel welcome and that they are in a warm and safe space. Use Table 4.1 to help you plan your physical environment. This table can help you think about those areas that are most important.

Table 4.1 Checklist for Organizing the Physical Environment

Physical Dimension	*Addressed*	*Not Addressed*
Arrange student desks to facilitate major instructional activity.		
Decide placement of teacher's desk.		
Identify major teaching stations.		
Provide easy access to all student desks.		
Free high-traffic areas of obstructions.		
Identify space and boundaries for different learning activities.		
Create ambiance that is businesslike, yet warm and inviting.		
Soften harsh environment with plants, wall decorations.		
Create sensory stimulation with wall decorations.		

MANAGING CLASSROOM TIME

Teachers never seem to have enough time. Most teachers complain that there is simply not enough time in the average school day and school year to accomplish all that needs to be done. Teachers often complain that contemporary demands such as completing paperwork leave them little time for teaching.

Time is a very important variable. Research has consistently indicated that student achievement is directly related to the concept *opportunity to learn* (Good & Brophy, 2003). Opportunity to learn is defined as providing the students with sufficient time to learn the instructional objectives. This only makes common sense. We cannot be expected to learn something unless time is set aside to work on it!

International comparisons of schools have revealed that, on the average, the United States has a shorter academic year than many other nations. As a result, some policymakers have proposed extending the academic calendar so that there are more days. Although this might be a valid proposal, a more immediate response is to consider how to better use the time that is available.

Studies have consistently discovered that there is a considerable amount of time in the average day when instructional time is lost. Managing time effectively is an important step in increasing learning time and in creating opportunities to learn. For example, let's suppose that by improving time management, you are able to claim 5 more minutes every day for instructional time. If we multiply these 5 minutes by the typical 180-day academic year, this would add the equivalent of 15 hours of instructional time to the year! In a typical secondary classroom meeting 50 minutes a day, this would be the equivalent of adding 18 more class periods! In the typical elementary self-contained classroom, this would be the equivalent of adding 3 full days!

Time management is not only important in improving student achievement; it is also an important element in preventing discipline problems. For example, when interviewing experienced teachers who have few discipline problems, it is common for them to state that they keep the students so busy that they do not have time to misbehave. There is a great deal of truth to this statement. Successful teachers are those who manage time effectively and keep a high number of students engaged in the lesson.

Defining Classroom Time

Understanding where time might be lost in the classroom begins with understanding how instructional time can be defined. Three different types of time can be identified: allocated time, engaged time, and academic learning time.

Allocated Time

Allocated time is probably most familiar. It refers to the amount of time that is allocated to teach the class. In a secondary classroom, 50 minutes a day might be allocated to teach a given class. Secondary teachers probably have little control over how much time is allocated for teaching their subject within a school day. Elementary teachers, however, usually have more discretion on how time is allocated. They are normally teaching in self-contained classrooms where they have to decide how to allocate time for the entire school day. However, the important decision those teachers must make, whether they are elementary or secondary, is how much time to allocate in order to teach a given concept or skill. These time allocation decisions vary from teacher to teacher. One teacher may allocate 30 minutes of the school day to teach a concept, and another might allocate an hour. Time allocation decisions should take into account the prior knowledge of the students, their interests and motivations, and the learning approach that is used. However, there is some evidence that teachers tend to make time allocation decisions based more on their interests and preferences than on student needs. For example, elementary teachers who are more interested and feel more competent in reading tend to allocate more time to reading and less time to other subjects such as mathematics. Good and Brophy (2003) discovered that elementary teachers who enjoyed mathematics allocated as much as 50% more time to teaching mathematics. Social studies teachers who like a particular historical era generally allocate more time to teaching about that era than about other time periods. A science teacher that enjoys lectures may allocate more time to whole lectures and less time to lab work. The important consideration when making time allocation decisions is to consider whether or not students are being provided an "opportunity to learn" the important content of the subject.

Although it is natural for someone to spend more time on something they find interesting, teachers need to remember that they have a professional obligation to teach the content they are assigned to teach. Furthermore, a problem arises when the students do not share the enthusiasm of their teacher. They may become bored if too much time is being allocated to content that is of little interest to them.

In summary, all teachers need to review the basis for their time allocation decisions. Are they basing them on sound principles of instruction and the needs of the students, or are they basing them more on the interests of the teacher?

Engaged Time

Whereas allocated time is the first type of time that needs to be considered, a more refined definition of time that is important in promoting learning is that of engaged time. Engaged time refers to the amount of time students spend focused on the instructional objectives. Engaged time is identified by subtracting from the allocated time, the time that is spent on activities other than focusing on the objective. For example, 30 minutes might be allocated to teach a concept. However, within those 30 minutes, materials are distributed, students move into groups, discipline problems are addressed, there is an interruption for an announcement from the office, and work is collected. These activities are not activities where the student is engaged in learning the objective. The time spent on these activities is then subtracted from the allocated time to get the actual amount of time that students are engaged in learning the instructional objectives.

Calculating the engaged time as a percentage of allocated time is useful in targeting places where time is lost. Some tasks, such as taking attendance or distributing materials, are necessary. However, time can be saved by finding ways of performing these noninstructional tasks quickly and efficiently. For example, one of us once supervised a student teacher who regularly took up to 10 minutes at the beginning of each class period to return homework. By changing the method for returning corrected papers, the entire 10 minutes could be saved and added to the engaged time.

Academic Learning Time

Academic learning time refers to the amount of time the students are engaged in learning the objectives with success. For example, a student might spend 20 minutes engaged in activities focused on the objectives but does not do so with success. This student has zero academic learning time. What is important then is that when students are engaged, they are also achieving success. This is the most important definition of instructional time. However, it is also one of the most difficult to measure. It is difficult to make sure that all students in a given classroom are achieving success. Increasing academic learning time requires that teachers remain active in monitoring student progress.

In summary, the beginning point for efficiently managing time requires that teachers first consider the allocation of time that is based on the abilities and the prior knowledge of the students, then maximize the engaged time by minimizing the portion of time that is lost on activities unrelated to the objective and constantly monitor students to ensure that they are achieving success.

Establishing Classroom Routines

One way of increasing engaged time is to establishing classroom routines for predictable and recurring events. Good managers, whether in the classroom or business, learn that establishing routines for predictable events and teaching them to students or employees helps them save time and allows them to devote their energies to "the exceptions" that require immediate attention. There are quite a large number of events that occur in classrooms on a daily basis. Those events involve such activities are taking attendance, distributing materials, collecting materials, and making announcements.

Emmer, Evertson, Sanford, Clements, and Worsham (1982) conducted a series of research studies that emphasized the importance of establishing clear classroom rules and routines. They observed a number of teachers during the first of the year and kept detailed records of their observations. As a result of observations during the rest of the year, they labeled the teachers as either effective or ineffective managers. When they then reviewed their records from the first of the year, they noticed some important patterns. Those who became effective managers took the first couple of weeks of the school year to establish classroom rules and routines and systematically taught them to the class.

Identify Recurring Events

The first step in developing routines that help you avoid wasting time is to identify those recurring and predictable events that occur in the normal course of a day. Once these are identified, then well-defined procedures for handling them need to be developed. This is an important activity that can take place before the school year begins. The good manager establishes the routines before the students arrive in the classroom, and one of the first orders of business is to teach these routines to the students. These events can then be handled automatically without much thought. Weinstein and Mignano (1993) suggest three different categories for classifying recurring events and developing routines. One category relates to the types of predictable events related to the nonacademic events that are necessary for running the classroom. These can be labeled *administrative routines.* A second category is those predictable events that take place during instruction. Those are labeled *lesson routines.* A third type of predictable event is interactions between students. These would be labeled *interaction routines.*

Classroom routines developed for these three types of recurring events should be simple, easily understood, and quickly performed. The routines should then be taught to the class as they are needed, with a special emphasis on teaching key routines during the first few weeks of school. Although some new teachers balk at spending time during the beginning of the year teaching these routines, the time will be well spent by avoiding considerable amounts of wasted time during the rest of the school year.

Administrative routines include all of those administrative duties that are required of teachers but are not a part of the academic program. These include entering the classroom and leaving the classroom, taking attendance, making announcements, handling tardy students, doing classroom housekeeping, getting materials, sharpening pencils, and participating in various safety drills. An especially important time is the beginning of the class period or the school day. It is important to handle routine administrative duties quickly so that students become engaged in learning activities as soon as possible.

One potentially troublesome administrative routine that requires some special thought is the routine that you will use when students need to leave the room. This may include going to the restroom, the library, the nurse, or special pullout programs. There are some important legal concerns that need to be addressed so that teachers can account for the time when students are out of the classroom and can make sure they are going where they are supposed to be going in a timely manner.

Lesson routines are those routines needed during a typical lesson. These include making assignments, collecting homework, making up missed assignments, turning in late assignments, returning corrected papers, distributing materials, and moving from one activity to another during the lesson. In addition, procedures need to be developed for how papers are to be headed, the margins, and the proper writing instrument to use.

An important instructional routine that needs special attention is to consider what students will do when they have completed their work. It is to be expected that different students in the classroom will work at different rates. Some students will complete assignments quickly, and others may need additional assistance. All students need to be given specific instructions concerning what is acceptable when they have completed their work. For example, you may require that students get approval from you before moving to another activity. This might be done to make sure that the student actually did the work and did it correctly. Then students might choose from a list of acceptable activities such as reading a book, completing other assignments, visiting a learning center, or participating in acceptable free-time activities.

Classrooms are generally materials-rich environments. Books, papers, reference works, audiovisual equipment, art supplies, lab equipment, and special machines are found in most classrooms. The constant use and distribution of supplies can be a source of wasted time. Routines need to be established related to the use of instructional materials.

The use of equipment in the classroom requires special consideration. Careful instruction is needed before allowing students to use the equipment. Not doing so is to invite legal charges of negligence should a student be injured. In addition, supervision of equipment such as paper cutters and audiovisual equipment is an absolute must.

Interaction routines are those related to interactions between students in the classroom. Probably the most common interaction routine is making contributions to classroom discussions and asking questions. Another common interaction routine is that of signaling the class when you need their attention. An important interaction routine is how students request assistance from the teacher. Do you want students coming to your desk to request assistance or will you go to them? If you go to them, how will you know who needs help?

One routine that is especially important is that of how and when students are to interact with each other. When are students allowed to talk with each other? How are they to be informed if the talk is getting too loud? These routines are often based on the preferences and individual comfort level of the teacher. Some teachers who might be insecure in their ability to control the classroom may try to prohibit nearly all talk between students. This is probably unrealistic, because students are social and want to interact with each other. It is most realistic to decide on those times when you will allow them to talk with each other and establish a routine to govern their interactions.

You may want to use the checklist in Table 4.2 and begin to establish routines for the items on the list. You may want to add some items that you need or you might want to delete items that do not fit your circumstances. If you do not yet have a classroom, you may discuss the procedures with experienced teachers to find out the routines they use.

Teaching the Routines

Once routines have been developed, they need to be taught to the students. This can be done as they are needed. There are some routines that need to be taught at the beginning of the year and others that can wait until the circumstances require them.

Routines are learned like anything else, through explanation, modeling, practice, and reinforcement. When introducing the routines to the class, you should identify the problem, state the rationale for the procedure, teach it step by step, have students demonstrate the procedure, and then have the class practice it. The practice should continue until you are certain that everyone understands how it is to be performed.

It is unrealistic to expect to teach a procedure during the first day or two of the class and have it followed perfectly for the rest of the year. Those who do follow the routines should be given occasional reinforcement; if the class begins to ignore the routine or become lax in its application, you will need to remind students of the routine and have them practice it again. These two actions signal that the routines are important and that students are expected to follow them. Establishing routines

Table 4.2 Checklist for Classroom Routines

Recurring and Predictable Events	My Routine

Administrative Routines
  Entering classroom
  Taking attendance
  Leaving classroom
  Going to restroom
  Sharpening pencils
  Handling tardies
  Coming to class without material
  Moving in/out of desk
  Conducting fire drill
  Conducting disaster/alert drill	

Lesson Routines
  Establishing guidelines for headings for papers
  Collecting assignments
  Distributing material
  Handling late assignments
  Assigning make-up work when absent
  Getting attention at the beginning of a lesson
  Establishing a signal for students to get
    teacher's attention	

Interaction Routines
  Participating in class discussion
  Requesting assistance from the teacher
  Participating in group work
  Talking to other students (When? How?)
  Using learning centers or stations
  Working with others (When? How?)
  Making student movement or transitions	

for recurring and predictable events, insisting on compliance, and monitoring students during the school year can result in more learning time, more positive relations between class members and the teacher, more teacher energy for dealing with the exceptions or the serious problems, and fewer behavioral problems.

Most teachers also believe that communicating these rules and routines to parents is just as important as communicating them to students. Elementary teachers usually accomplish this with a letter of introduction that they send home at the beginning of the year. Secondary teachers include them in the syllabus or "green sheet" and require that students have them signed and returned during the first week of class. They also might discuss them with parents during open house at the beginning of the year. This communication is an important part of the teacher–parent relationship and can help in the long term if you have difficulties with students.

Providing Assistance to Students

Another area where time can be lost is that of providing assistance to students who need help. The basic principle for providing assistance to students is quickly identifying those who need assistance, providing them with a minimum amount of assistance, and then moving on. Monitoring student work to make sure that there is the maximum amount of academic learning time requires interaction with as many students as possible. This cannot be accomplished if a great deal of time is spent with only one or two students. For example, let's suppose that you have allocated 20 minutes to independent student work. If you spend an average of 5 minutes providing assistance to each student, you can monitor only four students. Jones (1987) studied how teachers provide assistance and noted that teachers did spend an average of about 5 minutes providing assistance to each student. He developed what he called the *praise-prompt-leave procedure* that should be done in a minute or less. The procedure, with some modifications, is as follows:

- Provide models, charts, or displays of the assignment so that students can seek clarification independently.
- Develop a signal system so that those who need assistance can be quickly identified.
- When arriving at a student's desk, give a quick word of praise on something the student has done correctly, give a concrete prompt of what he or she needs to do next, quickly leave, and move to someone else.
- Check back in a couple of minutes to see if the prompt has helped. If not, give another concrete prompt and move away.

The rationale behind this procedure is that you do not want to create a dependency. If allowed, some students will let the teacher do all the work for them! However, the student, not the teacher, needs the practice. Therefore, giving a concrete suggestion or prompt and then moving on places the responsibility back on the student for doing the work.

Developing a signal system is an important part of the sequence. If students are sitting at their desk with their hand raised, they are not engaged in the lesson. In addition, when they are not working, they are more likely to be engaged in inappropriate activities, such as talking. In fact, disruptive talk with neighbors constitutes about 80% of the discipline problems in the typical classroom (Edwards, 1997). Therefore, many teachers have developed a signal system that might involve placing a colored card or some other symbol on the corner of the desk to indicate that they need assistance. The routine is for them to start on the next question or problem and keep working until the teacher arrives to provide assistance.

Managing Transitions

There are many times during the day when students have to make a transition between lessons or between activities within the lesson. Doyle (1986) estimated that there are about 30 major transitions every day in the typical elementary classroom. Although there are fewer transitions in the typical secondary classroom, there are still quite a few. A considerable amount of time can be lost during these transitions, and this is a time when many discipline problems occur.

Eliminating wasted time during transitions and keeping students engaged can be facilitated by planning your transition. Outline the steps of the transition, give clear directions to the students, provide signals to inform them of what they should be doing at specific points in the transition, and keep things moving at a brisk pace. If certain transitions occur frequently, develop them into a routine that you teach to them, and have them practice it.

REVIEW OF MAIN IDEAS

1. The physical environment of the classroom sets the stage for learning and influences student behavior. It is useful to think of the classroom as a behavioral setting where the physical environment communicates behavioral expectations to the students.

2. The arrangement of student desks needs to be done with attention to teacher goals and purposes and so that the teacher can arrive at any given student desk within seconds.

3. The action zone consists of an area nearest the teaching position. Students seated within the action zone participate more, have higher achievement, and report more positive attitudes toward the class. Teachers can maximize the action zone by teaching from different spots in the classroom or by moving the seats of students who are having difficulty into the action zone.

4. Although many teachers pay little attention to the location of their desk, its location in the classroom is important. It is best placed in a rather unobtrusive spot nearer the back of the classroom.

5. The classroom ambiance is the impression that is created by the environment on people who enter the classroom. Teachers should strive to create a classroom ambiance that is businesslike and orderly, yet warm and attractive.

6. One of the most critical aspects of classroom management is the management of time. Research has consistently indicated that student achievement is related

to the concept of "opportunity to learn." This means that students are given time to focus on the lesson objectives. In addition, making good use of time helps prevent numerous discipline problems.

7. The most important dimension of time is to maximize the amount of time that students are working on an objective with success. This is referred to as academic learning time. Academic learning time can be increased by establishing classroom routines for recurring and predictable events, managing transitions, and providing quick and efficient assistance to students.

APPLICATION AND ENRICHMENT

1. Visit several classrooms at different grade levels. Record your feelings when you first walk in the classroom. Does it feel comfortable and safe? Does it communicate a sense of order and purpose? What are the elements of the physical environment that influence your perceptions? Do you note any differences according to grade level or subject? What might account for these differences?

2. Observe a classroom in progress. Draw a simple seating chart and the location of the teacher. Note which students are called upon most frequently and those that participate most in the lesson. How many of those students are located in the action zone?

3. Take an existing classroom and draw up a floor plan. State your rationale for organizing the environment in this way.

4. Take a stopwatch to a classroom observation. Use the watch to record the amount of time spent during the class on things that are unrelated to the lesson objective. These would include attendance, announcements, returning and collecting papers, discipline incidents, and so forth. Suggest some actions that could be taken to reduce the amount of time spent on these activities.

5. Begin developing a plan for your first day of teaching. How will you introduce classroom rules? What routines will you need? How will you teach those routines to the students? You might develop a "First Day Checklist" that will help you prepare for this important day.

REFERENCES

Adams, R. L., & Biddle, B. J. (1970). *Realities of teaching: Explorations with videotape.* New York: Holt, Rinehart & Winston.

Becker, F. (1981). *Workplace: Creating environments in organizations.* New York: Praeger.

Brophy, J. (2006). History of research on classroom management. In C. M. Evertson & C. S. Weinstein (Eds.), *Handbook of classroom management: Research, practice and contemporary issues* (pp. 17–43). Mahwah, NJ: Lawrence Erlbaum.

Carter, K., & Doyle, W. (2006). Classroom management in early childhood and elementary classrooms. In C. M. Evertson & C. S. Weinstein (Eds.), *Handbook of classroom management: Research, practice and contemporary issues* (pp. 373–406). Mahwah, NJ: Lawrence Erlbaum.

Doyle, W. (1986). *Classroom management and discipline.* In M. Wittrock (Ed.), *Handbook of research on teaching* (3rd ed., pp. 392–431). New York: Macmillan.

Dykman, B., & Reis, H. (1979). Personality correlates in classroom seating position. *Journal of Educational Psychology, 71*(3), 346–354.

Edwards, C. H. (1997). *Building classroom discipline* (3rd ed.). New York: Longman.

Emmer, E., Evertson, C., Sanford, J., Clements, B., & Worsham, M. (1982). *Organizing and managing the junior high school classroom.* Austin, TX: Research and Development Center for Teacher Education, University of Texas.

Emmer, E., Evertson, C., Sanford, J., Clements, B., & Worsham, M. (2000). *Classroom management for secondary teachers* (5th ed.). Needham Heights, MA: Allyn & Bacon.

Gettinger, M., & Kohler, K. (2006). Process-outcome approaches to classroom management and effective teaching. In C. M. Evertson & C. S. Weinstein (Eds.), *Handbook of classroom management: Research, practice and contemporary issues* (pp. 73–96). Mahwah, NJ: Lawrence Erlbaum.

Good, T., & Brophy, J. (2003) *Looking in classrooms* (9th ed.). Boston: Allyn & Bacon.

Jones, F. (1987). *Positive classroom discipline.* New York: McGraw-Hill.

Probansky, H., & Fabian, A. (1987). Development of place identity in the child. In C. Weinstein & T. David (Eds.), *Spaces for children* (pp. 21–40). New York: Plenum.

Rosenfield, P., Lambert, M., & Black, A. (1985). Desk arrangement effects in pupil classroom behavior. *Journal of Educational Psychology, 77*(1), 101–108.

Smith, H. (1987). Nonverbal communication. In M. Dunkin (Ed.), *The international encyclopedia of teaching and teacher education* (pp. 466–477). New York: Pergamon.

Weinstein, C. (1979). The physical environment of the school: A review of the research. *Review of Educational Research, 49*(4), 577–610.

Weinstein, C., & Mignano, A., Jr. (1993). *Elementary classroom management.* New York: McGraw-Hill.

Chapter 5

MANAGING INSTRUCTION

CLASSROOM SCENARIO

Mike Williams was preparing to be a math teacher. Math had always seemed very logical to him, and he had always done well. He was impatient with some of the classes he took in the teacher preparation program because he firmly believed that the only thing a person needed to know to be a good teacher was the subject matter to be taught. He felt that a person who understood the subject didn't need a lot of time to prepare and organize lessons and units because an expert should already know more than the students and should know the organization of the subject. To him, motivation theory was just a waste of time:

> "Everyone knows that math is important. Students just need to know that they will either learn the math or they will fail. That's all the motivation they will need. By nature, math is a logical subject and there is really only one way to teach it: you start at the beginning and build a logical sequence. The teacher presents the concepts and explains them, and then the students practice them. There is no discovery or creativity in math. The content is already well established and has been subject to rigorous proofs. Maybe there is a need for inquiry and cooperative learning in other subjects, but not in secondary school math."

His position was, "Give me the book, so that I know what content needs to be covered, an overhead projector, and some marking pens, and I am ready to go."

CHAPTER OBJECTIVES

After completing this chapter, you should be able to:

- Define dimensions of lesson management that must be considered regardless of lesson format
- Identify examples of verbal behavior that interfere with teacher clarity
- Define management challenges that must be considered when using whole-class instructional approaches
- State how cooperative and group instruction changes the classroom dynamic and how the role of the teacher in managing instruction changes
- Define the issues associated with teaching in inclusive classrooms
- Explain different configurations for using technology in the classroom and the challenges created when using each configuration
- State how technology can be used to address the noninstructional management concerns of teachers
- State the principle that should be used when responding to incidents of misbehavior during a lesson

Two tightly linked major tasks are vital for successful teaching: delivering instruction and maintaining order. Teachers cannot deliver instruction unless there is order in the classroom, and good teaching facilitates good order. For example, beginning teachers are frequently advised to plan and deliver exciting lessons as a means of preventing misbehavior. Well-planned and well-executed lessons motivate students, help satisfy their need for achievement, promote on-task behavior, and prompt cooperation. However, planning and delivering lessons requires thought to several generic tasks such as gaining student attention, presenting content, distributing materials, keeping students involved, monitoring student progress, and concluding the lesson.

Minnick (1983) clearly identified the relationship between lesson management and discipline problems. In a study of an inner-city junior high school with serious discipline problems, Minnick found that teachers with a high incidence of discipline problems did a poor job of planning activities, had little variety in their lessons, infrequently communicated to students the importance of the lesson, rarely had students discuss or evaluate what they had learned, and did a poor job of monitoring student work.

One of the more comprehensive research studies on management and discipline was conducted by Kounin (1970). Kounin and his research team began their research by focusing on the response of teachers to discipline problems. They were interested in how successful teachers responded to incidents of deviant behavior and how their responses influenced the subsequent behavior of the student disciplined as well as other students. After some observations, Kounin became convinced that they were looking at the wrong variables. He was convinced that the differences between successful and unsuccessful teachers were not in their responses to deviant behavior but were in how they managed the class in order to prevent problems. The outcome was a number of management concepts that are very useful in planning and delivering instruction.

In this chapter, these concepts will be discussed and applied to the classroom. They will be discussed in the context of whole-group instruction, cooperative and group learning, and the use of technology. Each of these approaches poses management challenges that need to be addressed.

THE DIMENSIONS OF LESSON MANAGEMENT

Several generic dimensions of lesson management should be addressed regardless of your philosophy or method of instruction. Focusing on these generic dimensions is the beginning point in managing instruction.

Clear Objectives

No matter what the lesson content or the teaching approach that is used, you must provide one or more clear objectives. Clarity about lesson objectives provides direct guidance for organizing the classroom, determining activities and approaches that are most likely to bring about success in accomplishing the objectives, and making estimates regarding the amount of time you need to allocate. Furthermore, clear objectives help the teacher keep a clear focus and are useful in keeping a lesson on track.

Clear objectives serve yet another purpose. In fast-moving and unpredictable environments, teachers must make quick decisions. Keeping the purpose of the lesson in mind facilitates making good decisions. A lack of clear objectives often results in a lesson without cohesion and in student confusion.

Clear goals and objectives also have benefit for students. They help students understand the purposes of the activities and the content that is being covered. Clarity of purpose enhances student motivation and helps students make appropriate time and effort choices. In addition, clear goals become a framework, or advance organizers, for the material that is presented. Such a framework helps students organize and understand the material with greater comprehension and clarity.

This increased understanding facilitates student achievement and creates a climate of success. In addition, when students are informed of the objectives and they are clear regarding what is expected of them, their motivation is enhanced. They are better able to understand the logic of the lesson and the reasons for what is occurring in the classroom.

In summary, to be an effective manager in any part of life requires clarity of objectives. Good management is simply not possible unless teachers, as well as their students, know where they are going. Therefore, taking time to be clear about the objectives of a lesson is imperative.

Teacher Clarity

Another generic component that covers all of teaching is clarity. A lack of clarity will result in confusion, and confusion will lead to frustration and inappropriate student behavior. Classrooms are usually highly verbal environments. Therefore, clarity of verbal communication will have a profound effect on lesson success. Teacher messages that are confusing and garbled will result in off-task behavior. Although it is relatively easy to identify unclear messages, it is often more difficult to specifically identify what makes it unclear. Clarity involves a number of teacher behaviors and is made more difficult by the fact that it is a combination of what the teacher does and says and how students interpret the message (Gephart, Strother, & Duckett, 1981).

One specific factor that hinders lesson clarity is the use of vague and ambiguous terms. These terms include approximations (*about, almost*), ambiguous designations (*somehow, somewhere, someone*), bluffing (*everyone knows, it's a long story*), indeterminate quantification (*a bunch, a lot, a few*), and statements of probability (*frequently, generally, often*). Although these terms cannot be eliminated entirely, their repeated use during a lesson usually signals lack of teacher knowledge and leads to student confusion.

Communication mazes also block lesson clarity. Mazes are best compared to winding paths, including blind alleys, which must be navigated in order to get to the goal. These mazes occur when the verbal communications are disjointed and disconnected, taking listeners along a winding path with false starts and blind alleys. Verbal mazes are often verbal statements that lack logic or semantic sense.

Mazes and unclear communication are especially evident when giving oral directions. Directions are often given at the spur of the moment without much previous planning. It is common for teachers to give more than one direction at a time, resulting in student confusion and calls for repeated directions. Some students simply give up and will not do the work.

Giving Clear Directions

Providing clear directions helps get students to work quickly, avoids confusion, and prevents wasted time. Clear directions promote good lesson pacing and a smooth flow of classroom activities. While some teachers seem to have the ability to give clear directions, many do not.

If you seem to have difficulty giving oral directions and students are often asking for clarification, there are several steps you can take to improve the clarity of your verbal directions. One step is to write down the directions for activities when planning the lesson. This gives you an opportunity to read through them, making sure they are in logical order and are clear. They might be shared with someone else to see if they share your analysis that the directions are logical and clear. Written directions will also prompt you to be more concise and less wordy when giving directions. We have found it useful to write directions on a transparency and reveal it while giving directions so that students are not only hearing the directions but are also reading them.

Another step is to give oral directions and then randomly choose a couple of students to explain in their own words what they are supposed to be doing. If these students are unable to repeat the directions, it is best to restate the directions. Merely repeating the directions is seldom effective. It is better to think of several different ways to present the directions. Rather than merely repeating the same idea or concept, effective teachers try to find a new application, a new problem, or a new way of illustrating the main points of the lesson.

What Would You Do?

Read the following verbatim account of a middle school social studies lesson. Then rewrite the directions to increase their clarity.

Teacher: "Okay, we have identified four major points that we have listed on the board. However, this still doesn't give us the full picture of the event. I am certain that there will be a lot more about this incident in the newspapers over the weekend. I want you to do this for homework. Follow the incident over the weekend; there should be a complete article in the Sunday paper."

(The passing bell rings and the class starts putting away their books and papers.)

"Hold it!!! I didn't dismiss you yet. I want you to follow the incident and get as many facts as you can and then, first of all a paragraph or two. The most important part of the

---

(Continued)

(Continued)

> *assignment will be this: What will be the world opinion of the United States? In other*
> *words, will our position as a world leader be stronger or weaker? As an important nation*
> *in the world, our leadership role is critical in maintaining a stable world. "*
>> *Student: "What if I don't have a Sunday paper?"*
>> *Teacher: "That's a silly question. I'm sure you can get a Sunday paper."*
>
> - Exactly what are the students being asked to do for homework?
>
> - What interferes with the clarity of these directions?
>
> - How would you rewrite the directions to increase their clarity?

Withitness

Kounin (1970) coined the term *withitness*. In his observations of effective classrooms, he noted that teachers who were effective in managing the classroom had a high degree of awareness about what was happening throughout the classroom. The "with-it" teacher was one who knew what was going on in every corner of the classroom and who was on task and who was not. This high sense of awareness helped teachers to respond quickly and prevent problems from escalating into something more serious. Teachers who are "with it" are those that students describe as "having eyes in the back of their heads."

The with-it teacher also demonstrated some other characteristics. One characteristic was the ability to identify exactly who was involved in an inappropriate behavior. Kounin identified this as "being on target." In addition to being on target, with-it teachers also demonstrated good timing. They were able to promptly identify potential problems and respond before the problem grew in seriousness or spread to other students.

Withitness seems to be a skill that is acquired with experience and security. One of our friends commented on her lack of awareness as a new teacher by noting that one day during her lesson, a boy in the back of the room cut off his T-shirt to make a muscle shirt, and she didn't notice it until someone pointed it out. However, withitness can be enhanced if lessons are well planned and if the new teacher writes prompts, such as "Scan the room," right on the lesson plans to make sure that the need to be aware of all sections of the classroom is not forgotten in the hectic pace of activities.

WHOLE-CLASS INSTRUCTION

A large percentage of the lessons taught in the typical classroom are characterized by the teacher delivering instruction to the entire class. Although early childhood settings use more group and independent approaches, there is a portion of the time spent in the whole group. Managing the whole group presents some challenges. The teacher must be able to attend to whether the content being taught is understood, the pace of the lesson presentation, and the actions of all the students in the group. In addition to the generic dimensions of clear objectives, clarity, and with-itness, there are some other dimensions of management that need to be applied.

Lesson Momentum

One of the basic challenges of managing a whole group is to keep the lesson momentum. Lesson momentum involves keeping the lesson moving forward at a steady pace so that students do not become bored, yet not so fast that students do not understand or comprehend the material that is being presented. In a class with good lesson momentum, students move ahead at a relatively brisk pace and stay on task with no breaks in the flow of the lesson. Although unpredictable events, such as classroom visitors or announcements, have the potential to slow lesson momentum, teachers are the major offenders in breaking classroom momentum. Kounin (1970) identified two teacher behaviors that typically break lesson momentum: lesson fragmentation and overdwelling.

Fragmentation

Fragmentation, identified by Kounin as the major problem in maintaining lesson momentum, occurs in several ways. One typical type of fragmentation is breaking a lesson into several unnecessarily small steps when the task could be quickly accomplished in one or two steps. Many of us can relate to the situation where we have been given a task to do that we understand quite well. However, the instructor insists on doing only one small thing at a time, so we become impatient and frustrated. There are times when breaking a complex task into small steps is useful. However, teachers need to understand the students in the classroom and their prior knowledge so that the lesson does not become unnecessarily fragmented. Good examples of lesson fragmentation can be found in some individualized or programmed learning systems. Some of these programs break the content into such small steps that the person completing the program fails to see how the pieces fit together to make the whole and they become quite impatient and bored. Another commonly observed example of lesson fragmentation is when a student is called to the front of the room to solve a problem while the rest of the class sits and watches. This often produces boredom and provides an opportunity for students to focus their attention on something other than the lesson.

Overdwelling

Overdwelling, another enemy of lesson momentum, occurs when too much time is spent in needless repetition or elaboration of the content of the lesson or on giving instructions. It is true that repetition is important for learning to occur, but too much time spent repeating the same point over and over will bring lesson momentum to a standstill. Teachers do have a tendency to talk too much. This tendency, combined with overdwelling, often leads to a rambling discourse that can confuse even the most dedicated listener.

Another form of overdwelling occurs when an inordinate amount of time is spent on a minor or insignificant part of a task rather than on the main focus. When this occurs, students often get the message that it is the insignificant content that is important and they lose sight of the lesson objectives and major focus. They then become confused and angry when they are criticized for not understanding the main point or failing to achieve the lesson objectives.

Lesson Pacing

One of the most important elements of time management is the pace of activities during the lesson. The obvious result of any activity that proceeds too slowly is boredom. However, deciding on an appropriate pace for whole-group activities is difficult and is one of the common problems for novice teachers. There are several reasons for this.

One major reason is that classrooms are composed of students with diverse backgrounds, abilities, and learning styles. Some students may grasp a concept or master a skill very quickly while others struggle. Some students are impulsive learners who quickly decide they understand and want to move on. Other students are more reflective and want more examples and clarification before they feel comfortable moving forward. This creates a dilemma for many teachers. They want to make sure that all students have an opportunity to learn and thus are reluctant to move too quickly. However, moving too slowly runs the risk of losing the attention of those who quickly master the material.

Another issue is that some teachers are insensitive to the pace of the lesson. Some teachers seem to have an intuitive feel for moving at a rate appropriate for students, whereas others are nearly always moving too rapidly or too slowly. It is probable that those teachers who do seem to make appropriate pacing decisions do so based on something other than mere intuition. Some teachers just seem to be able to "read" the students and understand the cues that they are providing.

One aspect of "reading" the classroom is the formation of "reference groups" that provide clues to the teacher. The reference group is a group of students that the teachers attend to in order to gather data about what is occurring in the classroom. Although many teachers are unable to consciously identify particular students that serve as their reference group, a reference group is almost always present. Think of the times you are in front of a group. Do you not judge the pace and clarity of your presentation by observing the facial expressions and behavior of the listeners? Are there certain individuals that have more impact on you than others?

The influence of the reference group in pacing works like this: Ms. Garcia is teaching a difficult concept. As the concept is being taught, she is also attending to the nonverbal behaviors of the class. She observes the puzzled expression on the face of a high-achieving student and interprets this expression to mean that the student is confused. Because this is a high-achieving student, she infers that the difficulty must be in the pace of the instruction and not with the ability of the student. Because of her interpretation, she stops and asks some questions, reteaches some of the lesson, and slows the pace. Later on, Ms. Garcia notes an expression of boredom on the face of another student. This student is an academically able student, so she interprets this to mean that the student is bored and she needs to increase the speed of the lesson. Later, during another lesson, Ms. Garcia sees a puzzled expression on the face of another student. This time the student is one who is frequently off task. She doesn't interpret this to be a signal that she needs to change the pace of the lesson but attributes it to the attending behaviors of the student. Therefore, she does nothing to alter the pace of the lesson but moves to a closer proximity of the student.

The basic point is that it is important to be aware of the students being used as a reference group. If the reference group is primarily composed of those near the top of the class, the inferences drawn might be inappropriate for the majority of the class and widespread misunderstanding or failure is likely to occur. If, however, the reference group is composed of those who are usually the lowest achievers in the classroom, the danger is the pace will be so slow that the majority of the class will become bored. Teachers who are successful in managing a classroom and in establishing an appropriate pace are those who check their inferences and become more skilled at reading and interpreting the nonverbal behavior of a reliable reference group. Unsuccessful teachers attend to the wrong students or misinterpret student behavior.

A useful approach is to consciously identify those students at about the 25th percentile for your reference group. This means that the pace will be appropriate for 75% of the class. Although this pace may still be a bit slow for the more able learn-ers, it will keep the lesson moving at a moderate pace and provide for the success of most of the students.

Establishing a reference group at the 25th percentile does not mean that you ignore the bottom quarter of the class. You may have to reteach these students as a small group or arrange for peer tutors to assist them. The point is that nei-ther the slowest nor the fastest students should be the indicators for pacing decisions.

Overlapping

Overlapping is another concept Kounin (1970) developed to identify successful classroom managers. Overlapping refers to the ability to handle more than one task at a time. To some extent, overlapping is related to teacher withitness. A teacher skilled at overlapping is able to present lesson content to students, respond to a question, react to an off-task student, and handle unpredictable intrusions without missing a beat. It is the ultimate in multitasking. Teachers who lack the skill of overlapping simply get lost in the maze of events and lose control of the direction of the lesson. They have trouble getting much accomplished and find themselves frustrated at the end of each day.

An element of overlapping that is important is the judgment to identify which events need to be handled immediately and which can be ignored. Many novice teachers are unable to prioritize and focus on the most important or serious class-room events. Those that need immediate attention are overlooked while attention is directed to minor incidents. In a comparison of successful and unsuccessful teachers, researchers noted that successful teachers make rapid judgments during teaching, they group events into larger units in order to deal with them effectively, and they are able to discriminate among the events in terms of their immediate and long-term significance (Clark & Peterson, 1986).

Overlapping, like withitness, seems to be a difficult skill to teach. Some indi-viduals appear to have learning and thinking styles that do not allow for the con-sideration of multiple pieces of data at the same time. Therefore, they have difficulty focusing on more than one task at a time. Clark and Peterson (1986) indicate that it might be a skill acquired through experience. However, for experi-ence to be beneficial, teachers must develop a schema, or frame of reference, related to classroom teaching and learning that helps them select cues to attend to, understand the meaning of the cues, and make an appropriate decision. It is prob-able that a well-developed or context-appropriate schema is what makes teaching look so easy when demonstrated by outstanding teachers. Novice teachers often become painfully aware of this phenomenon when they take over the class of just such a teacher. What appeared to be so easy and natural when observed now is much more difficult and overwhelming.

Lesson Smoothness

Lesson smoothness, another concept developed by Kounin (1970), refers to flow of the lesson. Not only does a lesson need to move forward at an appropriate pace, but also parts of the lesson need to be thematically related so that one part of the lesson flows smoothly into the next. Two dimensions of lesson management that contribute to lesson smoothness are connected discourse and creative repetition. Factors related to lesson smoothness are thrusts, dangles and truncations, and flip-flops.

Connected Discourse

Connected discourse refers to the logic or connectedness of teacher talk. The parts of the lesson should be thematically connected so that there is a logical flow and the lesson makes sense. Some teachers have developed the bad habit of starting a lesson and then going off on a tangent. They then return to the topic of the lesson for awhile and then go off on another tangent. This causes confusion as students try to sort out the point that the teacher is trying to make. Although connected discourse is not one of the factors of lesson smoothness identified by Kounin, it has been identified as an important variable in research on teacher clarity and fits nicely with the concept.

Detailed planning can improve lesson smoothness. Trying to teach "off-the-cuff," or without giving much thought to the flow of major points, almost always results in a loss of smoothness. When planning, give thought to how parts of the lesson fit together in a logical and coherent manner. Do the pieces fit together to make a whole? Would it be easy for someone with limited knowledge of the subject to understand? Does it make sense?

Creative Repetition

A certain amount of repetition is necessary for learning to occur; telling students once is seldom enough. However, merely repeating the material over and over is a poor educational practice. If students did not understand it the first time, they are not likely to understand it if it is merely repeated. However, creative repetition at key points in the lesson helps clarify the material and assists the learner in comprehending and making meaning.

Another approach for using creative repetition is to provide internal summaries at key points in a lesson. This helps the learner understand the relationship of different parts of the lesson and how they fit together.

Thrusts

Another barrier to lesson smoothness is something Kounin called "thrusts." A thrust is best characterized as a verbal statement that is inserted, or thrust, into the flow of the lesson. For example, after getting a lesson started, the teacher suddenly remembers an announcement that needs to be made. Rather than waiting until the conclusion of the lesson, the teacher "thrusts" this announcement into the middle of the lesson. "Class, we have to remember to take the special announcements home tonight." A common thrust, one that disturbs many teachers, is announcements that come over the PA system while they are teaching. Everyone in the class has to stop and listen and then refocus on the lesson. The probabilities are high that some students will not refocus their attention. Some schools have developed policies that limit announcements to one particular time a day (for example, home room or the first 10 minutes of second period) in order to avoid unnecessary thrusts.

When teaching, it is important to try to eliminate unnecessary thrusts. Once a lesson is started, the momentum and the smoothness need to be maintained by keeping the class focused on the lesson. If you fear forgetting something, take a minute to write a note or establish a practice of placing important information in a particular region of your desk. You can then consult your notes before dismissing the class.

Dangles and Truncations

Dangles and truncations are other types of breaks in the lesson flow. A dangle occurs when the lesson is focused on a particular point or concept and then abruptly switched to something else, leaving the previous content sort of "dangling" without coming to a logical conclusion. If the focus never returns to the dangling content, that is a truncation. One of the common types of dangles occurs when the teacher, or a student, is reminded of a story or an incident that they share with the class. This is generally something that is not directly related to the lesson and leads to a digression away from the main point of the lesson. At times this digression becomes the major focus of the lesson and the main point is forgotten altogether. Even in the best-managed lessons, some digressions will occur. A skilled teacher understands how to accept the digression, maybe using it to illustrate some part of the lesson, and quickly focuses student attention back on the central objective. However, be aware that some students are very skilled at getting the teacher off on a digression that truncates the focus on the lesson objectives.

Another place where truncations can occur is when teachers forget to monitor the time. Suddenly they become aware that time has expired and they abruptly stop without bringing the lesson to a logical conclusion. One position in a lesson sequence that students remember best is the final part of the lesson. If that final part of the lesson is truncated without bringing it to a logical conclusion or providing a review of the main points of the lesson, a prime learning opportunity is missed.

Group Focus

Maintaining a focus on the group is another area identified by Kounin (1970) as important when managing a lesson. One of the issues associated with whole-group instruction is that the group is composed of diverse individuals. Decisions have to be made between keeping the group moving forward and assisting specific individuals who may be having difficulty. When teaching the whole group, it is important that the teacher focus on the group and keep the entire group focused and on task. There are several dimensions of group focus: gaining student attention, providing a variety of tasks and avoiding satiation, keeping individuals in the group alert and accountable, gaining the active participation of the students, and responding to misbehavior.

Gain Student Attention

Gaining and keeping student attention throughout the lesson is a central element of effective group management. Some teachers think that if they have students' attention at the beginning, the task is accomplished. However, when considering group instruction, attention needs to be directed to how to get initial student interest, how to maintain interest during the lesson, and how to enhance motivation at the conclusion of the lesson.

Gaining attention at the beginning of the lesson can be accomplished by appealing to the innate sense of curiosity or by starting the lesson with something novel or unique. Individuals will focus attention on something that they see as unique or something that does not correspond with the way they think things operate. Initial attention is also gained by relating the content of the lesson to student needs or interests. An effective technique for gaining student attention is to help create a need for the students to know the material that is to be presented.

However, initial attention is not enough. Teachers must also consider how to maintain attention once the initial interest begins to wane. Student attention during the lesson can be addressed by making the learning activities enjoyable and challenging. Keep in mind, however, that there is a difference between challenge and threat. Individuals are challenged by an activity when they perceive it to require some effort on their part but think it is still possible for them to achieve success. Threat occurs when individuals perceive a task to be not just difficult but impossible. The task of the teacher is to present lessons at an appropriate level of difficulty. This means the lesson activities need to require some effort or involve some challenge but not so much that the students feel overwhelmed. For example, in higher education, it is customary to provide the class with an outline the first day of class that outlines all the requirements for the entire term. If these appear to be overwhelming to some students, they will drop the class. However, because most college students have been successful, they are usually willing to persevere and attempt to meet the requirements. Many K–12 students are not confident learners, and such a practice would create stress and anxiety that would block learning and motivation. They would be threatened, not challenged. Keeping student interest during a lesson can be enhanced by reinforcing the progress that students are making. They need to perceive that they are making progress.

Another approach to maintaining attention during a lesson is to provide variety in the lesson sequence. This can be done by making sure that several different activities take place during a lesson. One modern language teacher had a rule of thumb that the students should not be engaged in any one activity for more than 15 minutes. That is a pretty good rule to follow. Students should not be expected to sit and listen or to work independently for extended periods of time. For example, in a classroom, they might be expected to read something for one segment, discuss the material as a whole class for another segment, and work with a small group or do independent work for a third segment.

Motivation at the conclusion of the lesson can be enhanced by reinforcing student success. They need to know what they did correctly and perceive that if they put forth sufficient effort, they can achieve success. Success is a powerful motivator, and if students believe that they are good at something, they will be willing to put forth more effort. One approach that is successful is placing an emphasis on what the student has done right in a lesson rather than what he or she has done wrong. For example, when students have completed a worksheet or a set of math problems, mark all correct items rather than all incorrect items. This is much more motivating for students, and you can note serious issues and reteach if necessary.

Keep the Group Alert and Accountable

Throughout a lesson, you need to make sure that all students are kept alert. This can be accomplished by holding the students in suspense so that they never know when they might be called on to respond to a teacher question or perform a task. Group alerting techniques, such as having all students signify their agreement or disagreement with a statement or question by holding up their hands, are useful in keeping students on their toes. If students believe you have started a lesson during which there is little probability that they will be called on to respond, their attention will wander and their involvement in the lesson will decrease.

Students in the back of the room are often overlooked.

© Photodisc

Keeping students accountable means letting them know that they will need to use what is taught in some manner. A good example of accountability can be observed in high school classrooms. For example, students often ask, "Will this be on the test?" This is their way of determining whether they will be held accountable for knowing the information. What happens if the teacher says, "No, this will not be on the test"? Pencils go down and students' attention begins to wander.

Testing students is not the only way, or even the best way, of making them accountable. Another technique is to stop at appropriate points of the lesson and have students summarize the material to a partner. Students can be given a worksheet following the

Table 5.1   Checklist for Lesson Management

Directions: Use this checklist to prepare and evaluate your lesson management.

Management Dimension	My Response
Objectives Are the objectives clear and focused on student behavior? Do the objectives provide a clear focus for the lesson?	
Teacher Clarity Is my language usage clear and precise? What terms or concepts might need clarification?	
Lesson Momentum How will I determine if the pace is appropriate? What will I do if students go off on a tangent? How will I handle unexpected intrusions?	
Lesson Smoothness Are the parts of my lesson logically connected? Is my verbal input connected? Where will I use creative repetition?	
Group Focus How will I gain initial attention? What can I do to keep attention during the lesson? How will I hold students accountable?	
Responding to Misbehavior How will I respond to minor incidents such as off-task behavior? How might I respond to intrusive incidents?	

teacher input and be required to use the information, or they might be required to write a short reaction paper. One useful approach is to have the students apply the principles or concepts presented in a lesson to a new situation. This avoids boring repetition and facilitates the transfer of their new learning to new situations. Use Table 5.1 to plan and/or evaluate the dimensions of lesson management in your own classroom.

COOPERATIVE LEARNING AND GROUP ACTIVITIES

In recent years, group work such as cooperative learning has increased in popularity. This trend has been supported by research that has indicated cooperative learning can result in some impressive achievement gains. Group work is not new and has been used more frequently in early childhood settings. More recently, though, specific cooperative learning approaches have provided guidance for classroom applications and can now be found throughout the curriculum.

However, cooperative and group work changes the dynamics of the classroom and the behavior of the students. Individuals often behave quite differently in groups than they do when they are working independently. In addition, there is a "chemistry" that develops as a result of a particular group composition. Sometimes this chemistry is helpful and sometimes it is detrimental to learning (Lotan, 2006). As a result, teachers using group approaches have discovered that managing groups presents different challenges than working with the whole class.

When working with the whole group, the teacher is directly in charge. Individuals are monitored for on-task behavior, and interaction between students is discouraged. However, in small-group and cooperative learning settings, much of the responsibility has been delegated to the students; student interaction is essential. The classroom environment is not as orderly, as there may be several groups working simultaneously on different tasks. When conceptualizing the role of the teacher in group and cooperative learning environments, we might characterize the role as that of an instructional manager. This implies that the role of the teacher is to manage the environment so that learning is possible rather than be directly in charge of delivering all the instruction.

The Role of the Instructional Manager

The role of the instructional manager involves assigning the students to groups, creating a responsive environment, monitoring group progress, watching for unequal participation, and mediating conflicts. Group and cooperative work usually requires more teacher planning and organization. How the teacher plans and organizes before the students begin work as groups determines the success of the group. It is also important to remember that successful cooperative learning and group work does not occur automatically. Students need to be taught the skills of how to work together.

Assign Students to Groups

This is one of the most critical components of the task of managing group work. Teachers need to have some understanding of the group dynamics of a specific group of students, their abilities, and their ability to work together. Lotan (2006) suggests making the assignment process open and public. This means that the teacher does the assignment process in class and allows student input. Allowing students some input helps make the groups more compatible so that there will be fewer problems and a better chemistry. Teachers need to make sure that groups do include a variety of abilities and skills. Make sure that the process does not end up like the common selection of teams on the playground, with the least talented publicly chosen last. It is a good idea to alter the group composition occasionally so that different students have the opportunity to work together.

Create a Responsive Environment

If cooperative learning and group work are to be successful, the groups must have access to the information and material they need. This is what is meant by "creating a responsive environment," one of the most important management tasks. Few things will reduce student motivation or group involvement more than not being able to find the material or information that is needed. Depending on the type of group task that is required, the teacher needs to gather the resources and place them in an easily accessible spot. This task involves a reallocation of teacher planning time. Rather than planning lessons, the teacher is involved in finding or gathering needed resources.

Monitor Group Work

In cooperative learning and group work, the teacher is not in front of the classroom delivering instruction. However, this does not mean that the teacher is not actively involved. The teacher must be very active in getting to each group and monitoring their progress. Students working in groups need to know that every few minutes the teacher will be showing up and observing what they are doing and they may have to answer questions about their progress. Groups that are not monitored carefully tend to get off task, and interpersonal conflicts increase.

Watch for Unequal Participation

In addition to monitoring group work, teachers need to be alert to unequal participation. One of the most common complaints about using group work is that a few students do all the work. One of the basic conditions of cooperative learning is important here: There needs to be individual accountability. In other words, evaluation needs to take into account the final group project as well as individual contributions.

During group work, teachers need to be alert to two important dimensions: They need to make sure that (a) everyone is contributing and (b) the group is not being dominated by one or two students. If this is observed, the teacher may need to talk with the individuals either privately or in the group to make sure they understand that participation of everyone is important and their role in the group will be recognized. Sometimes this involves problem solving by helping various members of the group define how everyone is to be involved.

Table 5.2 Planning Cooperative Learning Activities Checklist

Directions: Use this checklist to plan cooperative learning and group work.

Planning Dimension	My Response
Assigning Students to Groups	
What process will I use to ensure that groups are diverse yet compatible?	
Where will the groups meet?	
Creating a Responsive Environment	
What materials will be needed (books, handouts, pictures, videos, etc.)?	
Where will the materials be kept?	
How will students access the material?	
If students need to use the computer, how will they obtain permission?	
Monitoring Group Progress	
How will I monitor group progress?	
How often should I check with each group?	
What questions should I ask?	
What behavioral indicators do I need to watch for?	
Unequal Participation	
What will I do if a student is not participating?	
What will I do if a student is dominating the group?	
How will I evaluate individuals' contributions in order to hold all students accountable?	

Mediate Conflicts

There will always be some disagreements and conflicts within groups. Learning how to resolve these conflicts is one of the most important skills that students can learn. For example, one of the major reasons people are fired from their job is because they cannot get along with others. Throughout life, individuals will face many disagreements. Cooperative learning and group work provide an ideal setting for helping students learn how to resolve these conflicts. This is an opportunity for the teacher to serve as a mediator who helps students discuss the issues and decide how they are to be resolved.

In summary, group work is an important approach that can be used across all grade levels and all content areas. It can be very rewarding for both the teacher and the students. The quality of student work on interesting, worthwhile, and well-crafted group projects is often very exciting. However, successful group work does not just happen. It requires much teacher planning and skillful management. Table 5.2 provides ideas to help you plan group activities in your own classroom.

MANAGING INCLUSIVE CLASSROOMS

Educating students with special needs in regular education classrooms has been the norm for schools throughout the nation. This is the result of a number of federal regulations requiring this practice. One of the most important dimensions in managing special needs students in regular classrooms is the attitude of the teacher. Although teachers generally appear to be supportive of inclusive educational practices, many are skeptical of their ability to manage inclusive classrooms. Teachers often express a concern that they do not have enough time to give the special needs students the attention they need. However, they appear to grow in confidence with experience teaching in inclusive classrooms. Moreover, effective inclusion can have a positive effect on all students. When teachers note the positive benefits of inclusion for all students, they are more likely to accept special needs students and use more effective management processes (Soodak & McCarthy, 2006). Therefore, successful management of inclusive classrooms requires teachers who are confident about their ability to manage inclusive classrooms and who have support available when addressing questions and issues that might arise.

One of the basic requirements in inclusive classrooms is the need to differentiate instruction. Differentiation means altering the lesson in order to accommodate different needs and interests in the classroom. Differentiation might occur by altering the pace of lesson delivery, changing the mode of delivery from group to individualized learning, or altering the content of the lesson. Differentiation creates some management challenges. Many of the challenges are similar to those created when using cooperative learning. However, with special needs students, more attention needs to be paid to issues relating to the pace of the instruction and the criteria for assessing learning.

Some of the most successful approaches are those that do use differentiation in the classrooms. Some of those are what might be termed *peer-mediated strategies,* approaches such as cooperative learning and peer tutoring that increase time on task and academic engagement. This, in turn, reduces student frustration and discipline and management problems (Kamps, Leonard, Potucek, & Garrison-Harrell, 1995). In addition, peer-mediated strategies also have benefits for the students without disabilities. First, students develop an increased respect and appreciation for their special needs peers. They develop an increased sense of responsibility, and their own academic engagement and achievement improves (Cushing & Kennedy, 1997).

In general, there are some management practices that are effective when teaching inclusive classrooms. Those include the following:

- Using peer-mediated strategies, hands-on activities, and authentic assessment
- Establishing classroom rules that emphasize belonging

Students with a variety of disabilities are found in classrooms.

© Eyewire

- Establishing peer support programs
- Modeling acceptance of all students
- Providing positive verbal responses and supports
- Offering students choices about activities
- Training students in self-monitoring techniques (Soodak & McCarthy, 2006)

Since there are so many legal constraints that limit the approaches that can be used in responding to the behavior issues of students with disabilities, each local school district should develop a disciplinary policy for dealing with these issues.

These policies should then be distributed to all teachers and discussed in large group settings. Teachers must understand that students with disabilities may not be held to the same disciplinary standards and consequences as those applied to others in the classroom (Soodak & McCarthy, 2006). These restrictions often conflict with the current trend toward excluding students as a component of creating "safe schools." As a result, teachers in inclusive classrooms need to confer with school authorities and understand the parameters within which they can make management and disciplinary decisions regarding students with special needs.

In summary, teaching in inclusive classrooms is not something to be feared. It can be a rewarding experience for both the teacher and all the students. Learning how to differentiate instruction is not just a good practice for special needs students; differentiation is beneficial for all students and is simply good teaching. However, teachers must begin with their attitude and their feelings of efficacy. If they accept special needs students and believe that they can be successful in teaching them, they will normally experience success. Use Table 5.3 to help you think about different dimensions teachers must consider when working with special needs students.

TECHNOLOGY AND MANAGEMENT

One feature that sets contemporary classrooms apart from those of previous generations is the presence of technology. Technology, especially computers, has become a common tool for teaching and learning. Nearly all classrooms now have computers available. However, the use of computers in classrooms changes the classroom dynamics and presents new management challenges for the teacher. In fact, computers were identified by teachers as one of their greatest challenges (Bolick & Cooper, 2006).

On the one hand, computers have the potential to open up the classroom to new approaches to teaching and learning, to generate student excitement, and to increase student on-task behavior. On the other hand, computers in the classroom require rearrangement of the physical environment and the establishment of new rules and routines, create management problems when some students are working on computers and others are engaged in other tasks, require constant monitoring of their use, raise the potential for cheating, and increase worries related to the treatment of the hardware.

The most important management issue relating to the use of computers is how computers are used in a given classroom. In the beginning, due to cost, many schools had computer labs; students left the classroom and went to the lab in order to use computers. It is an effective configuration when students are learning about computer usage. The management problems associated with this type of computer use involve working the computer lab into the schedule and getting students to the computer lab.

Table 5.3   Managing the Inclusive Classroom: Planning Checklist

Directions: Use this checklist to help you plan for special needs students.

Management Dimension	My Response
Identification Who are the special needs students in the classroom? Is there an individual educational plan (IEP) for each one? What is my attitude toward each special needs student?	
Accommodation What are the specific needs of each student? How will instruction need to be altered to accommodate each need? Are there any special rules or routines that need to be developed? How can I model acceptance of special needs students?	
Peer-Mediated Strategies How might I use peer tutoring? Who would be the best students to be the tutors? How will the peer tutoring be implemented during the lesson? Where can cooperative learning be used? How will the special needs students be integrated into each group?	
Differentiation Does the pace of the lesson need to be changed for the special needs students? Is the content appropriate for the students, or does it need to be changed in order to motivate them? How might the content be altered so they are still working toward the primary objective? How will students working at a different pace, in different groups, or on different content be monitored?	
Evaluation Are the evaluation approaches appropriate for special needs students? What are the standards that will be applied to the special needs students? How will the evaluation of special needs students be conducted?	

Another typical configuration involves the placement of just a few computers, perhaps as few as one or two, in a classroom. This configuration raises management issues related to determining where the computers are placed, scheduling when students can use them, monitoring what students are doing, and minimizing disruptions that might be caused by noise associated with speakers, printers, and so forth.

A third configuration that is gaining in popularity is the use of mobile computers. This often consists of a cart of laptop computers that can be distributed to all members of the class. Some schools are now wired so that each laptop can be connected to the Internet. This creates other management issues. Usually the mobile computing cart needs to be shared with others, so there is the issue of working the schedule around the availability of the computers. There is also transition time associated with getting the computers into the classroom, getting them started, and making sure that everyone is connected.

Perhaps the most difficult management problems are associated with classrooms where there are just one or two computers. In fact, in one study, management problems significantly decreased when all students had access to computers (Bolick & Cooper, 2006).

There are a couple of issues related to technology use regardless of type of configuration. One of the most common problems is related to equipment failure. Many of the best plans are disrupted when the computer fails, bugs or viruses distort the software, or the printer stops functioning. Without a backup plan, this can be a management and discipline nightmare. This is extremely frustrating to both students and the teacher. Therefore, managing technology in the classroom requires a backup plan. Thought needs to be given to what can be done if there is an equipment failure.

Another problem, especially when the computers can be connected to the Web, is the possibility of students accessing inappropriate content. Sometimes by accident and sometimes on purpose, students access content that is violent, sexually explicit, or inaccurate. In addition, there is a dark side of technology that includes child pornography, kidnapping, and cyberbullying. In order to combat these problems, teachers need to make sure that the school has an acceptable use policy and that the students and the parents are informed of the policy. Then students need to be educated about the dangers related to inappropriate use and what to do when they access inappropriate sites.

The following guidelines have been suggested by technology specialists (Bolick & Cooper, 2006):

- Always go through a technology application before using it in the classroom.
- Teach students a signal system to use when they need assistance (e.g., a red cup placed on the monitor or desk).

- Have backup plans for the event of equipment failure.
- Establish that all monitors are to be off when the teacher is giving directions.
- Have typed directions for common computer operations at each computer.
- Use student helpers as "technology assistants" to help set up computers, answer common questions, check hardware, and properly turn off equipment at the conclusion of the lesson.

Noninstructional Use

In addition to the possibilities of using computers to enhance and extend instruction, computers have the potential to help teachers become better managers. Bolick and Cooper (2006) estimate that teachers spend over 11 hours per week on noninstructional activities. Computers have the potential to help teachers reduce the amount of time they spend on these noninstructional tasks or at least make the time spent more productive.

Spreadsheets and database programs for keeping classroom records are common uses of technology. These tools allow teachers to do things such as create class lists, keep attendance, organize a schedule of activities, track student progress, and calculate grades. This helps eliminate some of the paperwork, making it easier to keep up with noninstructional tasks.

A growing use that has the potential for impacting classroom management is using the Internet to contact parents. This tool makes it easy for the teacher to communicate to the parents regarding events at school, the curriculum, and classroom assignments. Some teachers have found that sending a message to all parents every couple of weeks regarding the curriculum and classroom objectives has been well received by parents. It helps keep them involved and informed and increases the possibility that they can support the curriculum with supplemental activities. In addition, sending a quick note home when there is a problem can help develop a linkage between parents and teachers as partners in the education of the student. There is some evidence that frequent e-mails between the teacher and the parents have a positive impact on student behavior (Bolick & Cooper, 2006). The downside to this is that you can spend many hours each day sending and responding to e-mails. We suggest that you set aside a certain amount of time each day. Respond to as many e-mails as possible, starting with the serious ones first. Budgeting your time is extremely important.

In summary, computers allow for exciting teaching and learning opportunities. As teachers become more familiar with computer use in the classroom, their management concerns are diminished. In addition, computers have noninstructional uses that can help teachers with their management responsibilities. They can assist in record keeping and paperwork that many teachers find overwhelming. The prevalence of computers in society has also made it possible to communicate with parents on a more frequent basis. Good use of e-mail keeps parents informed and increases the probability that they can assist and support the teacher.

RESPONDING TO INCIDENTS OF MISBEHAVIOR

Good lesson management will prevent many incidents of misbehavior. However, misbehavior will still occur. Responding to misbehavior is the major focus of later chapters, but we also need to mention it in the context of lesson management. Unfortunately, teacher responses to misbehavior during a lesson may destroy lesson smoothness, divert student attention from the instructional objectives, and result in a considerable loss of instructional time.

The major principle for responding to incidents of misbehavior during a lesson is to respond in a manner that keeps the attention of the class on the lesson content rather than focused on the misbehavior and the teacher responses. If possible, respond to incidents of misbehavior in an unobtrusive manner that gains the attention of the offending student but does not divert the attention of the rest of the class. This is not always possible, because there is some misbehavior that is so intrusive or serious that the lesson might need to be stopped in order to maintain control. However, some teachers are guilty of responding to each minor incident in such an obtrusive manner that the attention of all students is focused on the misbehavior. The lesson becomes fragmented, with a series of stops and starts that are interspersed with teacher control statements. Unfortunately, the students will remember the control statements rather than the lesson content.

Deciding how to respond to an incident of misbehavior must take into account the intrusiveness of the behavior and the likelihood that it will spread. If the behavior is not intrusive and it does not seem to be attracting the attention of other students, the behavior might be ignored for the time being or handled unobtrusively, such as moving closer to the misbehaving student.

However, if the behavior is intrusive and is attracting the attention of others, it cannot be ignored. Quick action is needed in order to prevent it from spreading. Even in this situation, though, the reaction needs to be performed quickly and the attention of the class quickly refocused on the lesson. Later chapters will provide you with some concrete suggestions on how to choose an appropriate response.

REVIEW OF MAIN IDEAS

1. Managing the classroom is one of the major responsibilities of teachers; good lesson management is absolutely essential to student learning.

2. Research by Kounin found that a major dimension of successful teaching was not in the way teachers responded to incidents of misbehavior, but rather in the way teachers managed lessons in order to prevent problems.

3. There are several dimensions of lesson management that need to be considered regardless of the approach used in the classroom. These include having clear objectives, demonstrating verbal clarity, providing clear directions, and demonstrating *withitness*.

4. When teaching the whole group, direct attention to maintaining lesson momentum, deciding on the pace of the lesson, learning how to attend to more than one thing at a time, developing lesson smoothness, and maintaining a group focus.

5. Cooperative learning and group approaches, when properly implemented, have a positive effect on student learning. However, these approaches pose management issues for teachers. They change the dynamics of the classroom interaction and the roles of the teacher and the students.

6. The role of the teacher in cooperative learning and group approaches might be best characterized as that of "instructional manager." The instructional manager assigns students to groups, creates a responsive environment, monitors group work, watches for unequal participation, and mediates conflicts.

7. Inclusive classrooms are the norm across the nation. The beginning point for success in inclusive classrooms is the attitude of the teacher. Teachers must believe that they can make a difference and understand that inclusion has benefits for all students. Differentiation of instruction and the use of peer-mediated approaches are two of the most effective approaches for inclusive classrooms.

8. Specific challenges are associated with using technology as a teaching tool. In fact, managing technology in the classroom has been identified by teachers as one of their greatest challenges.

9. Management issues related to technology depend on the way technology is used in the school. Different challenges exist when there are only one or two computers in the classroom as opposed to when all students have a computer. Some of the general challenges are related to organizing the physical environment, equipment failure, and student access to inappropriate content.

10. Noninstructional applications of technology can help teachers deal with management tasks. Computers can assist teachers with tasks such as record keeping, attendance, student progress, and grading. One of the more promising areas is the ability to communicate with parents.

11. Even in well-managed classrooms, misbehavior will occur. It is important that teacher responses to misbehavior minimize lesson disruption and time off task.

APPLICATION AND ENRICHMENT

1. Withitness is an important aspect of classroom management. Brainstorm with a group of individuals those things that indicate teacher withitness and what teachers can do to develop this important skill.

2. Observe a lesson from beginning to end. Identify how the teacher tries to keep momentum and smoothness in the lesson and handles those aspects of teaching that can interfere with smoothness and momentum.

3. Observe a classroom where cooperative learning or group learning is being used. Identify specific management issues that need to be addressed when using these teaching approaches. Note how the teacher assigned students to groups, created a responsive environment, handled conflicts, and dealt with unequal participation.

4. Interview teachers of inclusive classrooms. Have them identify what they feel are the greatest challenges to teaching inclusive classrooms, the approaches they have found most successful, and what they see as the benefits.

5. Determine how schools in your area use technology in the classroom. Identify rules and procedures that you would use if you were in a similar classroom.

6. Obtain a copy of an acceptable use policy from a local school district. Identify the elements of the policy and describe how you would present this to students and parents.

REFERENCES

Bolick, C., & Cooper, J. (2006). Classroom management and technology. In C. M. Evertson & C. S. Weinstein (Eds.), *Handbook of classroom management: Research, practice, and contemporary issues* (pp. 541–558). Mahwah, NJ: Lawrence Erlbaum.

Clark, C., & Peterson, P. (1986). Teachers' thought processes. In M. C. Wittrock (Ed.), *Handbook of research on teaching* (3rd ed., pp. 255–296). New York: Macmillan.

Cushing, L., & Kennedy, C. (1997). Academic effects of providing peer support in general education classrooms on students without disabilities. *Journal of Applied Behavior Analysis, 30*(1), 139–151.

Gephardt, W., Strother, D., & Duckett, W. (1981). Practical applications of research. *Phi Delta Kappa, 3*(3).

Kamps, D. M., Leonard, B., Potucek, J., & Garrison-Harrell, L. (1995). Cooperative learning groups in reading: An integration strategy for students with autism and general education peers. *Behavioral Disorders, 21*(1), 89–109.

Kounin, J. (1970). *Discipline and group management in classrooms.* New York: Holt, Rinehart & Winston.

Lotan, R. (2006). Managing groupwork in the heterogeneous classroom. In C. M. Evertson & C. S. Weinstein (Eds.), *Handbook of classroom management: Research, practice, and contemporary issues* (pp. 525–539). Mahwah, NJ: Lawrence Erlbaum.

Minnick, D. (Ed.). (1983). Student disruption: Classroom chaos linked to teacher practices. *Research and Development Center for Teacher Education Review, 1,* 2–3.

Soodak, L., & McCarthy, M. (2006). Classroom management in inclusive settings. In C. M. Evertson & C. S. Weinstein (Eds.), *Handbook of classroom management: Research, practice, and contemporary issues* (pp. 461–489). Mahwah, NJ: Lawrence Erlbaum.

Chapter 6

WHEN MISBEHAVIOR OCCURS

CLASSROOM SCENARIO

There just seem to be certain groups of students that are difficult to manage. At the end of the school year, one experienced elementary school teacher wrote of the frustrating year that she had experienced:

> "I've enjoyed my 11 years as a teacher and have seldom questioned my ability. However, this past year made me stop and evaluate what I am doing. The year was a nightmare! The students in the classroom never came together as a group. They were arguing and fighting with each other all year. Just the smallest incident acted like spontaneous combustion that would result in all sorts of problems. It seemed like every day I had to act as a referee trying to resolve differences between students. I was surprised because the class was composed of quite a few high-achieving students. Perhaps that was a part of the problem. The students were always competing with one another and delighted in trying to tear each other down.

> "I had expected to have a very pleasant and satisfying year. That might have been another problem because I started the year assuming that I would not need to be as firm and demanding as usual.

> "The year was so trying and frustrating that by the end of the year I was questioning my teaching ability and was thinking that maybe I needed a change of professions!"

CHAPTER OBJECTIVES

After completing this chapter you should be able to:

- Explain how teacher attitudes and motives influence the choices they make when responding to problems
- State the basic question that should guide teacher responses to the misbehavior of a specific student
- Define basic principles that can help teachers determine an appropriate response when confronted with a behavior problem
- State the factors that should be considered when developing a list of alternative responses to discipline problems
- Explain the organization that undergirds a range of responses to problems

---

Management is the prevention dimension. Good management practices prevent many discipline problems. However, students, like all human beings, will misbehave at times. No degree of skill on the part of the teacher can prevent all problems. Even the best teachers have to respond to inappropriate behavior at times. So, while prevention is the first dimension of management and discipline that needs to be addressed, the response dimension is the next. The response dimension is, in fact, the one that most concerns new teachers. They often ask, "What should I do when . . . ?" Although this is an important question, there are no simple answers. Humans are complex organisms with a variety of wants, needs, and motivations. What might address one student need might not address another. Simple suggestions on how to respond to incidents of misbehavior are not satisfactory for all situations. The sobering fact is that teaching is decision making, and making decisions about how to respond to incidents of misbehavior is one of the most important. What is needed is information on how to make these decisions.

Decision making begins with an understanding of basic principles that provide a framework for making decisions. This chapter will present some basic principles that can be helpful in making decisions about how to respond to specific incidents of student behavior. In addition, categories of different levels of teacher responses will be defined in order to help the reader begin developing a range of alternative responses that could be used.

TEACHER ATTITUDES AND MOTIVES

The beginning point in making a decision about a response to inappropriate behavior is the attitude of the teacher and the teacher's motives in choosing a specific response.

In the past, a common response to misbehavior was to subject the student to humiliation.

© Corbis

Teacher attitudes regarding their view of their students and their ability to teach and control the students are of critical importance. Teacher motives relate to the reasons why they choose a particular response. Teachers who are unaware of their attitudes and motives will have difficulty evaluating options and choosing ones that are appropriate for the situation.

Teacher Attitudes

Several questions can help you identify the attitudes and beliefs that might influence your own attitudes. For example, do you expect students to be inherently good or bad? Do you expect students to be constantly looking for opportunities to misbehave? Do you think students want to learn and succeed, or do you think they need to be forced to learn? What do you see as the role of the teacher in dealing with inappropriate behavior? Do you see misbehavior as a deliberate attempt to challenge your authority? Thinking about these questions can help you begin to identify your attitudes and what will influence the choices you make.

Effective and ineffective teachers typically exhibit different attitudes. Generally, effective teachers have more positive attitudes toward the students and their ability to respond to them. For example, effective teachers tend to view inappropriate behaviors as important opportunities to help students learn from their mistakes and develop increased self-control. They also believe that students can make good choices.

On the other hand, ineffective teachers generally view inappropriate behaviors as direct challenges to their authority. They often choose responses designed to "teach them a lesson" or to make them "an example." Their choices tend to be those designed to demonstrate their power as teachers.

One of the basic differences between effective and ineffective teachers can be noted in the types of concerns they express. Ineffective teachers usually express primary concerns about self. They are interested in maintaining their role and authority as teacher and are afraid of losing control. On the other hand, effective teachers generally express primary concerns about their impact on students. They are more interested in how a particular response will help the student grow and learn. In other words, when they choose a specific response to an inappropriate behavior, teacher concerns boil down to two questions: "What is best for maintaining my authority as teacher?" or "What is best for the student?"

Teacher Motives

Research by Brophy (1985) found that the types of responses teachers make to inappropriate behavior are related to their motives. He identified seven different motives that guide the responses teachers make to inappropriate behavior. These motives also reflect those teacher attitudes mentioned previously:

1. *Survival, or personal authority.* This motive relates to concerns about self. Teachers with this motive are merely trying to survive another day and trying to maintain their status as teacher. They tend to view students as threats and consequently interpret inappropriate behavior as a direct challenge to their authority. About 12% of the teachers in Brophy's study cited this as the primary motive for their response to inappropriate behavior.

Think about how individuals with these motives would be likely to respond to student misbehavior. They are likely to feel threatened and angry. They interpret classroom incidents as a personal challenge. Their responses are not based on a concern for the students and their needs and feelings but on a concern for their own needs and feelings. We might predict that they would attempt to deal with classroom incidents through the use of teacher power. Probable responses might include scolding, blaming, and threatening. Teachers who cite survival as a motive seem to lack an understanding of alternatives for dealing with misbehavior (Brophy, 1985).

2. *Anger and irritation.* Teachers with this motive cited that their basis for responding to a behavior is specific to the student who is misbehaving. Often they are personally angry with the student or indicate that they do not like the student. This usually is an extension of the survival and power concerns of the teacher. They see the student as a threat to their survival or as someone who is challenging their authority and power. Teachers often have the perspective that what the student has done is so bad that something bad needs to be done in return. This was the primary motive selected by about 11% of the teachers.

The responses teachers use when they have this motive are usually designed to seek revenge and psychologically, or even physically, hurt the student. They often choose responses that involve shame and ridicule or that are demeaning to the student. There is no concern for the needs of the students or for any long-term positive impact. Teachers with this motive are unable to help students learn self-control because they are not exercising self-control.

3. *School rules.* Teachers choosing this as a motive simply stated that their responses are chosen based on the violation of a school rule and therefore they had no choice but to respond. This might be defined as the "law and order" motive. This was the primary motivation of about 11% of the teachers responding.

Although it might be argued that the concern of teachers with this orientation is focused on helping students, the focus is actually on teaching them obedience to the rules. There is no attempt to take into account the concerns of the students, and there is little thought to developing interpersonal relationships with students. In fact, some teachers with this orientation state that they avoid developing interpersonal relationships with students because it interferes with their ability to apply the rules objectively. Concern about self, especially personal power, is the primary characteristic of teachers with this motivation.

The responses of these teachers tend to be impersonal and routine. The responses are generally the same for all students and might be varied in severity according to the gravity of the rule that is violated. Teachers with this motive usually do not accept any responsibility for misbehavior. It is up to the students to follow the rules and there are no excuses.

4. *Time on task, or an instructional concern.* The motive here is to increase the time the students are working toward the accomplishment of lesson objectives. The major concern is to get through the lesson and cover the content. About 24% of the teachers responded that this is a primary motive when choosing a response to misbehavior. It is possible that this percentage would be even higher if the study were conducted today. When the original study was conducted, there was not as much emphasis on standards and content coverage as there is today. In many schools, the current emphasis is on covering the content rather than understanding the needs of students.

Teachers with this motive usually do not consider the causes of the behavior. Although this response might be interpreted as a concern for the students and their learning, it is more often related to the self-concerns of the teacher to "get through the lesson." The needs of the students are still placed second to content coverage. Teachers with this motive tend to rely more on responses that are impersonal and somewhat automatic. Their responses tend to be the same regardless of the type of behavior or the needs of a particular student. Choices such as individual conferences and counseling would seldom be used because they take too much time.

The focus of these teachers is not on the individual but on the group. They are more likely to focus on prevention measures and more long-term changes in behavior. The methods used often focus on group appeals and group sanctions to get the student to comply.

5. *Group continuity and safety.* This concern begins to show a shift in teacher concerns from self to others. The motive is to keep the lesson moving and not let anything interfere with group learning. However, the concern is for the larger group and not for individuals. Specific students are not allowed to interfere with the smooth operation of the class. This is the most common motive cited by teachers. About 61% of the teachers responding to the research study cited this as a primary motive. This is certainly a solid motive for choosing a response. However, take care to make sure that the needs of an individual are not overlooked.

The choices of teachers who act with this motive in mind tend to focus more on the prevention of problems and on long-term changes in behavior. The choices often include the use of group sanctions and peer pressure.

6. *Concerns about the student.* Teachers who cited this as a motive for their responses indicated that they place the needs of the students first. Their motive is to help individual students learn to solve their own problems and develop self-control.

This motive indicates that teachers have made a shift from concerns of self to concerns for students. This was another popular choice of teachers in the study. About 46% of the teachers cited this as a primary motive for choosing a response.

Teachers who have this motive are more likely to tailor their responses to individual students rather than having automatic responses that are applied to all students and all behaviors. They are more likely to choose a response that they consider most appropriate for a particular student. Maintaining respect for the student is a major concern. Individual counseling and guidance are examples of responses that are often chosen.

7. *Future life.* Teachers choosing this as a motive cited a concern about future learning and the long-term success of the student. Long-term and permanent change in behavior is the goal. Immediate or temporary compliance is not a major concern. They are willing to sacrifice short-term benefits, such as content coverage, in order to help students develop changed attitudes and behavior. These teachers cited that they are concerned that students who are not corrected will fail, drop out, or have difficulty with authorities. About 12% of the teachers chose this as a primary motive for their responses. This motive also indicates that the teacher concern has shifted from self to that of the impact of their actions on students.

A common goal of teachers who choose this motive is that of developing positive relationships with the students. They emphasize student–teacher interaction and joint problem solving. Probable responses to inappropriate behavior include individual conferences, counseling, one-on-one discussion of behavior and consequences, and personal attention.

What Would You Do?

Read the following incident and state how you would respond.

I teach physical education and coach basketball. Our school district, like many others, is fiscally strapped. The district did find the money to refinish the basketball floor. I strictly enforce the policy of no street shoes on the floor because I know it will be a long time before we can expect another refinish job.

Wally was an insolent 10th-grade student who seemed to hate school and made a habit of breaking the rules and defying teachers. When I came out of the locker room, I saw Wally standing in the middle of the basketball court in his street shoes. I sort of lost it.

"Wally, get off the floor!" I yelled. "What's wrong with you?"

(Continued)

(Continued)

> *Wally started for the door and as he neared the edge of the floor he looked directly at me and deliberately scraped his shoes on the floor. I grabbed him by the arm and pulled him off the floor.*
>
> *Wally violently jerked his arm out of my grasp and shouted. "Leave me alone, you ignorant jock, or you'll wish you had!"*
>
> - What appear to be the primary motives of the teacher in this incident?
>
> - What mistakes did the teacher make in his response?
>
> - How could the incident have been kept from escalating into a major confrontation?

In summary, it is important for you to consider your attitudes and your motives when responding to inappropriate behavior as they limit or expand responses when misbehavior occurs. It is the beginning point in making choices. If you are able to move beyond needs of self and power and consider the needs of students and the impact your choices will have on them, you will be able to make better choices that more likely will result in a productive social environment. Table 6.1 lists some helpful and harmful attitudes and attributes. Use this list to perform a self-assessment.

THE PURPOSE OF DISCIPLINE

At this point, it is useful to focus attention on the purpose of discipline. The focus of this book is that management and discipline do have a purpose that goes beyond that of maintaining order in the classroom so that content can be covered. Our assertion is that one of the most important lessons individuals need to learn is how to exercise self-control and accept responsibility. Elias and Schwab (2006) support this emphasis when they note that having socially responsible individuals, those who are self-disciplined, is of critical importance to society.

However, self-control is something that is learned. It is learned as we experience the consequences of our choices and actions. The role of the teacher, therefore, is to help students reflect on their choices and the consequences of their actions. Teacher concerns should not be concerns of self; they should be concerned about the impact of their actions on their students' development of self-control. In this

Table 6.1   Discipline Self-Appraisal

Performing a self-appraisal is helpful in establishing a foundation for developing the attitudes and skills necessary for becoming successful in managing classrooms and responding to misbehavior. If you are currently teaching or have the opportunity to work with students, use this checklist to reflect on your teaching.

Helpful Attitudes and Attributes	*Harmful Attitudes and Attributes*
Consistent	Inconsistent
Clear expectations	Lacks trust in students
Fair	Pessimistic
Noncombative	Places priority on teacher power
Creative	Defensive
Patient	Fearful
Well organized	Disorganized
Tolerant of frustration	Easily intimidated
Enjoys teaching	Relies on threats
Accepts responsibility for classroom leadership	Neglects responsibility for classroom leadership

context, discipline problems are not things that teachers should fear. They should be viewed as opportunities to teach toward a critical objective.

Having a clear understanding of the purpose of discipline leads to a basic question that should be asked whenever a response to inappropriate behavior is required: "What response will help move this student in the direction of increased self-control?" This question should take priority over other concerns such as covering the content or maintaining a quiet classroom. This does not imply that these are unimportant concerns. There are times when a response is required that will stop a behavior so that a lesson can continue. However, this response needs to be followed with actions that will help the student move toward self-control in order to avoid future problems. In the long run, helping students learn self-control will result in more time to teach and increased opportunities to learn.

Keeping the primary purpose of the development of self-control at the forefront also helps teachers evaluate the choices they make. As the academic year progresses, if students are not demonstrating increased self-control, then your choices need to be questioned.

Keep in mind that learning self-control can be a lengthy process. Students who do not have much self-control should not be expected to demonstrate improvement in a day or even a week. There are times when students may appear to have regressed. In fact, some students who have been so used to getting their own self-centered desires met may get worse before they start to improve. They have always been able to get their own way through misbehavior, so when that doesn't work, they misbehave even more, expecting the teacher to eventually give in. Therefore, evaluating the growth toward self-control needs to be done over weeks and months. Do not expect immediate and dramatic change. Growth and learning can be a slow process. Some students who have not developed much self-control are not likely to demonstrate much improvement in a week or even in a month. However, over several months, there should be some evidence that the class is progressing toward increased self-control.

BASIC PRINCIPLES TO CONSIDER WHEN CHOOSING A RESPONSE

As indicated earlier in the chapter, there are no simple answers on how to respond when a problem occurs in the classroom. If there were simple answers, discipline problems would not be one of the major concerns cited by teachers or one of the major reasons teachers are dismissed.

There is no shortage of suggestions on how to respond. However, what works for one teacher may not work for another. What works in one context might not work in another. What works for one class might not work for another. This simply means that managing the classroom and responding to discipline problems is a matter of decision making. Making good decisions requires that you are able to evaluate the situation, you understand alternatives that are available to you, you understand the unique needs and motivations of the students you are teaching, and you have some basic principles that will guide your decision making. The following are some principles that can assist you as you make decisions about an appropriate response to misbehavior.

Preserve the Dignity of Students When Responding to Their Behavior

First of all, respecting the dignity of students should be a priority for all teachers. Teachers are engaged in a helping profession that values human diversity and the uniqueness of each individual. Teachers need to realize the potential impact they can have, for good or for bad, on the individuals in the classroom. Furthermore, teachers need to remember that they are working with what most parents consider their most prized possession, their children. Individuals who do not respect the dignity of other human beings should not be involved in teaching.

One of the places where the dignity of students is often overlooked is when responding to discipline problems. Teachers who are more concerned with issues of self rather than concerns for their impact on students have a tendency to choose responses that do not respect the students as valued individuals.

However, in addition to the moral imperative to value students, there are practical and concrete reasons why it pays to respect the dignity of students. When individuals believe that their dignity is being challenged, the tendency is to strike back. Therefore, rather than correcting a misbehavior and helping students move toward increased self-control, responses that do not respect the dignity of the student usually lead to other misbehaviors, often more serious ones. Docking (1987) emphasizes this when he points out that students often see maliciousness as a way of restoring their self-dignity when confronted by situations in which they feel that they are not being treated as persons. Their misbehavior is often retaliation for being insulted by the teacher. In fact, a significant percentage of secondary students state that this is precisely why they misbehave. They believe that the teacher is not respecting them as a person and is assaulting their self-respect and dignity. Therefore, they strike back by showing disrespect for the authority and the dignity of the teacher.

Solving behavior problems is very difficult if there is not a positive relationship between the teacher and the student (Kohn, 1996). Students need to trust and respect their teachers, and they need to believe that the teachers have their best interests at heart. This will not occur if they have been humiliated or demeaned. When students feel disrespected, the stage is set for a power struggle, one that is difficult for a teacher to win. Teachers and students become adversaries rather than collaborators reaching for the same goal.

Private Correction Is Preferable to Public Correction

This principle is related to respecting the dignity of the student. When correction is done in public in front of others, embarrassment and anger are usually the result. For example, we have heard teachers complain about a supervisor or administrator who corrected them in front of others. Students are no different. They do not like to be singled out or corrected in front of others. Those who may seem as though they welcome public correction probably want attention, and public correction is only reinforcing their belief that the only way to get attention is to misbehave. For example, one of the authors once had a particularly difficult student state, "Everyone in school knows me because I'm always in trouble. But, what do you get for being good?" In other words, his inappropriate behavior was seen as having a payoff, increased attention. Although some of us might find it hard to understand, students who believe that they cannot get attention through constructive channels may resort to destructive behavior. For them, any reaction is preferable to being ignored!

Public correction has several potential dangers. As stated previously, public correction has the potential for humiliation and the reinforcement of inappropriate behavior. In addition, public correction focuses attention of the entire class on inappropriate behavior. It provides a model for inappropriate behavior rather than a model for appropriate behavior.

In addition, public correction can complicate the situation for the teacher. Many of us have seen teachers correcting students in public and yet the students refuse to change. The teacher is now on the spot. In essence, the authority and the skill of the teacher have been challenged in front of the entire class. Everyone is now watching to see how the teacher will respond. A typical response to this public challenge is to escalate the power struggle and the conflict by getting tougher. What originally started as a minor incident has now become a major confrontation that is played out in front of an audience. The fact that the situation even reached this stage is a blow to the credibility of the teacher.

Private responses remove the audience. The student will not get more attention by challenging the teacher, and the need for the student to save face in front of an audience is removed. Most situations can be dealt with relatively quietly and unobtrusively so that the dignity of the student and the teacher are preserved.

Indeed, there are times when a private response is not possible. For example, if inappropriate behavior is disrupting a lesson and interferes with your ability to teach and the students' ability to learn, something needs to be done to stop the behaviors so that the lesson can continue. However, when public correction is needed, it needs to be done as quickly, as unobtrusively, and as unemotionally as possible. Then, when it is possible, talk with the student privately to try to prevent further occurrences.

Respond to Incidents of Misbehavior Consistently and Fairly

Implicit in this principle is the assumption that incidents of misbehavior require a response. Few problems will disappear by pretending they do not exist. However, there are some well-meaning authorities who counsel that ignoring misbehavior will eliminate it because withholding attention deprives the student of the reinforcement they desire. This may work if the goal of the student is attention and if the teacher is the only source of reinforcement. However, this is rarely true in the classroom. Other students provide reinforcement for behavior, and the type of reinforcement they provide might be valued over that of the teacher.

One key concept that permeates advice to teachers about their response to student behavior is that of consistency. It is important to define consistency, including all of its dimensions. The first dimension of consistency focuses on responding to incidents of misbehavior over time. If something is against the rule on one day, it is against the rule every day. Responding to behavior should not be dependent on the mood of the teacher. Students need a clear understanding of what the rules are and that there will be consequences if they violate the rules. If students do not perceive that rules are going to be enforced on a consistent basis, they will constantly test the rules to see if the teacher is going to enforce them. In other words, enforcement of the rules needs to be predictable.

A second dimension of consistency is related to following through on promises or threats. Students need to know that if something is promised it will be delivered. This means that teachers should not make promises (or threats) they cannot keep. Idle threats or promises erode the credibility of the teacher.

Fairness means that the rules apply to all students and all experience the consequences of their actions. There is a tendency for teachers to note the inappropriate behavior of some students and respond to it while ignoring the inappropriate behavior of other students. This uneven treatment leads to resentment. Not only do students lose respect for the teacher, their resentment often is directed to those students they believe are getting preferential treatment. Teachers need to make sure that if cute little Sarah misbehaves, she will experience a consequence just as surely as Barbara, the perennial problem.

Identify the Causes of Misbehavior

There is a great deal of emphasis on how to respond to misbehavior. However, it is just as important to identify what is causing the misbehavior. Identifying the causes of misbehavior can be uncomfortable because teachers may discover that they are the cause of the misbehavior. Identifying the causes of misbehavior requires an attitude of inquiry. Teachers need to address not just what students did, but why they behaved as they did. Kohn (1996) notes that the adult's role in an unpleasant situation begins with the diagnosis of what has happened and why.

Attempts to correct behavior often fail because the underlying reasons causing the behavior are ignored. This failure to identify causes almost always results in a recurring pattern of misbehavior. It is probable that persistent misbehavior signals some deeper, more fundamental, problems either with the organization and climate of the classroom or with some personal issues being experienced by the student. Merely responding to the surface behavior may temporarily stop the behavior, but it will not solve the problem. You can be sure that misbehavior will recur and might even take a more serious form.

It has been our experience that persistent misbehavior is often a desperate call for help. Nearly all students want to be successful and do not want to misbehave. However, if students are experiencing serious social or emotional problems, they may be unable to change their behavior until the underlying issues are addressed.

Understanding that persistent misbehavior may be a desperate call for help rather than a deliberate challenge of your authority can help you choose a response that not only eliminates the problem but also results in great professional and personal rewards.

Being willing to search for the causes of misbehavior requires a professionally and personally secure teacher. Teachers must be willing to consider the possibility that their choices might be causing the problem. However, research indicates that teachers do not readily recognize that they might be a causal factor of student misbehavior (Brophy & Rohrkemper, 1981). There is a tendency to blame students when things do not go well. For example, they are not motivated, they don't care, they haven't had the proper upbringing at home, they are lazy, and on and on. However, blaming students is unproductive. We need to ask why they are not motivated or why they don't seem to care.

It is sometimes difficult to look beyond the surface problem and raise questions about one's own practice. However, that might be exactly what is required in order to find a solution (Kohn, 1996). Perhaps the students do not have the prerequisite knowledge they need to be successful, the teacher's directions are confusing, lessons are poorly planned, reactions to students are demeaning, the teacher has created a climate of fear and anxiety, or the teacher is responding inconsistently and unfairly. We need to make sure that the students are not blamed for all problems. Probing for the causes of the misbehavior can lead to professional improvement and growth. Table 6.2 lists some indicators of troubled schools that can be useful in searching for solutions.

CHOOSING A RESPONSE TO MISBEHAVIOR

With these basic principles in mind, it is time to consider specific responses to misbehavior. One of the problems faced by teachers, especially inexperienced teachers, is that they are unaware of the options that they might choose when responding to misbehavior. Some new teachers fail to respond to misbehavior simply because they are uncertain about how to respond. The same responses are not appropriate for all problems, and relying on a limited number of responses often leads to their ineffectiveness. Being an effective teacher includes having a range of alternative responses that can be applied to the classroom and knowing when to implement them.

Choosing a Personal Response

One of the variables that makes discipline difficult is the personal dimension. Both teachers and students have different personalities and different interpersonal

Table 6.2   Signs of Troubled Schools and Classrooms

Environmental Factors	*Teacher Actions*	*Student Behavior*
A noticeable lack of care of the physical facilities	Little indication of lesson planning	High rate of truancy
Few displays of student accomplishments	Little evidence of established routines	Many displays of disruptive behaviors
Few indicators of school pride	Teacher verbalization of frustrations	Appearance of boredom
Disorganization	Teacher yelling and screaming	Failure to work productively
Classrooms cluttered	Little evidence that teacher attempts to interest students in lessons	Constant challenges to authority
Rules stated negatively	Little or no differentiation of instruction	Little adherence to established routines
	A large amount of time spent on behavioral control	Lots of off-task behavior
	Teacher unawareness of the IEP goals of special needs students	
	Emphasis on low-level outcomes rather than on conceptual understanding	
	Teacher direction of most activities from teacher's desk	

SOURCE: Adapted from The Melissa Institute for Violence Prevention and Treatment (2007).

skills and strengths. Each group of students is different, and each group develops a different group dynamic. This dynamic is often overlooked by those individuals who think they can enter the classroom and simply emulate one of their favorite teachers. The truth is that they have a different set of interpersonal abilities than those of the teacher. Therefore, the successful teacher is one who understands the personal dimension and is able to be flexible when working with diverse groups of students.

Students bring their previous experiences with them to the classroom. Advanced placement students who have high expectations of success and an academic orientation will respond to teacher correction somewhat differently than will students who have had difficulty achieving success in school. Not all students arrive at your classroom door motivated, enthusiastic, and positive. Some may have experienced considerable difficulty in school and have no expectation that things will be different. Fear of failure can be a serious barrier to success. Others may come from home environments that are not helpful to them. Others may enter the classroom with language difficulties and a high level of anxiety. Although the background and previous experience of students cannot be changed, it should not be a reason to give up. One of the great rewards of teaching is to see the frightened, hesitant, reluctant student become excited and confident and know that you had a role in changing his or her life.

Students come to school with different cultural and social values concerning the importance of school and appropriate behavior in the school environment. Contemporary teachers need to know that in the diverse society in which we live, they probably will not be teaching students like them. This diversity will not only include ethnicity but also socioeconomic status, language, religion, gender, and learning disability. As one of our professors used to remind us, "In the schools, we teach all the students from all the families."

To begin the search for alternative responses, it is important to consider your values and your beliefs. Consider how your background influences your interpretations of behavior and what is comfortable for you. The following are some questions that can help you consider responses that might be most comfortable for you:

1. *What are your values and beliefs about the nature of learners and your role as a teacher?* The attitudes and beliefs that teachers hold toward learners will have an important impact on the way they choose to respond to incidents of misbehavior. A key question is whether you view students as basically good or basically bad. If teachers believe, for example, that the students they are teaching are not capable or trustworthy, then their response to misbehavior is likely to be one that is heavy on teacher power and low on student choice. If, on the other hand, teachers believe that students should be given freedom because they can be trusted to make appropriate choices, then approaches to misbehavior are likely to be ones that deemphasize teacher control and emphasize student responsibility.

One of the values you need to consider is your attitude toward the use of rewards and incentives. A rather prevalent belief in our society is that individuals should do what is right with no expectation of a reward. Individuals holding this perspective view the use of reinforcements as inappropriate and even unethical. For example, there are those that claim that rewards are contrary to student growth and contend that students are "punished by rewards" (Kohn, 1993).

Those who hold this view will not consider responses that involve rewards and reinforcements. However, there needs to be a clear definition of rewards and reinforcement. For example, are grades reinforcement? What about teacher comments? Does this mean that neither positive nor negative comments are appropriate?

On the other hand, others see rewards and reinforcement as a part of daily life. They point out that few of us would continue in our professions if we were not rewarded for our efforts. They contend that we learn by receiving reinforcement regarding our performance and behavior. They point out that it is not the process of using rewards and incentives that has a negative impact on individuals, it is the inappropriate application of rewards and incentives.

If the use of reinforcements and punishments is acceptable, how and when should they be applied? What are the limits of using reinforcement? What can be done to make sure that students do not become dependent on the reinforcements rather than developing an intrinsic appreciation for the value of good behavior and learning?

Interpretations of the learning process also influence teacher responses. Teachers who view the learning process as hard work that takes place in a strict, no-nonsense environment will define discipline problems differently and will respond to incidents of misbehavior differently than those who consider learning a process of activity and exploration that involves making mistakes.

What is your understanding of the learning process and how individuals learn? Do they need to be coerced to learn or do individuals naturally want to learn? How much freedom and independence is appropriate?

Individuals often enter teaching with very well-established views of the role of the teacher. After all, most of us have spent thousands of hours in classrooms as students and have observed hundreds of teachers. Is the role of the teacher that of the "boss," or the authority in the classroom that should be obeyed without question (legitimate authority)? Is the primary role of the teacher one of communicating content and meeting standards rather than worrying about the social and emotional needs of students?

Secondary-level teachers often choose teaching because of their love of the subject. Their primary interest is in teaching that subject. Some of them become very impatient with the emotional concerns of students and see them as the responsibility of school counselors.

However, some authorities point out that ignoring the social and emotional needs of students and reducing discipline to what needs to be done to generate student compliance actually limits the use of responses that can lead to successful learning (Slee, 1995).

At all levels of education, the emotional and social needs of the students will impact their learning. Students do not leave their personal lives at the classroom door. Nor can it be expected that school counselors can solve their problems. In fact, most students look to a favorite teacher for help in the social-emotional area rather than to a school counselor. Those who see the role of the teacher as one of simply delivering content often find the role of the teacher frustrating and unrewarding.

2. *What is the maturity level of the students?* Most teachers understand that the responses chosen for inappropriate behavior are different for primary-level students than for secondary-level students. Some responses to inappropriate behavior require more maturity than others. Some of the approaches, like student conferences, might require abstract reasoning or the ability to assume the perspective of others, which simply are not present in young children.

However, care needs to be taken not to make the assumption that age is a reliable indicator of emotional and moral maturity. There are students in the secondary schools who have not developed the moral maturity to understand the function of rules and laws in society or to accept social and moral responsibility for their behavior.

3. *What are the cultural backgrounds and the values of the students?* In recent years, a great deal of emphasis has been placed on the multicultural characteristics of contemporary education. The cultural dimension does not end with the content of the curriculum of various learning styles. Culture also plays an important role in management and discipline. Rothstein-Fisch and Trumbull (2008) point out that students whose home values conflict with school values may become very confused as to what constitutes appropriate behavior. In addition, teachers who do not understand the cultural values that shape student actions may misinterpret the actions of the students. This, in turn, can lead to an increase in problems. Rothstein-Fisch and Trumbull (2008) state that the key to good management is an awareness of the key values of the home and school cultures so that students are not placed in the position of choosing one system over another. What is needed is culturally responsive teaching and management.

One way of beginning to understand cultural differences and their impact on classroom management and discipline is to look at two broad cultural values systems. The two systems are based on the framework of the emphasis placed on individual versus group well-being. One of the systems is labeled individualism and the other collectivism (Rothstein-Finch & Trumbull, 2008). Keep in mind that these are broad frameworks and that elements of each can be found in any culture. The defining characteristic between the two is not the presence or absence of individual or group well-being, but rather the emphasis placed on an individual's well-being or on group well-being.

The basic values in the individualism system include the following:

- The well-being of the individual and responsibility for one's self
- Independence and self-reliance
- The accomplishments of the individual
- The importance of self-expression and a willingness to take independent positions
- A primary focus on getting the task completed
- Self-esteem and the self-importance of the individual
- Emphasis on cognitive ability and intellectual attainment

The collectivism system values the following ideas:

- The well-being of the group as primary and responsibility of the individuals to preserve the group
- Cooperation and working interdependently with others
- Emphasis on the accomplishments of the family or group above those of the individual
- Modesty in individual accomplishments and respect for the accomplishments of others
- A priority on preserving the social organization of the group as opposed to putting the task first
- Emphasis on social skills and social intelligence (adapted from Rothstein-Fisch and Trumbull, 2008, p. 9)

In general, schools in the United States tend to reflect the individualism value orientation whereas many immigrant groups, as well as Hispanics, Native Americans, and African Americans, tend to emphasize collectivism (Rothstein-Fisch & Trumbull, 2008). These differences can lead to misunderstandings and conflicts in several areas.

Teachers with an individualistic value orientation place emphasis on the growth of the individual whereas students and parents with a collectivism orientation are more interested in how the individual is contributing to the group. Teachers emphasize how well the student is doing compared to the group and give individual praise, whereas students and parents may be embarrassed by praise and attention given to individual accomplishments. Teachers value individual self-expression and contributions, whereas students and parents emphasize quiet listening and respect for authority (Rothstein-Fisch & Trumbull, 2008).

In summary, as teachers consider how to respond to classroom behavior, they need to consider the cultural perspectives of the students. Otherwise, they may choose responses that are incompatible with the values of the students, forcing them to choose between two different value systems. It may well be that the students will reject the values of the teacher, and attempts to create an effective classroom environment will not be successful.

4. *What are the previous school histories of the students in the classroom?* Responding to this question requires a high level of professionalism and care. Previous school history can be used in destructive as well as constructive ways. For example, if the previous histories of students are used to label them, lower expectations for them, and limit their opportunities for growth, that is destructive

and unprofessional. However, if reviewing the previous history helps identify the causes of certain student behaviors, that would be constructive and professional.

When a student demonstrates persistent or serious behavior problems, it would be a professional action to review records and look for events or patterns of behavior that might lead to understanding. Some of the patterns that might be explored are the following:

- Has the student had some illnesses in the past? It might be that the period of illness caused some significant gaps in learning so that the student is unable to achieve success.
- Does the student have a history of moving from school to school? He or she might feel afraid and lonely.
- Was the student retained? He or she might have poor self-esteem and perceive himself or herself as a failure.

5. *How can you gain support of the parents?* Nearly all parents want their children to be successful, and most parents are more than willing to help. However, many parents do not know how to establish a partnership with the teacher in order to support the development of the student. Many parents are initially fearful and defensive when contacted by a teacher. Unfortunately, this is because when parents are contacted by the teacher, it is usually bad news. They rarely are contacted about something good. Because many of us take the failures of our children personally, we tend to become defensive when someone else criticizes them, because the criticism is taken as criticism of our values and parenting skills.

To overcome this defensiveness and to develop parents as allies rather than adversaries, positive contacts with parents are important. They need to be kept informed and they need to be invited to get involved in the school program. Efforts should be made early in the year to make contact with the parents with positive information. For example, some elementary teachers have found it useful to make a brief contact with parents by phone just to introduce themselves and communicate an interest in the child. Secondary teachers may find that they can use the Internet to communicate with parents and keep them informed. Sending positive notes home throughout the year worked well for one of us who was a secondary teacher. It not only built good parent–teacher relationships but it also enhanced the teacher–student relationships.

6. *When choosing a specific response, how much time and effort is required?* Some responses require more investment of time than do others. Some approaches may require a meeting or a counseling session with the student. There are situations in the classroom when this time is simply not available. When this occurs,

you need to choose, at least temporarily, a less desirable approach. Some approaches, such as behavior modification, require a large investment of out-of-class time to develop the reinforcement plan and considerable in-class time to implement. An elementary teacher with a class of 30 students or a secondary teacher with several different preparations simply does not have the time to implement behavior modification plans for several students. Keep in mind that you may have to respond one way in the interest of time. However, you must find long-term solutions or you will continue to deal with the behavior over the course of the academic year.

7. *Does the response require resources, and are they available to you?* Resources include time, space, and materials. Some approaches, such as providing reinforcers and plotting data for behavior management, require time and material. Is there time and opportunity to plot the data and to provide the reinforcers? What are appropriate reinforcers for these students? Other approaches, such as time-out, where students are isolated from the rest of the class, require appropriate space. Some approaches might require preplanning and cooperation from the school administration or other teachers in order to implement them effectively.

8. *What support can be expected from the school administration?* It is important that teachers understand the expectations of the school administrators and the support they can expect when dealing with inappropriate behavior. Canter and Canter (1992) state that teachers have a right to expect support from the school administration. This may be true, but the type of support that can be expected from school administrators varies tremendously from school to school. In addition, teachers have different interpretations as to what this means. For example, some teachers interpret support from administrators to mean that they should be able to send any problem to the office and expect the administrators to solve it. Other teachers interpret this to mean that the administration trusts the teachers and will become directly involved if there is a serious problem. For the most part, school administrators expect teachers to manage the classroom and take care of minor problems. However, they certainly want to be involved if there is a major problem that might involve others or the safety of students and teachers.

One of the first acts of a teacher new to a particular school building should be to have a conference with the school administrators. This might involve the principal or the associate principal in charge of discipline. It is important to know the expectations of the school administrators regarding the role of the teacher in responding to various types of problems and to clarify the conditions under which a student is to be sent to the office. In addition, the teacher needs to share the discipline plan he or she has for the classroom so that the administrator can provide guidance and understands how the teacher will respond when problems do occur.

This is an important conference that should be held as soon as possible. The conference provides guidance to the teacher in selecting a response and can help prevent serious misunderstandings. Keep in mind that the discipline dimension, if not handled appropriately, can lead to problems with parents and with other school professionals. There are some legal issues involved in discipline, and this is one of the areas where lawsuits can easily arise if not handled professionally.

DEVELOPING A RANGE OF ALTERNATIVE RESPONSES

One of the greatest fears of new teachers is not knowing how to respond when a problem occurs. As indicated in the previous sections, there is no one correct response for all problems. Choosing a response that is best for the student and the situation requires an awareness of alternatives. Therefore, taking into account the questions raised in the previous section, it is useful to develop a range of alternative responses. New teachers might want to take time to develop a range of alternatives and to write them down. Having this list close at hand can be useful when problems occur and the mind seems to go blank. A quick look at the alternatives can restore some confidence and assist in choosing a response that is likely to have the desired impact. More experienced teachers often have an informal range of responses that they have used and found to be successful.

One way of developing a range of alternatives is to organize them into categories. One way of categorizing responses is to arrange them according to their degree of intrusiveness. The first category can be those responses that require minimal effort and are relatively unobtrusive. Subsequent categories include responses that are more intrusive and require more teacher effort.

Minor problems can be addressed by using the least intrusive responses. Recurring, serious problems usually require more severe and more intrusive responses. As a general rule, the least intrusive and least severe responses should be tried first. If they do not have the desired impact, the more intrusive and more severe responses should be tried.

We suggest three categories that can be helpful to you as you begin to develop your range of alternative responses. In subsequent chapters, we will provide some concrete responses for each of the categories. These three categories include the following: (a) low-profile approaches that support self-control, (b) more intrusive teacher intervention, and (c) responses for serious and persistent misbehavior.

Low-Profile Approaches That Support Self-Control

This category includes two basic kinds of responses: (a) positive responses that are intended to support incidents of appropriate behavior and (b) teacher responses

Teachers must respond to misbehavior while maintaining lesson flow.

© Photos.com

directed toward minor offenses. The responses grouped in this category allow students considerable freedom and choice. Their intent is to communicate in an unobtrusive way to the student that there is a problem. The student is then given the opportunity to exercise self-control and correct the problem. By allowing the student the freedom to choose to exercise self-control and then reinforcing this choice, a positive environment is developed that shows respect for the student and supports growth in self-control and the acceptance of responsibility.

The specific responses that fit into this category are those that are relatively simple and low profile and that require a minimal amount of teacher effort. Teachers who are skilled in managing a classroom often respond with such unobtrusive responses that observers and even other students in the classroom are unaware that there was a problem.

More-Intrusive Teacher Intervention

Low-profile responses do not always work. Sometimes the behavior is so disruptive that it interferes with the ability of other students to learn and the teacher to teach. In addition, some students simply have not learned how to exercise self-control, and low-profile responses seem to have little impact. In these situations, more direct and intrusive teacher responses are needed.

Responses in this category might be as simple as a firm command or a rule reminder or might involve more complex actions such as a teacher–student conference.

Behaviors that persist over time and that are destructive to the learning process might be addressed through a behavior modification plan. This requires considerably more time and effort but can prove to be very worthwhile in stopping a behavior and putting the student back on the track toward self-control.

Responses for Serious and Persistent Misbehavior

The responses in this category should be reserved for the very serious and persistent problems. If used too frequently, these responses begin to lose their effectiveness. The responses in this category involve the use of teacher power and authority. As a result, they often result in student anger and resistance. However, there are times in the classroom when these more severe responses need to be implemented.

When these more serious responses are used, it is important to keep the focus on student responsibility. The students need to know that this action is a consequence of their behavior and that the student can choose to change the behavior and therefore choose not to experience the consequences. Establishing a link between behavior and the consequence is important if growth is to occur. Unfortunately, some students attribute the consequences to actions beyond their control. Therefore, they have no responsibility for their actions, and responses are viewed as unfair action by teachers who do not like them and who are just getting revenge.

When possible, the type of response chosen in this category should be related to the nature of the problem. In other words, there should be a logical connection between the behavior and the response. For example, if the behavior results in wasted time, they make up the time. If it involves the destruction of property, the response should involve restitution.

Some of the responses grouped under this category include isolation, removal from class, detention, suspension, and parent conferences. When behavior problems are persistent and serious, it is important that the appropriate school administrators be informed and involved.

REVIEW OF MAIN IDEAS

1. Even the best teachers encounter incidents of misbehavior in the classroom. There are no responses that fit every situation. Therefore, teachers need to develop alternative actions that they might choose that would be consistent with the situation.

2. Teacher attitudes and motivations play an important role in the choices they make in response to problems. These attitudes and motives are often related to teacher concerns. These concerns are related to concerns about self or concerns about the impact they have on students.

3. The major purpose of discipline is to develop self-control and responsibility, and decisions about responses should keep this goal in mind.

4. Respecting the dignity of students is an important consideration when choosing a response. Students often report that their misbehavior is the result of their perceptions of not being respected.

5. Public correction of students has some potentially negative side effects. Therefore, private corrections should be used whenever possible.

6. Teacher consistency and fairness are key elements in developing respect for the teacher and in creating a climate that decreases incidents of misbehavior.

7. If the causes of the misbehavior are not identified and addressed, it is not likely that the problem will be removed. However, identifying the cause of misbehavior can be uncomfortable because the cause might be the actions of the teacher.

8. Choosing responses to problems has a personal element. Teachers need to choose responses that are consistent with personal values and beliefs.

9. Responses to individual students should take into account the maturity level of the student, his or her prior experience, and his or her cultural background.

10. Elements that influence appropriate responses are related to the availability of resources, the amount of effort required, and the support of the school administration.

11. It is useful to develop a personal range of alternatives that can be used when responding to problems. The range of alternatives should be ordered from low-profile and unobtrusive responses to those that require more intrusive teacher intervention.

APPLICATION AND ENRICHMENT

1. Develop a range of alternative responses that would be consistent with your values and beliefs. Organize this range of alternatives using the framework suggested in the chapter from low-profile responses to more intrusive responses.

2. Interview some students at the grade level of choice regarding their views of discipline. What do they think are the common misbehaviors that occur in the classroom? Why do they think they occur, and what do they think effective teachers do when confronted with discipline problems?

3. Observe in several classrooms. Note the types of misbehavior and the responses that teachers make to them. What percentage of the behaviors would you classify as minor and what percentage as serious? Which teachers seem to have the most positive results? What do you think accounts for their success?

REFERENCES

Brophy, J. (1985). Teachers' expectations, motives and goals for working with problem students. In C. Ames & R. Ames (Eds.), *Research on motivation in education, Vol. 2: The classroom milieu* (pp. 175–214). New York: Academic Press.

Brophy, J., & Rohrkemper, M. (1981). The influence of problem ownership on teacher perceptions. *Journal of Educational Psychology, 73*(3), 295–311.

Canter, L., & Canter, M. (1992). *Assertive discipline: Positive behavior management for today's classroom.* Santa Monica, CA: Canter.

Docking, J. W. (1987). *Control and discipline in schools: Perspectives and approaches* (2nd ed.). London: Harper & Row.

Elias, M., & Schwab, Y. (2006). From compliance to responsibility: Social and emotional learning and classroom management. In C. M. Evertson & C. S. Weinstein (Eds.), *Handbook of classroom management: Research, practice, and contemporary issues* (pp. 309–341). Mahwah, NJ: Lawrence Erlbaum.

Kohn, A. (1993). *Punished by rewards.* Boston: Houghton Mifflin.

Kohn, A. (1996). *Beyond discipline: From compliance to community.* Alexandria, VA: Association for Supervision and Curriculum Development.

Melissa Institute for Violence Prevention and Treatment. (2007). *Indicators of troubled schools.* Retrieved Nov. 12, 2007, from http://www.teachsafeschools.org/trouble-schools.html

Rothstein-Fisch, C., & Trumbull, E. (2008). *Managing diverse classrooms: How to build on students' cultural strengths.* Alexandria, VA: Association for Supervision and Curriculum Development.

Slee, R. (1995). *Changing theories and practices of discipline.* Washington, DC: Fanner Press.

Chapter 7

WHEN PROBLEMS ARE MINOR

CLASSROOM SCENARIO

A 20-year veteran of teaching discusses changes in teaching since she started and imparts some advice to a group of student teachers:

> "It seems to me that over the years there has been a shift of responsibilities from parents to teachers. I heard one parent remark, 'I'll be glad when Johnny goes to kindergarten so that he will learn how to behave.' Things that used to be taught in the home and the family are now left to the teacher. What this means is that teachers cannot assume that students coming to school know appropriate behavior. While this is obvious to those of us who teach in elementary school, I have secondary teacher friends who are also amazed at how even high school students seem to be unaware of appropriate behavior and are surprised when they are disciplined.

> "However, I do believe that students respond to structure and direction. They want the security of knowing what is expected of them and how to achieve success. Much of their misbehavior in the classroom is relatively minor, and some teachers make the mistake of making every minor misbehavior a major offense. Teachers must be patient and not overreact to every incident. They need to realize that the student may not know any better. This means that teachers need to spend time teaching students appropriate and expected behaviors and need to respond in ways that help students learn what is acceptable."

CHAPTER OBJECTIVES

After completing this chapter you should be able to:

- State the importance of reacting to incidents of misbehavior
- Define the role of the teacher in building a supportive community
- Define the difference between defensive communication and supportive communication
- Explain the difference between punishment and consequences
- Develop a list of low-profile and nonintrusive responses that can used when misbehavior is minor

---

One of the encouraging facts regarding student behavior in the classroom is that the majority of the misbehaviors occurring in the classroom are those that would be classified as minor. Most of the misbehaviors involve minor infractions such as talking, making noise, inattention, or out-of-seat behavior. One study estimated that about 80% of behaviors identified as problems were nothing more than students talking to one another (Jones, 1979). Although these behaviors are defined as minor, they still require a teacher response. To simply ignore inappropriate behavior does not help the student or the class. Everyone needs to learn that there are consequences for his or her actions. The world needs to be accepted as it is, not as we wish it were. Individuals who behave badly toward others are rejected; individuals who do not act responsibly are not given responsibility. We might hope that others in the world would excuse our poor behavior, but they do not always do so.

When individuals are shielded from the consequences of their actions, an opportunity to help them learn valuable lessons is missed. Students need to understand that developing as a productive citizen in society requires the acceptance of responsibility. There is not an innate acceptance of responsibility or knowledge of what is right or moral; it is something that is learned. Moral values such as respect, responsibility, honesty, and cooperation are learned through concrete experiences with people they respect. Teachers who earn the respect of students are in a position to help students develop their social and moral knowledge in "safe" environments where there is an opportunity for reflection and growth.

Misbehavior in the classroom can interfere with the rights of the teacher to teach and other students to learn. Behaving responsibly means that individuals don't act in ways that interfere with the rights of others. In addition, a ripple effect usually develops when inappropriate behavior is not stopped. The behavior starts to spread and other students, and soon a whole classroom, is out of control. The result is a minor problem escalating into a major problem that is very disruptive and harmful to the learning climate.

It needs to be remembered that student behavior is purposeful and is related to their interpretations of classroom life and their relationships with teachers. They choose to comply or resist the rules, or to ignore or acquiesce to teacher requests. One study of high school students indicated that students made their choices depending on their perceptions of the teacher. If teachers were perceived as mean and cold, students were more likely to engage in resistant behaviors. They identified their behaviors as ways of "getting even" with teachers whom they perceived as ineffective (Hoy & Weinstein, 2006).

This implies that teachers, as classroom leaders, need to earn the respect of the students and create a safe environment. They need to respond to incidents of misbehavior in ways that respect the dignity of the students and preserve positive relationships with students and a constructive classroom climate.

One of the common mistakes observed in classrooms is when teachers interpret every incident of misbehavior as a challenge to their authority and then overreact, so that minor problems soon become major problems. Anger and frustration are the result, and the opportunity to learn is lost. Classrooms need to be safe so that students are allowed to make mistakes and learn from them.

This chapter presents information on how to respond to incidents of misbehavior that might be classified as minor. We will make suggestions for a range of alternative responses that are consistent with respecting the dignity of the student and creating a positive learning climate.

DEVELOPING A SUPPORTIVE COMMUNITY

Student behavior takes place in a social context. A good beginning point for considering responses to incidents of misbehavior is to consider the group context. Watson and Battistich (2006) contend that a supportive, relational community is necessary if the classroom is to be a safe one where students can learn to take responsibility for their behavior. Students want to belong and be accepted, and they are often seeking the approval of the group. In fact, the approval of the group might be more important to them than the approval of the teacher. Therefore, their actions need to be interpreted in the group context. Individuals simply behave differently in groups than they do when they are alone. Successful teachers need to build a supportive community so that their actions will have the desired impact.

It is the responsibility of the teacher as the classroom leader to begin the process of building a supportive community. The conditions under which a supportive and caring community can develop include treating students with respect, allowing students a voice, sharing classroom responsibilities, and involving students in the decision making. These conditions are facilitated if the teacher role is viewed as that of lead management, as discussed in earlier chapters. Ginott (1972) clearly articulates the impact of the teacher:

> I've come to the frightening conclusion that I am the decisive element in the classroom. It is my personal approach that creates the climate. . . . As a teacher, I possess tremendous power to make a child's life miserable or joyous. I can be a tool of torture or an instrument of inspiration. I can humiliate or humor, hurt or heal. In all situations, it is my response that decides whether a crisis will be escalated or deescalated and the child humanized or dehumanized. (pp. 15–16)

In addition, the actions of the teacher need to communicate that developing responsible individuals is as important as developing good students, and that social-emotional goals are at least as important as academic goals. Think about it. What good would it do to educate members of society to a high level of academic competence if there is an absence of self-control and responsibility? We need only to look to history to find that some of the greatest atrocities of modern times were committed by highly literate individuals and societies who acted without regard to moral values and social consequences.

Several actions can contribute to building a supportive community. Those include the following:

- Evaluate the quality of teacher interactions with students. Are they positive and constructive or negative and disrespectful?
- Evaluate the curriculum. Is it relevant and important? Is it at the appropriate level of difficulty for the students? Is the pace too fast or too slow?
- Involve students in problem solving. Do students have a voice? Are they treated as respected individuals? What do the students see as the problems? What solutions do they suggest?
- Reduce reliance on extrinsic rewards. Help the students choose behavior based on what is right rather than the rewards it brings.
- Insist that students respect each other (adapted from Hardin, 2008, p. 143).

Building a supportive community also requires a celebration of success. Unfortunately, many teachers tend to focus on the negative and respond to incidents of misbehavior and ignore examples of good behavior. Mendler (1997) contends that teachers fail to recognize about 95% of the appropriate behaviors. All individuals, regardless of age and circumstances, want to feel that their efforts are recognized. Few of us will remain in a job if the only feedback we receive is based on our mistakes, and our accomplishments are never recognized. A supportive environment is a positive one where everyone feels he or she can be successful.

To be sure, there is more to creating a supportive climate than just giving abundant praise. In fact, several authorities have cautioned about the inappropriate use of praise. Some have even gone so far as to condemn the use of praise. It is true that praise can be used so indiscriminately that it becomes ineffective and counterproductive. However, everyone has a need for achievement. We all want to know that we are growing and improving. Well-earned praise helps meet that need and is effective if it meets certain criteria.

For praise to be effective, it must be genuine and earned. Students will quickly see through praise that is not genuine. It will then be viewed as meaningless. Praise should not be given indiscriminately but earned instead. Indiscriminate and overly effusive praise can be embarrassing and counterproductive. If praise is not linked to something earned, then it does not serve the purpose of informing the students that they are improving.

Communication in a Supportive Classroom

A key ingredient in establishing a supportive classroom climate is the communication style. Nearly all proposals for responding to misbehavior involve communication, both verbal and nonverbal, as a central element. One of the major contributors to behavior problems is a breakdown in communication. The language used by teachers when interacting with students verbally sends messages that have profound effects on students' behavior and self-concept. In addition, communication theory emphasizes the importance of nonverbal communication, including facial expressions, gestures, touching, and paralanguage components such as voice tone and emphasis and rate of speech.

Nonverbal communication forms the frame of reference for the verbal communication and heavily influences the message that is received. In other words, we may think that we are sending a clear message by the use of our words. However, students may interpret the message quite differently based on the nonverbal behaviors of the sender. This is especially true when the verbal message and the nonverbal message are incongruent. The nonverbal behaviors are often viewed by those receiving the message as the accurate message because they are sent by an unaware sender and a very aware receiver. In other words, we are often unaware of our nonverbal behaviors such as smiling or frowning, but it is very much a part of what the students receive, and they tend to trust our nonverbal message as the one that is accurate. For example, if a teacher is praising a student while frowning, the message is often interpreted as sarcasm rather than genuine praise. On the other hand, if a negative verbal message is being sent and the teacher is smiling, it is often interpreted as insincere. Therefore, your responses to inappropriate behavior will be influenced by your communication styles. It is not just what is said but it is also how it is said.

Nonverbal behavior is an important component of communication.

© Photos.com

Teachers typically establish one of two opposite communication styles: a defensive style or a supportive style. The supportive style is problem oriented, spontaneous, descriptive, and empathic (Borisoff & Victor, 1998). *Problem oriented* means that the communication is clear and the person has a desire to cooperate to solve the problem rather than controlling or manipulating the other person. *Spontaneity* refers to responsiveness and openness rather than predetermined, automatic speech or the presence of hidden agendas. In other words, the communication style needs to be open and honest and indicate a willingness to listen. *Descriptive* means that communication describes and informs rather than judges and evaluates. This communication style opens the door for additional communication. *Empathetic* communication means that there is an effort to understand the other. If students feel that they are being disrespected and their feelings or perspectives are unimportant, they generally become defensive. This does not mean that teachers have to agree with their perspectives. Rather, it means there is an openness that allows them to share their perspectives with someone who is willing to listen with an open mind.

The defensive style of communication is based on a lack of respect for the other and the need to exercise one's power. There are several types of communications that contribute to a defensive communication climate (Borisoff & Victor, 1998).

Sarcasm

Sarcasm seldom has a place in the classroom. It is often an insidious tactic for criticizing others. Some teachers contend that it is just an expression of humor. However, if it is an attempt at humor, it is humor at the expense of another. The person who is the target of sarcasm is frequently humiliated. This undermines student trust and the creation of a safe environment. In addition, young children usually do not understand sarcasm and easily misinterpret the message.

Reprisals and Threats

Reprisals and threats are forms of coercion that create barriers to a supportive communication climate. By their very nature, they are destructive to collaboration. Reprisals and threats are characteristic of a person with power threatening to use that power to impose pain unless the other person conforms. Teachers who use threats often find themselves in difficulty when the student challenges them to deliver on their threats and they are unable to do so. The inability to follow through reduces teacher credibility and power. Reprisals and threats usually turn into no-win situations. If you follow through on threats and reprisals, relationships are destroyed; if not, credibility is lost.

A useful alternative to reprisals and threats is to calmly ask students to identify what happens when people continue to violate the rules. Let them know that they are choosing to experience those consequences if they continue. Keep the responsibility on the student and on the inappropriate behavior rather than making a threat that switches the responsibility from the student to the teacher.

Hostile Questioning

A typical response to misbehavior is to direct a question at the misbehaving student. There are instances when this is effective. However, some questions communicate a hostile intent. These questions are often loaded questions or carry accusations. For example, "Don't you want to grow up?" carries the accusation that the person is immature. The tone of voice and emphasis often communicate hostile intent as much as the words that are used. It is okay to use questions to get information to help solve a problem. However, hostile questions are not intended to solve the problem; they are intended to put down or embarrass somebody.

Students become adept at using hostile questions to deflect teacher focus on the major issue. For example, a student might ask, "Don't you know anything about feelings?" The intent is to make the teacher feel guilty and shift the focus from the misbehavior of the student to the actions of the teacher. This neat switch of responsibility often works, and the teacher ends up on the defensive.

Personal Attacks

It is difficult to separate the behavior from the person. However, this is what needs to be done. Students need to understand that while a particular behavior is unacceptable, they are still respected as a person. Therefore, take care to ensure that responses to misbehavior are not personal attacks on the person. Personal attacks such as "You are just immature" do not focus on the inappropriate behavior and do not open the door for learning. They just create additional anger and a need for the student to defend his or her dignity.

In summary, the communication style in a classroom is an important ingredient in establishing a supportive and caring classroom. Those types of responses that create a defensive style of communication need to be eliminated. This is sometimes easier said than done, because some teachers are unaware of their responses and how they might be interfering with the establishment of a supportive and caring climate.

WHEN MISBEHAVIOR OCCURS

As previously indicated, it is important that teachers respond when incidents of misbehavior occur. However, responses need to be carefully chosen. Thoughtless responses can be destructive. Building a supportive community requires that encouragement needs to accompany consequences (Albert, 1996). Students who do experience the consequences of their choices also need to believe that they can improve. Few things are more destructive to a supportive environment than student feelings of hopelessness. Therefore, when students have experienced consequences for inappropriate behavior, they also need to be encouraged in their ability to do better. The basic point is that the goal is not only to weaken unacceptable behaviors but also to strengthen desired behaviors.

Consequences and Punishment

At this point, it is important to distinguish between consequences and punishment. Some individuals have a difficult time understanding the difference. Punishment is something that is administered with the intent to be psychologically or physically hurtful. It often has a component of "getting back" at the student for his or her behavior. Punishment usually has the unpleasant side effect of creating tension, and results in a break in the relationship between the teacher and the student (Marshall & Weisner, 2004).

In our society, there seems to be a strong sentiment that punishment is good for us. However, although punishment may be effective in stopping a particular behavior, the effects are usually temporary. Punishment may inform an individual of what is inappropriate, but it does not teach what is appropriate. Punishment tends to generate fear and anxiety, conditions that block learning. There is a general consensus among most authorities that the disadvantages of punishment far outweigh any potential advantages. Table 7.1 identifies the role punishment plays in a classroom.

Consequences are best defined as logical or natural responses to actions. For example, if students choose to waste time in the classroom, they make it up on their own time. If they make a mess in the classroom, they clean it up. If they are unable to work quietly with others, they are removed from the group. There is a place where consequences can turn into punishment. For example, if a student makes a mess in the classroom, cleaning up the classroom is a consequence. Being required to pick up trash on the playground is a punishment. When a student wastes time and fails to complete work, having him or her complete this work rather than another preferred activity would be a logical consequence. Having him or her serve detention or stay after school would be a punishment.

Table 7.1   The Role of Punishment

- Punishment may temporarily stop a behavior.
- Punishment does not teach appropriate substitute behavior.
- Punishment should only be used as a last resort.
- Punishment usually signals that the teacher has no other options.
- Punishment damages the relationship between teacher and student.
- Punishment should never be used when the student goal is revenge. It only justifies revenge as a response to a hurtful environment.
- Punishment actually results in a negative ripple effect so that there is likely to be more misbehavior after the implementation of punishment.
- When implemented, punishment should be administered in relationship to the seriousness of the misbehavior.

Reinforce Appropriate Behavior

As noted previously, good behavior tends to be ignored by teachers. One of us once worked with a student who was a chronic discipline problem. The student stated in a conversation, "Everyone in school knows me because I'm always in trouble. But, what do you get for being good?" It was clear that he had a need for attention and had found it was easier to fulfill that need through misbehavior than through constructive ways. Although most of us who have had successful school experiences might find this difficult to comprehend, we must remember that for some students, any kind of attention, even negative attention, is preferable to being ignored.

What do students get for being good? This is one of the questions all teachers should consider. One simple rule that can change the classroom climate and contribute to a supportive group is to "catch them being good." Some teachers are caught up in the role of enforcer and see their role as catching students misbehaving. This game of "cops and robbers" creates a destructive environment where students are trying to see what they can get away with and teachers are trying to catch them. Teachers can't win this game. There are simply too many students and too many opportunities for students to get one up on the teacher. Those teachers who do think they are successful in being the heavy-handed enforcer often discover that misbehavior is only transferred to other places and other times. The only choice is to gain student cooperation. Gaining their cooperation requires that they believe the teacher is interested in them as individuals and is supportive. This is enhanced if the teacher provides recognition when the student is doing something right.

Choose a Thoughtful Response

When discipline problems occur in the classroom, teachers need to give some thought to the causes of the problem prior to responding. Remember that not all misbehavior is the result of willful disobedience. Sometimes conditions created in the classroom facilitate inappropriate behavior. In other words, sometimes the cause is related to the teacher or the curriculum. Misbehavior in the classroom is often a sign that something is wrong. So, rather than blaming students and immediately implementing a consequence, a teacher should diagnose the classroom situation. There are a couple of questions that need to be answered:

1. Self-evaluate and ask, "Is there something that needs to be changed?" It could be that the students are having trouble achieving success because they lack the prerequisite knowledge, or the pace of the lesson is too slow or too fast so that they are getting bored. Perhaps their anxiety might have been raised to the point

that their ability to exercise self-control is hindered. Perhaps the directions or the purposes of the activity are unclear and students are frustrated.

2. A second question is designed to prompt a hypothesis about why the student is engaging in misbehavior. What is the goal of the student? Is it just an outgrowth of youthful exuberance? Is the goal to seek relief from boredom? Is it to gain attention? Are the students trying to gain status in the group? To be sure, this question results only in hypotheses, and they might be wrong. However, it does provide a starting point for choosing an appropriate response. If some thought is not directed to the possible goals of the student, there is a real danger that the responses of the teacher might reinforce the inappropriate behavior.

What Would You Do?

Read the following incident and suggest what you would do.

Keith is not really a serious behavior problem. He wants to please and is very likable. His work is always at an acceptable level. The problem is that Keith is a constant talker. Whenever the class is working independently, he is constantly talking. If there is no one around, he talks to himself! It isn't loud talking, but it is noticeable. It is as if talking is just a normal part of his behavior and he is unaware that it creates a problem. Others seated near him sometimes get angry and tell him to be quiet.

- Is this a problem that requires a response? Why or why not?

- What might be some responses that you would try?

- What would be your criteria in choosing a response?

LOW-PROFILE RESPONSES

When misbehavior is minor, the best responses are those that are low profile and noncoercive. These responses need to be chosen with an emphasis on the needs and goals of the student and the need to maintain a positive classroom environment. The advantages of low-profile approaches are that they are generally easy to use, do not require a lot of teacher effort, maintain respect for the student, and help prevent power struggles between the teacher and the students. Responses in

Most incidents of misbehavior involve minor problems such as talking and lack of attention.

© Photodisc

this category keep the responsibility for correcting the problem with learners and provide them with an opportunity to self-correct and practice self-control.

As a general rule, when minor problems occur in the classroom, the first responses should be from this category of responses. If this response does not have the desired effect, then more intrusive responses might be needed.

There are a number of low-profile and noncoercive responses that can be used. We suggest a few in Table 7.2. You might want to add others to the list as you observe them in the classroom.

Table 7.2 A Selection of Low-Profile Responses

Nonverbal Responses	Low-Profile Verbal Responses
Facial expressions	Reinforcement of appropriate behavior
Eye contact	Use of the student's name in the context of the lesson
A wait for compliance	Redirection of the student
Gestures	A quiet word
Proximity control	Rule reminder
Distraction removal	Classroom meetings

The purpose of low-profile techniques is to communicate to students that their behavior is noted and that it is inappropriate. It gives them an opportunity to self-correct and practice self-control. Low-profile messages need to be as unobtrusive as possible so that the focus of other students in the classroom remains on the lesson and not on the inappropriate behavior.

Nonverbal Responses

Borisoff and Victor (1998) estimate that as much as 65% of the meaning of a message is communicated nonverbally. Because these nonverbal messages are so important in communication, they are very useful in responding to misbehavior in ways that are not disruptive to the classroom. One study (Weinstein & Mignano, 1993) found that nonverbal signals stopped misbehavior 79% of the time!

One dimension of nonverbal behavior that can be useful in sending messages to students is body language. Charles (1992) contends that about 90% of discipline is body language. When in front of a group of students, what does your body posture communicate? Does it communicate confidence, poise, and security? Or does it communicate fear, tension, and uncertainty? Your posture and the way you stand, walk, and gesture communicate messages about your confidence and poise. When a problem occurs, how do you react? Does your body slump in resignation? Does your walk signal uncertainty? Do you avoid eye contact?

When responding to a problem, an erect and confident carriage communicates confidence. Simply standing up, placing hands on your hips, making eye contact, and moving toward the problem area communicate to students that you are not intimidated and that you mean business. Nervous movements, darting eyes, and a hesitant stride are quickly interpreted as a sign of uncertainty and invite additional challenges.

Teachers need to evaluate their nonverbal messages. They may discover that they are sending unintended messages to students. Since nonverbal messages are sent from a largely unaware sender, increasing our understanding can be difficult. This is where videos can be helpful. These need not be long segments but relatively short episodes that capture typical actions. It is sometimes useful to eliminate the sound so that the focus is on the nonverbal actions rather than the words. What is the body language? Does it communicate poise and confidence? What gestures are used? What is the pattern of eye contact? When sound is included, what is the voice tone? What is the style of communication? Is it supportive or defensive?

Facial Expressions

Facial expressions are an important part of the messages sent. Those listening to messages are often interpreting the message by watching facial expressions. Facial expressions without words can be very effective as low-profile

responses to problems. There are a number of facial expressions that can communicate disapproval. Those can include frowns, the unsmiling face with tight
lips, or the look of puzzlement. Some teachers use facial expressions very naturally and easily. Others have difficulty. If you are someone who has difficulty,
consider coaching and practice. Some individuals have found that taking a the-
ater arts class helps them learn how to use body language and facial expressions
to communicate effectively.

Eye Contact

Eye contact has long been recognized as a powerful means of communicating.
When someone is misbehaving, catching his or her eye and maintaining eye contact is often enough to stop the behavior. When eye contact is established, keeping
the gaze steady and focused on the student until after the student has returned to
the appropriate behavior is most effective. A typical sequence is the following: A
student is off task or engaging in inappropriate behavior, he or she looks up and
sees the teacher looking at him or her, the student returns to appropriate behavior
for a few seconds and then looks up again. If the teacher has moved on and is no
longer paying attention, the student resumes his or her off-task behavior. However,
if the teacher is still alert and focused on the student, the student decides he or she
had better remain on task.

Gestures

Gestures are more direct forms of nonverbal communication. They can be
viewed as a form of conducting. Effective teachers soon learn that teaching
involves an element of conducting, just as a musical conductor uses gestures to
communicate with the orchestra. Effective teachers use gestures to communicate
with students, and these gestures are often interpreted by students as an indication
of teacher enthusiasm.

Gestures are effective communication devices that can be used without interfering with the regular flow of classroom activities. Holding up a hand as a stop signal,
pointing down to indicate the student should be focusing on work they are supposed
to be doing, a finger on the lips to indicate silence, pointing to the clock to indicate
that time is being wasted, or a thumbs-up to indicate approval are all tools used by
effective teachers. Hand gestures can communicate both positive as well as negative
messages. Without words, they communicate expectations to students.

As with other nonverbal behaviors, some teachers are very good at using gestures and some are not. However, they can be learned through practice. Viewing
videos of teaching with a special focus on gestures can be helpful. Watching how

others use gestures and then practicing in front of a mirror are all steps that can help teachers learn how to use gestures more effectively.

Proximity Control

Proximity control refers to controlling behavior by being in the area where the inappropriate behavior is occurring. It is difficult for students to misbehave when the teacher is standing next to them. One example of proximity control is when one or more students are off task while the teacher is teaching a lesson. The teacher casually and somewhat unobtrusively moves next to the students without interrupting the lesson. If possible, it is effective to move right behind the students. Many of the other students are not aware of the reason for your movement. However, the off-task students are aware of the teachers' presence and most certainly know why the teacher is there. If there is a need for added emphasis, placing a hand on the desk or on the back of the chair leaves no doubt in the mind of the student that the teacher means business. Caution should be exercised in placing a hand on the student because that might be interpreted as a violation of personal space and can provoke a reaction.

Establishing eye contact and giving a disapproving look will also add emphasis. The message is very clear: "I know what is going on and you need to stop." Once the student is back on task, the teacher might slowly move away. Glancing back to make sure the student has stayed on task reminds the student that the behavior is being monitored.

Remove Distractions in an Unobtrusive Manner

One of the causes of misbehavior is when there is something that is distracting the attention away from the lesson. This might be an iPod, a text message, a cell phone, or other reading material. The trick is to remove the item without creating a power struggle with the student. Sometimes simply just stating, "I'll keep this safe until after class," is all that is needed. Another approach is to use the object in the context of the lesson. One of us observed a student reading an inappropriate magazine during one of our lessons. While continuing with the lesson, she slowly moved next to the student, reached down, and took the magazine out of the student's hands. She then used it to illustrate a point she was making in the lesson. After making her point, she placed the material on her desk and continued on with the lesson. She not only removed the object in an unobtrusive way, but she also captured the student's attention with her illustration! The problem was efficiently solved without a word. The student was left with no opportunity to protest and had no option but to pay attention. After class, she and the student discussed the problem outside the audience of the whole class.

Wait for Compliance

Another effective nonverbal approach is simply to stop the lesson and wait until everyone is back on task before continuing. This is often a good choice when several students are off task. Continuing to teach when students are off task means that they are not learning. Usually they will need to be retaught or at least will have many questions that waste valuable class time. In addition, continuing to teach without the attention of the students communicates that what you are saying is unimportant. Simply stopping, using facial expressions to indicate disapproval, and waiting usually have the desired effect. One teacher we observed kept a stopwatch on his desk. When he had to stop and wait, he picked up the stopwatch and clicked it on. He focused on the stopwatch until the class was quiet and the attention of the group was focused on him. He then clicked the stopwatch off and noted how long it took. The click of the stopwatch almost always caught the attention of the class and led to a prompt cessation of off-task behavior.

It is useful to have a signal that indicates that students need to focus on the teacher. This is especially true at the beginning of a lesson or when getting the attention of the students back after group activities. It might be something such as turning off the lights. Some early elementary teachers use hand signals that the students duplicate in order to show they are paying attention. Once the attention of the class is secured, move on.

Low-Profile Verbal Responses

If nonverbal responses do not have the desired result, low-profile verbal responses may be needed. One again, the emphasis of low-profile verbal responses is to draw as little attention as possible to the misbehavior and to provide the student with the opportunity to exercise self-control. Many teachers do not understand this principle. Their verbal response is intrusive and focuses the attention of the entire class on the student and the inappropriate behavior. If the goal of the student was to get attention, the teacher has just reinforced the idea that getting attention is best obtained through inappropriate behavior. In addition, the student has now been placed in the spotlight and may feel the need to save face. This might be done by challenging the teacher with some back talk so that the problem moves from a minor disruption to a major one.

Reinforce Appropriate Behavior

This might be one of the first steps used when noting inappropriate behavior. The approach is that rather than focusing attention on inappropriate behavior, the teacher provides reinforcement to those who are demonstrating appropriate behavior. This response is especially useful in the elementary grades where students place a high value on approval of the teacher. However, used wisely, it is also effective in secondary classrooms. It is most appropriate when there are a number of students off task. The technique is simply that of looking for someone in the room who is behaving and reinforcing them. For example, at the secondary level it might involve stating, "Bill, I appreciate you getting right on that task." At the elementary level, it might take the form of "I like the way Group 1 is ready." The advantage of this technique is that it gives attention to appropriate behavior and lets students know that their good effort will be noticed.

Use the Student's Name in the Lesson

One interesting and low-profile approach is to use the name of the student in the context of the lesson. For example, the tendency of a teacher who notes a student off task is to state, "John, I want your attention right now!" All the students are now focused on John and the confrontation between John and the teacher. However, the teacher can get John's attention and communicate an awareness of his behavior by slipping his name into the context of the lesson. If the lesson was focused on the discovery of the New World, the teacher might say, "If John were a member of the crew, he would have noticed that . . ." When John hears his name, the tendency is to look up. Then you can make eye contact and use nonverbal messages to communicate to him that you're aware of his behavior and he needs to refocus. The student is not put on the spot, the inappropriate behavior is not emphasized, and the lesson has continued without interruption. This is often all that is required to change the behavior from unacceptable to acceptable.

Redirect Student Activity

Redirecting student activity is where the teacher notes that a student is engaged in unacceptable behavior. The challenge is to redirect the student to an acceptable alternative without rewarding the student for inappropriate behavior. Teachers who work with younger students tend to become very adept at doing this. However, it can be done throughout the grades.

This approach requires a high level of teacher awareness. The teachers need to be aware when a student is beginning to move away from the focus of the lesson and respond quickly. This approach is often used when students are working independently. They may be having difficulty and are beginning to lose their focus because of frustration or they may have been working on a task to the point of boredom. In some instances, a good approach is to ask the student to engage in an activity such as performing a housekeeping task, gathering material, delivering something to another teacher, or completing another task designed to give the student a quick break. Then, when the student returns, there is an opportunity to focus on what the student is doing and give some assistance to help him or her reengage in the appropriate activity.

Another example of redirecting student activity is to have the student engage in an alternative activity to accomplish the instructional goal. For example, a student might be having trouble completing a math assignment and is getting anxious and frustrated. The teacher might state, "John, could you help me by creating a way to visually represent these problems?" Giving the student some concrete objects to manipulate can change the activity without demeaning the student and while keeping the focus on the lesson objective.

One word of caution: Redirecting an activity should not be viewed by the students as a reward for inappropriate behavior or as a way to avoid assigned work. Redirecting student activity works best when you catch a potential problem in its beginning stages.

Quiet Word to the Individual

This response is usually most appropriate when students are working independently. The technique is that of quietly informing that student that their behavior is unacceptable and they are expected to change. The teacher simply goes to the student and, as quietly and unemotionally as possible, gives the student a command. This can be as simple as a quiet "Back to work" or "Save the talking until later." Once this is done, the teacher can move away while maintaining eye contact until the student returns to the appropriate activity. The intent is to keep it soft enough that only a few nearby students are aware that you have said anything and to keep it brief and focused on what the student should be doing. At this point, you are not interested in engaging in dialog or in student excuses. The purpose is to communicate that you are aware of the behavior and you are reminding them of the acceptable behavior.

Rule Reminder

Rule reminder is simply that of either asking the students or pointing out the classroom rule that is being violated. This response can be useful if several students are engaged in the behavior. When you use a rule reminder, you can simply ask, "When is it appropriate to be out of your seat?" A variation might be to ask a student to read the appropriate rule. The rule reminder communicates to the class that you will enforce the rules and they are being given a chance to correct their own behavior without any further consequences.

These low-profile responses are very effective in stopping incidents of misbehavior and providing students with the opportunity to self-correct. They respect

Table 7.3 Checklist for Handling Minor Problems

	Often	Seldom
1. I model respect and courtesy.	____	____
2. I have student attention before beginning a lesson.	____	____
3. I provide clear directions for assignments.	____	____
4. I circulate around the classroom when students are working.	____	____
5. I send nonverbal signals when responding to misbehavior.	____	____
6. I avoid sarcasm, threats, and personal attacks.	____	____
7. I look for students being good and reinforce them.	____	____
8. I look for the causes of misbehavior.	____	____
9. I use proximity control when I notice someone misbehaving.	____	____
10. I use a rule reminder when students are off task.	____	____
11. I use a quiet word to individuals as a low-profile response.	____	____
12. I attempt to keep the focus on the lesson and not the behavior.	____	____

the dignity of the students and communicate a belief that students do have the ability to exercise self-control. Generally, these responses are useful in addressing those minor incidents of misbehavior that constitute a large percentage of problems that occur in typical classrooms. Table 7.3 provides a checklist to help you consider your actions as you handle the minor problems in the classroom.

REVIEW OF MAIN IDEAS

1. Student behavior takes place in a group context. Therefore, teachers need to be aware of group dynamics and actively build a supportive community in order to respond to problems effectively.

2. Communication is a central element of the classroom. A major contributor to problems in the classroom is a breakdown in communication.

3. Teachers can develop a communication style that is supportive or one that is defensive. A defensive communication style is built around the exercise of teacher power and communicates lack of respect for the students.

4. There is a difference between punishment and consequences. Punishment carries the intent to be hurtful to others. Consequences are the logical or natural result of actions. All individuals need to learn that their actions will have consequences.

5. Rather than blaming students for all problems in the classroom, the teacher needs to be thoughtful in analyzing the situation and identifying how other factors might be the root of the problem.

6. The majority of the problems that occur in the classroom are those that could be classified as minor. The appropriate response for minor problems is one that is low-profile and unobtrusive.

7. It is useful for teachers to develop a range of nonverbal and verbal responses that can be chosen when minor behavior problems occur.

APPLICATION AND ENRICHMENT

1. Observe in a classroom. Make an observation tool with two columns. On one side, keep track of the minor discipline problems that occur in the classroom. On the other side, keep track of what you consider major discipline problems. What percentage of the problems were minor and what percentage were major? Did the teacher respond to the problems differently? What were the techniques most often used by the teacher?

2. Begin developing a list of low-profile responses that you would feel comfortable using in the classroom. Share your list with a peer and get his or her reactions to your list.

3. Interview at least one or two students who are currently having difficulty in school. Ask them to identify what they believe to be the causes of their difficulties. Do these students perceive a relationship between their behavior and the consequences of their behavior?

4. Nonverbal behaviors are usually sent from an unaware sender to an aware receiver. How aware are you of your nonverbal behaviors? You may ask peers or video yourself teaching and analyze your nonverbal behaviors. Pay special attention to your facial expressions, your body language, and your gestures.

5. Observe in several classrooms. In these classrooms, try to identify whether the communication style of the teacher is supportive or defensive. What do the teachers do to develop a supportive communication style and what do they do to develop a defensive communication style?

REFERENCES

Albert, L. (1996). *Cooperative discipline.* Circle Pines, MN: American Guidance Service.

Borisoff, D., & Victor, D. A. (1998). *Conflict management: A communication skills approach* (2nd ed.). Boston: Allyn & Bacon.

Charles, C. M. (1992). *Building classroom discipline* (4th ed.). White Plains, NY: Longman.

Ginott, H. G. (1972). *Teacher and child.* New York: Avon Books.

Hardin, C. (2008). *Effective classroom management: Models and strategies for today's classrooms.* Upper Saddle River, NJ: Merrill Prentice Hall.

Hoy, A., & Weinstein, C. (2006). Student and teacher perspectives on classroom management. In C. M. Evertson & C. S. Weinstein (Eds.), *Handbook of classroom management: Research, practice and contemporary issues* (pp. 181–220). Mahwah, NJ: Lawrence Erlbaum.

Jones, F. (1979). The gentle art of classroom discipline. *National Elementary Principal, 58,* 26–32.

Marshall, M., & Weisner, K. (2004). Encouraging responsible student behavior. *Phi Delta Kappan, 87,* 498–507.

Mendler, A. (1997). Beyond discipline survival: Reclaiming children and youth. *Journal of Emotional and Behavioral Problems, 6,* 41–44.

Watson, M., & Battistich, V. (2006). Building and sustaining caring communities. In C. M. Evertson & C. S. Weinstein (Eds.), *Handbook of classroom management: Research, practice and contemporary issues* (pp. 253–280). Mahwah, NJ: Lawrence Erlbaum.

Weinstein, C. S., & Mignano, A. J., Jr. (1993). *Elementary classroom management: Lessons from research and practice.* New York: McGraw-Hill.

Chapter 8

RESPONDING TO PERSISTENT MISBEHAVIOR

CLASSROOM SCENARIO

Wilma is a constant problem in the 10th-grade English class. She has an insolent attitude, makes an obvious display that the class is a waste of time, makes fun of other students, and constantly challenges teacher authority. Frankly, the class runs much smoother when Wilma is absent. Today, a full 5 minutes after the class has begun, Wilma comes sauntering into the classroom, slamming the door behind her. The attention of the whole class is on Wilma. For Ms. Baker, this is the last straw.

"Wilma, why are you tardy?" snapped Ms. Baker.

"I had to go to the bathroom. Is that okay with you?" was the sarcastic reply.

"Wilma, I don't appreciate your attitude!"

"Well, I don't appreciate your attitude, either, so I guess we're even."

"Wilma, I've had enough of you!!! Take this note and go to the office, right now!"

CHAPTER OBJECTIVES

After completing this chapter, you should be able to:

- Explain why teacher persistence is required when students do not respond to teacher attempts to stop inappropriate behavior

- Identify a range of alternative responses consistent with your values and beliefs
- List steps that can be used in keeping responsibility for behavior on the student
- Model how to respond to misbehavior with clarity and firmness
- Describe the process of limit setting
- Define preferred activity time and state how it can be used as a response to misbehavior
- Explain when time-out might be an appropriate response to behavior problems
- List the steps of behavioral problem solving and the development of behavioral improvement agreements
- List the steps that can be used in helping students learn to modify their own behavior
- Model a parent–teacher conference
- Define the uses and the potential problems associated with detention

There will always be students who lack self-control or who meet their personal needs through misbehavior. Students like Wilma cause teachers stress and sleepless nights. These students dominate teacher thoughts and interfere with the satisfactions of teaching. These students seem to have a knack for pushing the right buttons to upset the teacher. The feeling is often, "This would be a good class if _____ was not a member." On the other hand, it can be extremely rewarding to see students who are persistent behavior problems change their behavior and begin learning self-control. One of us once taught a "behavior adjustment" class of middle school students. These were students with persistent problems who were referred to the class from several nearby schools. It was one of the most professionally rewarding experiences in this teacher's career.

Low-profile responses to the misbehavior of these students do not seem to have much impact. These students require more direct and firm teacher action. However, direct and firm teacher intervention is not without some difficulties. Direct responses take more time and thought. They are more disruptive to the learning process and focus student attention on inappropriate behavior. If not handled with care, they may reinforce the inappropriate behavior rather than teaching the appropriate alternative.

Elias and Schwab (2006) contend that the type of responses applied to problem behaviors is an important component of the management and discipline process. They state that the system of responses used can either "make or break" the entire discipline system. Therefore, the system of responses needs to be considered carefully and needs to be planned out in advance. Since it is difficult to predict the types of misbehavior that can occur in a given classroom, teachers need to be aware of a variety of responses and when they might be appropriately applied.

Responses to persistent misbehavior require a good deal of teacher persistence. The students have developed their behavioral patterns over a period of time, and immediate changes should not be expected. Students who demonstrate persistent behavior problems have discovered that they can achieve personal goals of attention and power through inappropriate behavior. Because they have developed these responses as a means to achieve personal goals, they may just try harder when teachers attempt to get them to change their behavior. Therefore, initial responses to persistent behavior problems may result in the problem getting worse before it gets better. Teachers need to be persistent and avoid giving up if initial attempts to change behavior do not work as well as anticipated.

Another potential problem associated with responses to persistent behavior problems is that they create conditions that can result in power struggles. Students have been used to getting their way, and they will resist teacher attempts to stop the behavior. When these power struggles get out of hand, they are disruptive to the relationships between the teacher and the students, and they harm attempts to build a supportive community.

We subscribe to the approach of using a range of consequences when responding to persistent behavior. The consequences implemented need to be based on the needs and the goals of the misbehaving student, the ability of the student to exercise self-control, and the severity of the offense. Effective consequences are clear and specific, they preserve the dignity of the student, and they teach the student that there are consequences to misbehavior (Hardin, 2006).

In this chapter, we provide suggestions for a range of alternative responses for persistent misbehavior. These alternatives have been used by teachers to respond effectively to persistent misbehavior. The responses to persistent misbehavior are more intrusive and require more effort and planning than do those for minor problems. They should be used when other, low-profile responses have not had the desired effect or when the problem is serious enough to warrant a more direct and intrusive response.

It is important for each teacher to identify responses consistent with personal values and beliefs. This list should be used as a beginning point for developing a personal range of alternatives. You need to think through these alternatives ahead of time. It is difficult to respond appropriately in the midst of a complex and fast-moving classroom. Developing a personal discipline plan with a range of alternatives can be extremely valuable in providing you with an increased sense of security and confidence and in helping you choose an appropriate response. It would be useful to consider what alternatives might have been applied to the scenario at the beginning of the chapter.

A RANGE OF RESPONSES FOR PERSISTENT BEHAVIOR PROBLEMS

Many new teachers have difficulty responding to persistent misbehavior. They become frustrated because their previous responses seem to have had little impact. They spend considerable time worrying about the problem and frequently feel as if their power and authority is being challenged. Unfortunately, there are no easy answers, because one response does not fit all students and all situations. What works with one teacher in one environment might not be as effective in the classroom of another teacher and with another group of students. Students are different; consequently, the causes of their misbehavior are different. Teachers, too, are different, as are their personalities and strengths. A strict prescription or a "one size fits all" approach will not succeed.

Although the needs of teachers are seldom addressed when specifying approaches to inappropriate behavior, they are an important consideration. Teacher responses need to be consistent with the values and the beliefs of the teacher. If certain responses are uncomfortable for teachers and inconsistent with their values or beliefs, they will be reluctant to use those responses and will run the risk of ignoring inappropriate behavior or appearing to be inconsistent. These conditions will only make the problems worse. In addition, if teachers are uncomfortable with a response, they are likely to do a poor job of implementing the approach and it is likely to be more harmful than helpful. Therefore, you need to be aware of a range of alternative responses that are consistent with your values, your personality, and your strengths. Table 8.1 lists a variety of direct teacher interventions from which you might choose.

Focusing Responsibility for the Problem

Anyone who has spent any time in a classroom is familiar with the scenario. The teacher notes a student engaged in inappropriate behavior and responds with,

Table 8.1 A Selection of Direct Teacher Interventions

- Focus responsibility
- Respond with clarity and firmness
- Set limits
- Limit preferred activity time
- Provide a cost-benefit analysis
- Give a time-out
- Rearrange the environment
- Have a teacher–student conference
- Use behavioral problem solving
- Write up a behavioral improvement agreement
- Teach the student to modify own behavior

"Mary, why are you out of your seat?" Mary responds, "Helen didn't know what to do and needed help." Or, a teacher reacts to misbehavior with, "John, stop talking!" John responds, "Billy was bothering me and I was just telling him to stop so I could go to work!" Very clever! In both instances, the student has tried to evade responsibility for his or her behavior by blaming it on someone else. They have attempted to change the focus from their actions to the actions of someone else or to describe their actions as helpful. Unwittingly, in these examples, the teacher response has opened the door for students to evade responsibility for their actions. Frequently, these tactics are successful and the attention of the teacher is diverted from the inappropriate behavior.

As previously discussed, it is important for students to learn to accept responsibility for their behavior and there needs to be a clear relationship between their actions and the consequences. In the scenarios described in the previous paragraph, the reactions of the teacher have made it more difficult to keep the responsibility on the student who is demonstrating the inappropriate behavior. In considering how to respond to persistent misbehavior, we need a response that does not allow students to evade responsibility and keeps the focus on the relationship between their actions and the consequences. When responding to incidents of misbehavior, it is useful to do so in a way that does not allow the student to make excuses. Our chosen response should be one that keeps the focus on the action of the student. However, keep in mind that teachers often have to deal with a problem quickly and do not have time to engage in extended responses. A relatively simple process that can be useful has been adapted from the approach originally proposed by Glasser (1965) a number of years ago.

Ask the Student to Describe Behavior

The first step is critical and involves a change of emphasis on the part of the teacher. The first response needs to be phrased so that it takes away the opportunity for the student to come up with an excuse. This is done simply by asking, "What are you doing?" The emphasis is on what the student is doing and not why they are doing it. The *why* question opens the door for rationalization, excuses, and a debate about the behavior. The purpose is to get students to describe their behavior quickly in a way that forces them to take responsibility. To be sure, students who have learned to play the classroom game will try to respond with an excuse. When this occurs, the teacher simply ignores the response and focuses back on the student. "Mary, I asked what you were doing." Other students may try to play the ignorance card by responding with, "Nothing." Others may try to shift the focus by identifying another behavior such as "I'm just sitting here." If the student persists in trying to avoid identifying their behavior, the teacher can simply state, "I saw you . . ."

Get the Student to Identify the Consequences

Once the inappropriate behavior has been identified, simply ask, "What happens when individuals do that?" The intent is to establish a clear link between the behavior and the consequences. The students need to understand that it is their behavior that is leading to the consequence and not the whims of a vindictive or angry teacher. An understanding of the link makes it possible for students to comprehend that their behavior is a matter of choice and the consequences that they experience are also a matter of choice. This step works best if there is a set of rules and procedures that has been established, and the class has either identified or discussed the possible consequences for violations.

If a student refuses to identify consequences of responses with the typical, "I don't know," the teacher identifies the consequences for the student. This requires that the teacher have some consequences ready to implement. Frequently, just asking the student to identify the behavior and the consequences of the behavior is enough to stop the behavior. This exchange need take no more than a minute or two. If the behavior persists, implement the consequences.

Have the Student Make a Value Judgment About the Behavior

If the student does not change, a one-on-one conference needs to be held when there is an opportunity to do so. In this conference, review what the student was doing and the consequences that follow such a behavior, and then ask the student to make a value judgment. This is accomplished quite simply by asking the student if he or she wants to continue to experience the consequences of his or her actions. Another question that can be posed is, "How are these actions helping you?" The purpose of getting students to make value judgments is to get them to identify that there is a linkage between their actions and the consequences. They also need to consider how this behavior is harming them, not helping them meet their needs.

Some students may persist in defending their actions by making statements such as, "Yeah, that's okay with me." At this point, the teacher should not engage in a prolonged discussion or try to argue with the students. The teacher can respond by calmly stating, "I wanted to make sure that you understood the choices you were making and the consequences." Students are often bluffing and trying to engage the teacher in a power struggle; by keeping the responsibility for the behavior on the student, the teacher can avoid unnecessary power struggles.

Develop a Plan With the Student for Changing the Behavior

If students respond that they do not want to continue to experience the consequences of their behavior and that they recognize that their behavior is not helping them, the door is open for developing a plan to change their behavior. This does not mean it needs to be a time-consuming step that results in a complex plan; the best plans are those that are easy to implement and that cover a relatively short period of time. It is important that the plan be one with which the student has a high probability of success. Once students attain success in following a plan, then they should be reinforced for their success.

The purpose of this step is to help students establish a plan that will help them fulfill needs in a productive way. This step can be implemented simply by asking the student, "What can we do to make sure that this will not happen again?" If a student is reluctant to answer, an appropriate response is to state simply, "You think about it, and I will return in a few minutes and discuss it."

When the student does identify a plan, the student needs to be asked why he or she thinks this will work and what should be done if it does not. The teacher might make suggestions but should not attempt to force a plan on the student. The student must make a commitment to the plan, and this commitment may be only a superficial one if the student believes he or she has no choice but to follow the teacher's plan.

If the student is unable to complete the plan successfully, another conference can be held with the student to develop a new plan. It may well be that several plans will need to be developed before the student realizes that the teacher means business and is not going to give up.

Return to the scenario at the beginning of the chapter. How might the teacher have used this approach with Wilma? How might that have changed the dialog and the power struggle between Wilma and the teacher?

Responding With Clarity and Firmness

A verbal response is one of the most frequent teacher responses to persistent misbehavior. However, many verbal responses are ineffective. Those verbal responses often take the form of vague and generic statements such as, "Please behave" and "Let's get back to work!" In some classrooms, the entire lesson is filled with intrusive and ineffective verbal responses of this sort. Kounin (1970), in his extensive study of classroom management, found that for verbal responses to be effective, they needed to have clarity and firmness.

Clarity involves sending a verbal message that identifies who is misbehaving, what that person is doing, and what he or she should be doing instead. A verbal message involving clarity might be as follows: "Betty, stop your talking and begin working on the assignment." This message indicates that Betty is the target, her talking is the inappropriate behavior, and working on the assignment is the acceptable alternative. In this message, there is no question about for whom the message is intended and what is required. Verbal messages such as "Class, let's all behave" fail the clarity test.

Firmness involves nonverbal messages. When the verbal message is delivered with clarity, it is accompanied by tone of voice and body language that indicate that the teacher means business. As the message is delivered, eye contact is established with the student, the facial expression is stern, movement is toward the student, and posture is erect and rigid. If the verbal message is accompanied by smiling and laughing and the tone of voice is light, a mixed message is sent and it is most likely that the student will receive the nonverbal signals, which are likely to be interpreted to mean that the teacher is insincere and the verbal message is not very important. Then if the teacher responds with a consequence, the student feels betrayed.

Limit Setting

Limit setting is another effective response to persistent misbehavior. It is proposed by Jones (2001) as an approach to rule enforcement that is relatively quick, emphasizes body language, and conveys an "I mean business" demeanor. Jones calls limit setting the gentle use of personal power.

This means that teachers are exercising their personal power in an assertive, yet gentle manner. An important prerequisite to limit setting is to remain calm throughout the process. Jones contends that emotions are contagious. If the teacher is upset, the student will be upset. Clarity and firmness are also important conditions for effective use of limit setting.

Jones defines limit setting as moving in, dealing with back talk, and moving out. A prerequisite to limit setting is teacher awareness of behavior throughout the classroom. This is the withitness described by Kounin (1970). Jones emphasizes that disruptions need to be identified as soon as they begin and there needs to be a swift response. Once misbehavior is noted, Jones states that the teacher needs to stop teaching and focus on the misbehavior. If the misbehavior does not immediately stop, the teacher implements the process by moving in.

Moving In. If you are working with the whole class, calmly state to the class, "Excuse me, class." If you are working independently with another student, tell the student you will be right back. Next, make sure your body language communicates disapproval and a full commitment to dealing with the problem. Take a couple of deep breaths to relax yourself and call the student's name in an unemotional or bland manner. Then walk directly to the edge of the student's desk. Do not focus on anything other than the misbehavior. The intent is to inform the student that he or she has your undivided attention and you mean business. When arriving at the student's desk, body posture should be erect, and eye contact established. Then it is useful to pause for a couple of seconds to take a couple more deep breaths. Once again, this is calming, and it gives the student an opportunity to think and make a decision. If the student makes a commitment to return to work, nothing needs to be said and the teacher can then proceed to the moving out phase.

If the student does not make an obvious commitment to return to work, then a verbal and a physical prompt is used. The physical prompt involves bending at the waist, placing one hand on their desk and using the other hand to indicate what the student should be doing. This might involve placing a pencil in the student's hand, moving the work to a direct location in front of the student, or removing a distracting object. The verbal prompt is a command or directive using clarity to tell the student to stop what he or she is doing and what he or she should be doing instead. If this does not elicit the desired result, both hands are placed on opposite sides of the desk, the teacher leans over to be at eye level, and eye contact is maintained until the student gets back on task. Then the teacher remains for a few seconds and begins the moving out phase.

Back Talk. Some students will attempt to display their power and take control of the situation through back talk. *Back talk* is defined as verbal statements intended to change the subject, divert attention from their behavior, and get off the hook. Back talk is not always hostile or confrontational. It may even appear to be a compliment. For example, some students are really adept at diverting the teacher with statements such as "You look nice today." Other forms of back talk are denial of any wrongdoing, blaming others, profanity, insults, or even crying. All forms of back talk have the same purpose; they are diversionary tactics designed to elicit a reaction from the teacher that will change the focus. Jones contends that back talk will starve if not fed. Therefore, a good approach is simply to stay quiet and ignore it.

Jones suggests that the first step in dealing with back talk is *camping out.* Camping out means that the teacher settles into proximity and takes up residence at the student's desk. This is done by lowering weight on the hands and elbows so that the face of the teacher and the student are on the same level. The facial expression and body posture of the teacher should communicate indifference or boredom. When the student stops the back talk, the verbal prompt is repeated. The intent is to communicate that you were not listening and are not going to allow attention to be diverted to something else. If back talk resumes, when the student has stopped, the prompt is delivered yet again. This is what is called the *broken record* technique. If three or four attempts at repeating the prompt do not stop the back talk, then a more serious consequence may need to be used.

Moving Out. The intent of moving out is to communicate to the students that they are expected to stay on task and their behavior will be monitored. The first step in moving out begins when the student returns to acceptable behavior. It involves quietly thanking the student for returning to work, taking a couple more deep breaths to stay calm, and staying in place for a few seconds before slowly standing.

If moving out is done too quickly, a return to off-task behavior usually follows. Not moving away too quickly is intended to send the message that the teacher means business. Stand slowly but do not move away. Continue to monitor the student for a few seconds and then slowly move away.

If a second student was involved in the inappropriate behavior, the same process should be repeated to make sure that student gets the message and is on task. It is important that each student be dealt with independently.

If the teacher is engaged in whole-class instruction, return to the teaching position, take a couple more deep breaths to stay calm, look at the student, and, if the student shows signs of not being committed to attending to the lesson, wait a bit longer before resuming the lesson. If everything is back in order, resume the lesson. However, make sure the student is kept in the field of vision.

Jones states that this whole process needs to be a deliberate one that is much more slowly paced than is normal in the classroom. The contention is that much more time will be lost if the behavior is not stopped. The most difficult task may be taking a couple of deep breaths before each move. However, this step is important because it helps calm the teacher so that composure is maintained, and it establishes an appropriate pace.

Preferred Activity Time

In just about any classroom, there are activities that are preferred by the students. Allowing students to engage in these activities helps make the classroom experience enjoyable. Everyone likes to have some fun. Jones (2001) suggests that preferred activities are relatively easy to use and have an educational purpose. These activities might be educational games or videos. In addition to the preventive effect of preferred activity time, the loss of an opportunity to engage in preferred activity time is an especially effective consequence. This can be a logical consequence for those who wasted time or who were off task. In elementary schools, students enjoy taking responsibility for different tasks in the classroom, and losing that preferred activity is especially powerful as a consequence for misbehavior.

However, this approach will work only if there are regular times in the classroom when students do have the opportunity to engage in some preferred activities that can be removed. Therefore, teachers need to consider places in the school day when the student can engage in "fun" activities and ways of allowing students some classroom responsibilities.

For example, some secondary school teachers have discovered that students like to listen to music while they are engaged in seatwork. This is a privilege that can be withheld as a consequence of misbehavior. Secondary students also love to socialize, and providing an opportunity for some of them to quietly engage in conversation with others once they have finished their work is another privilege that can be withheld if necessary.

One elementary teacher had a particularly difficult group of students. She found an activity that most students enjoyed and informed the class that time would be set aside each day to allow the students to engage in that activity. However, time wasted responding to misbehavior would be deducted from this time. When the group leader tested the system and realized that wasted time did mean a loss of the privilege, the class members put pressure on each other to follow the rules. In a short time, the problems almost totally disappeared (Jones, 1987).

Cost-Benefit Analysis

Many behaviors that cause teachers difficulty can be handled rather easily by letting students know that there is a cost associated with their choice. For example, elementary teachers are often at a loss regarding what to do with constant requests to go to the restroom. They feel that it is cruel to deny students permission if they really need to visit the restroom. However, when there are frequent requests, there is a suspicion that the request is really an attempt to avoid work. A common issue in secondary classrooms is when students "forget" to bring appropriate material to class. The solution to these and other similar situations is to shift the responsibility to the student. This is accomplished by associating a cost with the privilege and allowing the student to make the choice.

For example, when students repeatedly requested permission to visit the restroom, one teacher responded with a cheerful "Sure." Then the teacher made a point of marking down the time. The student was then informed, "Check in with me when you return so that I can mark down the correct amount of time that is missed. You can make that up during preferred activity time" (Jones, 1987). The students are now provided with a clear choice. If there is a legitimate reason to visit the restroom, they will do so. If, however, it was only an excuse to take a break, they have to decide if they are willing to pay the cost. A secondary teacher worked out a "rental" program for students who could not seem to bring material to class. For example, if they did not bring a book to class, they had to leave something with the teacher until they returned the item. Sometimes this would be one shoe. With seniors, it worked well to have them leave their driver's license. This was a highly prized object that they did not want to have out of their possession. Not surprisingly, this class seldom forgot their books! This clear cost-benefit choice is consistent with logical consequences and keeps responsibility with the students.

Time-Out

Time-out has been a popular response to inappropriate behavior. It has been used more in elementary schools than in secondary schools. Most secondary-level classrooms do not have enough space to set aside a time-out zone. When it is used in secondary schools, it is almost always used schoolwide. These secondary schools often have designated a time-out area for the whole school that is staffed full-time. This is the contemporary equivalent of being sent to the principal's office.

An isolated desk is set aside as time-out space.

© Corbis

In elementary schools, time-out usually involves setting aside an area in the classroom. This is generally a desk or a chair that is separated from the rest of the students. The purpose of time-out is to move the student to an area where he or she will not be able to continue to disturb others. This is not intended as a punishment but as a place students can be removed to in order to remove the stimulus for misbehavior and to allow them time to calm down and reflect (Glasser, 1977). Time-out can be effective when the behavior has been disruptive and when the teacher cannot deal with it.

Students stay in the time-out area until the teacher has an opportunity to meet with them. At this time, conduct a conference and ask the student to identify the behavior that resulted in his or her removal. Second, ask the student if he or she is ready to return to the whole class and what the consequences should be if he or she continues the inappropriate behavior. If the student states he or she is not ready to return, then the conference is terminated and the teacher returns to work.

Time-out can be effective for those students who have attention needs. They want to be a part of the group. They cannot get attention if they are in time out. Most of the time, these students will choose to modify their behavior in order to return to the group.

A word of caution: Students should never be sent to the hall, the playground, or an area where they will not be under direct observation. If students are in a place where they are not supervised, they can engage in dangerous activity or even leave the school grounds. In these situations, the teacher can be held legally liable for any harm that might occur. For example, one student wandered off to watch other students playing ball and was injured by a student throwing rocks. Another left the school grounds and was injured by a car. In situations like this, the teacher who placed the student outside the scope of supervision is placed in a position of high legal risk. However, in spite of this legal risk, we still see the practice of sending students to the hall as a form of time-out in many schools.

Rearrange the Environment

If misbehavior persists, it might be necessary to consider altering the classroom environment in order to remove distractions and make it easier for the students to exercise self-control. Jones (2001) suggests that this is one of the most effective actions that can be taken. Changing the arrangement should take into account several considerations. One focus should be on increasing the ease of using proximity control. Simple changes in the seating arrangement can be done that allow a teacher to quickly get next to every student desk. Another point of focus is to look for dimensions of the environment that might be causing difficulty. Is the student close to the door and tempted to interact with those passing by in the hallway? Is the student in a position so that he or she can be distracted by what is outside the windows? Perhaps the student is too near the major traffic center in the classroom and he or she is tempted to interact with everyone who passes by. Sitting near the teacher's desk might distract some students because they have to listen in on every teacher conversation. Another choice in rearranging the environment would be to move individuals who are frequently off task into the action zone. This makes it easier for the teacher to monitor their behavior, decreases the distance between the student and the teacher, and usually results in a reduction of off-task behavior. Finally, some students simply cannot sit next to each other. They stimulate each other and may need to be separated.

Teacher–Student Conference

If problems persist in spite of several efforts to change them, it is time for a teacher–student conference. A conference with a student can be relatively short and is best done where there is some privacy. If others are listening, some students feel a need to preserve their image.

The conference, as with other responses, needs to be approached calmly. If the teacher is angry, it is best to remove the student to a time-out area and then wait until the anger subsides before meeting with the student. The purpose of the conference is to engage the student in seeking a solution. It is not to berate, threaten, or shame the student. It is hard to achieve this purpose if the teacher and the student are angry.

During the conference, the teacher needs to start by getting student participation. It is best to begin with questions that focus on what the student was doing. The student should do much of the talking. Teachers can use questions such as "What is the problem?" "What suggestions do you have for preventing the problem?" "What can I do to help you?" and "What do you think I should do the next time this happens?" Some students will try to ignore the teacher or avoid participating and getting involved in the discussion. If they do so, the behavior should be identified with statements such as "I saw you . . ." Communication should be with clarity and firmness, and teachers should share their feelings with statements such as "When I am interrupted when talking, I get frustrated because I have to waste time by stopping the lesson." If the student is reluctant to suggest solutions, the teacher can suggest solutions that the student would definitely not like. When the student protests, the responsibility should then be shifted back to the student to suggest some other alternatives. The student might be given time to return to his or her seat and write out several alternatives. The teacher needs to be firm and should not let the student get by with superficial responses. For example, if a student states, "I just won't do that again," a response such as "That is not good enough; what if you forget?" forces the student to think more deeply about appropriate consequences.

What Would You Do?

Louis is a teacher's nightmare. He is a handsome boy that initially is polite to adults. He doesn't overtly challenge the authority of the teacher. But he appears to be the instigator of many of the disturbances. When he thinks the teacher is not looking, he will knock someone's books on the floor. He will deliberately elbow students in the back and try to hurt them. One day, he deliberately snapped in half some new pencils of another student. He tries to instigate fights between other students.

- What would you do?

- What do you think Louis is trying to accomplish by these behaviors?

- What specific steps would you take to try to prevent his misbehavior?

- What are some responses that you would use when he does misbehave?

Behavioral Problem Solving

A natural extension of the student conference is that of behavioral problem solving. However, behavioral problem solving can be (and sometimes should be) a whole-class activity. Coloroso (1994) suggests that teaching problem solving is a critical element in helping students develop self-control and inner discipline. Coloroso defines a six-step process for behavioral problem solving. The goal is to use this process with students until they learn how to implement the process on their own. The six steps are as follows:

1. *Define the problem.* The most important step in behavioral problem solving is that of defining the problem. The way in which the problem is defined can stimulate or can inhibit the search for solutions. For example, if a problem is defined simply as a student bothering others, it may miss the root of the problem. In this

situation, the search for solutions might be limited to how to keep the student from bothering others. However, if the root of the problem is that the student is lost and fears failure, then a more rewarding solution would be to find ways of helping the student get the assistance needed in order to achieve success. Defining the problem might take some time for the teacher to question students and allow them to reveal their feelings.

2. *Brainstorm solutions.* Brainstorming involves listing all possible solutions without judgment. This may take some time, and students might need the opportunity to reflect and think about possible solutions. As much as possible, the solutions should come from the students.

3. *Evaluate the possible solutions against a set of criteria.* The role of the teacher is to help the students think through the possible consequences of actions. Coloroso (1994) suggests that the solutions should be evaluated using the criteria of whether or not the consequences of the possible solution are unfair, hurtful, unkind, or dishonest. Other criteria might be that the possible solutions respect the dignity of everyone involved and do not interfere with the rights of others.

4. *Select an option.* After the consequences of all solutions have been explored, those involved in the problem need to choose an option that best addresses the problem, meets the criteria for a good solution, and meets the needs of everyone, including the teacher.

5. *Plan the implementation.* The discussion now needs to center on how the option can be implemented. Again, there should be some criteria for the implementation. It needs to be accomplished without interfering with the rights of others and should be something that can be done easily. Complex plans are almost certain to fail. The implementation needs to maximize the probability of success.

6. *Review the problem.* This step is like a summary. It is a review of the problem definition, the proposed solutions, and what will be done in the future to avoid similar situations. The summary helps students pull the process together and provides them with a model to follow.

Behavioral problem solving obviously takes some time. Therefore, it should not be implemented with minor problems. It should be reserved for more serious problems that interfere with the rights of others. Behavioral problem solving can be implemented with individual students or it can be used in a classroom meeting with the entire class. Classroom meetings are very useful if the problem is relevant to the entire class or if it involves a number of students. The role of the teacher in classroom meetings is to exercise leadership in making sure the process is implemented and not to dominate the meeting.

Behavioral Improvement Agreements

Behavioral improvement agreements are written agreements between the teacher and the student. When behavioral problem solving has been implemented and students do not follow through, then it might be time to develop a behavioral improvement agreement.

The process is similar to that of behavioral problem solving. If there is more than one behavior that is causing difficulty, the behavioral improvement agreement should focus on the one that is causing the most difficulty. It is important not to try to solve all the problems with one agreement.

The advantage of the written agreement is that it makes the expectations very clear and specifies what each person will do and lists the consequences if the agreement is not kept. These written agreements are especially useful in a conference with the parents or with other professionals. It is important to make sure that the agreement is one that allows the student to succeed. It does not need to be overly complex.

If the agreement is not kept, then the consequences need to be applied and a new agreement developed. Some students will continue to test the teacher until they realize the teacher is not going to give up. If several agreements are tried and are not successful, then additional action needs to be taken. Table 8.2 provides an outline for a behavioral improvement agreement.

Table 8.2   Behavioral Improvement Agreement Form

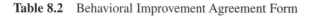

Student_____

Teacher_____

Date_____

We have met and developed the following agreement to improve the learning climate.

I, (Student name), agree to do the following in order to improve my behavior.

I, (Teacher), promise to help by doing the following:

Failure to follow this agreement will result in the following consequence:

Signatures

_____   _____

Teaching Students to Modify Their Own Behavior

Some students have difficulty with self-control. They do not engage in serious misbehavior, just numerous incidents of minor misbehavior. A useful response is to help these students monitor their own behavior and learn how to take appropriate action to prevent getting into trouble. Several studies have shown that teaching students to monitor their own behavior is effective and has several advantages (McLaughlin, 1976). One advantage is that the students become more aware of their behavior and the control of the behavior is left with the students. Another advantage is that it relieves the teacher from always playing the role of the enforcer.

There are several methods that can be used to teach students to monitor their own behavior. One technique is to provide the students with a series of questions they learn to ask themselves when they are faced with temptation or when they begin to feel anxious or angry. The questions might include the following:

- What is causing me to feel this way?
- What will happen if I don't control myself?
- Is this what I want to happen?
- What can I do to calm down and gain control?

In response to the last question, you might work with the student to identify acceptable responses. For example, some students might be given the freedom to choose to go to the time-out area for a short time voluntarily. They could be allowed to put their heads down on their desks and think of favorite activities or happy thoughts or begin counting and, when they begin to relax and calm down, resume working.

Another method is to have students keep a record of their behavior. For example, they can keep a tally of every time they get out of their seats or every time they talk without permission. They can be prompted when to record. Some students respond positively to this approach. At the conclusion of a given period of time, the teacher and the student review the records. Some students are surprised at the prevalence of the behavior. They are then allowed to set goals and decide how they will reward themselves when they improve.

Implementing self-monitoring requires more than just talking about it. It is useful for the teacher to model and demonstrate the technique. For example, you might model the process by identifying with the class something you would like to change. Some teachers fall into bad verbal habits such as overusing terms such as "okay." This can be discussed with the class. In fact, they might help identify the behavior that needs change. A tally sheet can be kept on the desk and the class can help keep the tally. After a period of time, the tallies can be reviewed with the class and a plan established to change the behavior. As they observe the teacher modeling the process of changing behavior, students will learn how to apply it to their lives.

Parent Conferences

If misbehavior persists and teacher responses seem to have little impact, it might be time to have a conference with the parents or guardians. Parent conferences often cause teachers a fair amount of anxiety. As a result, many teachers are reluctant to have parent conferences. However, the majority of parents want their children to be successful in school. Although they may initially appear somewhat hostile because they see the actions of their children as a reflection on them and their parenting skills, properly handled parent conferences can have a positive impact and can help teachers and parents become collaborators rather than adversaries.

Parent conferences are most effective if a positive relationship has been established between the teacher and the parent. The problem is that the only time many parents hear from the school is if there is bad news. They need to receive positive comments about their children and the progress they have made. Although this is easier for elementary teachers, who have fewer students and more contact with all students, secondary teachers also need to find ways of establishing positive communication with parents. Some teachers have developed support by sending our regular notes to parents through e-mail.

Effective parent conferences need to be planned. They do not just happen. The first step is to step back and consider the perspectives of the parent. Parents want teachers who are concerned about their children. They want teachers who are firm but fair. Parents also approach meetings with teachers with a certain amount of anxiety. Parents of students who have been chronic discipline problems have usually had several negative experiences with parent conferences and may approach the conference with a definite lack of enthusiasm. Sometimes they are simply frustrated and do not know what to do.

This means that teachers need to make sure that the focus of the conference is on the child and what is best for the child. Teachers need to make sure they are not angry or hostile or blaming the parents. Teachers need to be good listeners and be willing to let the parents share their perspectives and their ideas. This does not mean that the teacher needs to agree to all of their ideas. However, their comments might reveal the causes of the problem so that a more effective plan can be developed.

Teachers need to do some homework before the conference. They need to review records regarding the student, the successes as well as the problems, and look for patterns of behavior and information about the family. Having knowledge about the student and the family will communicate a sense of professionalism and that the conference has been taken seriously. One other piece of homework might be to keep anecdotal records on the student. These can easily be done by just jotting the date, time, and description of the behavior on note cards. The cards might be shared with parents who try to minimize the misbehavior and believe that the teacher is not being objective. After doing some homework, establish some clear goals for the conference and what you would like from the parent.

Parent conferences need to be conducted in a comfortable spot. Parents may feel that their dignity is assaulted if they are required to sit in a small chair appropriate for primary-level students while the teacher sits in a regular chair behind a desk. The tone for the meeting needs to be one that is cordial and friendly, yet businesslike and professional. This is not the place for gossip or small talk. It also means that you need to consider your body language and nonverbal communication. Such things as lack of eye contact or slouched body posture communicate to the parents that you are not really interested in what they have to say.

The teacher can start the conference in the right direction by thanking the parents for taking time to come to the conference and by communicating his or her concern for the welfare of the student. Inform the parents that you are interested in their perspectives and you would like their advice and assistance. Do not be preachy or hostile. State simply that there is a problem and briefly describe the problem. Then get the parents involved by asking if they can offer any insight as to why the problem is occurring. As with behavioral problem solving, the critical issue is to make sure that there is a good definition of the problem. The teacher should not dominate the conference and should allow ample time for the parents to participate. If a parent is critical of the teacher or the curriculum, clarify the criticisms and express an interest in addressing any mistakes that you might have made and refocus the discussion on the behavior of the student. It is important to keep the conference focused on the problem and not criticisms of the teacher, other teachers, the school, or the other parent. Although those might have a relationship to the problem and might be taken into account when developing a plan of action, the accountability needs to remain with the student. Even though there might be negative dimensions of the student's life, the student still needs to learn that it does not excuse behavior that interferes with the rights of others.

Provide adequate time for the conference so that the parents do not feel rushed. They need to feel that their child is a priority and that the teacher is serious. Make sure that the parents have your undivided attention and that you are listening to their comments. However, do not prolong the conference beyond what is necessary. Always end the conference on a hopeful note. Summarize what has been discussed and identify a plan of action that will be taken by both the parents and the teacher.

After the conference, write down a summary of the conference and the agreements that were made. Then, in a few days, contact the parents and ask if there are any additional questions. Any changes in the behavior should be shared.

Good parent conferences can help build a positive relationship between the parents and the teacher. They can be effective in helping diagnose the problem and in making sure that everyone is working together. Remember, the goal is to help the student, not demonstrate teacher power or win an argument. If you encounter hostile parents, the suggestions in Table 8.3 can help you deal with them in a positive, stress-free way.

Detention

Detention is a time-honored response to serious or persistent behavior problems. Staying after school has long been viewed as the appropriate response when

Table 8.3   When Parents Are Hostile

Some parents come to conferences with a hostile attitude. The probabilities are that they have had negative experiences with schools and want to find a place to place the blame. Hostile parents can evoke impulsive and defensive behavior on the part of the teacher. When it is apparent that a parent is hostile, the teacher needs to exercise a great deal of self-control and remain calm and professional. The following are some considerations in dealing with hostile parents.

1. Be a good listener. Look the parents in the eye, and use nonverbal signals to indicate that you are listening and understand.

2. If the parent displays feelings and emotional distress, show empathy. Use statements such as "It must be difficult for you," "I know that there are many challenges parents face today," and "I understand that you are unhappy."

3. If the parent has a legitimate complaint, become his or her ally. Write down their complaint and state that you will work to make sure changes are made.

4. Do not take criticism personally. Ignore any attacks, and redirect the conference back to the student. Use statements such as "I'm sorry you feel that way about my efforts. However, we are here to discuss _____."

5. Ask for parent input: "What would you suggest?" or "How do you think we could solve this problem?" Be open to valid suggestions from the parent.

6. Be firm and businesslike, not hostile and emotional. It is useful to have data on the behavior of the child. Just state, "Let me share with you information about the behavior," and present the information. Be firm in letting the parents know that the behavior is unacceptable and changes must be made.

7. If parents continue to be hostile and abusive, end the conference. You cannot let parents assault your dignity and self-esteem. Simply state, "It is clear that we are not going to be able to resolve this issue. This conference is over and we will schedule another meeting with the school administration."

students misbehave. However, detention should be exercised with care, as there are several potentially negative outcomes.

First, detention is usually a punishment and not a natural or logical consequence for inappropriate behavior. Therefore, detention creates anger and hostility and may provoke a desire to get revenge. In addition, because detention is not a logical consequence, it does not help the student develop more self-control. For example, one of our student teachers noted that one particular student was kept after school day after day. He sat in the classroom and cried, but his behavior did not improve. It is clear that detention in this case was not working and had more negatives than positives. While it instituted punishment for behavior, it was not teaching the student appropriate behavior.

Finally, detention requires consideration of safety and logistics. The world has changed considerably in the past several decades, and it may not be safe for students to make their way home alone. Harm that can come to them on the way home can result in legal challenges. Parents are more concerned about safety and may become quite disturbed if their children do not arrive home when expected. In many schools, there are transportation issues so that if the bus is missed, there is no transportation home. If after-school detention is to be used, parents need to be notified and arrangements made to make sure that the student does have a safe way to get home.

One elementary school changed detention from something negative to something positive. They established what they called a "Kindness Club." The Kindness Club evolved out of the concept of a traffic school. It was an after-school activity that lasted 4 weeks and included students from several classrooms. Students with persistent misbehavior were referred to the Kindness Club. A teacher volunteered to operate the club as a part of her extracurricular duties. She developed a curriculum that focused on anger control, conflict resolution, and reconciliation. Students engaged in role-play and practiced taking the perspectives of others. They learned how to make concrete apologies so that they did something tangible rather than using empty words to restore friendships and reconcile with those they had offended.

Prior to the club meeting, the teacher met with the parents and explained the curriculum. She solicited the help of the parents and had them sign an agreement to make sure the students attended the club meetings. At the end of the month, each student developed a plan about how he or she was going to change. There was a ceremony where certificates were distributed and student growth was celebrated. Because of the interactive nature of the club, students rarely missed the meetings. The Kindness Club had a positive impact on the whole school and was accepted by teachers, parents, and the students (Powell, McLaughlin, Savage, & Zehm, 2001).

If detention is used, it should be used only as a last resort. It should never be applied until there is a conference with the parents so they understand when and how detention will be applied. Students in detention should be engaged in an educational activity. It should not be a time where they are just expected to sit and do nothing.

Involving Others

There are other professionals in the school who can assist teachers when all else seems to fail. Teachers need to realize that they are not psychologists or trained psychiatrists and cannot be expected to solve all problems. Some students in schools have serious problems and need additional help. Seeking assistance is not a sign of failure and is the professional thing to do when problems are serious. Allowing a student to continue on a path of self-destruction is not professional or compassionate. The welfare of the student should be placed ahead of the ego of the teacher.

The beginning step to involving others is to consult with the person in the school who handles serious discipline problems. In most elementary schools, this is the school principal. In secondary schools, it might be an assistant principal or a school counselor. However, before consulting with the person, a description of the problem and steps that have been taken need to be documented. The administrator or counselor needs as much information as possible so he or she can clearly understand the problem and determine how serious it might be. Sometimes there are teachers who simply become overly frustrated and seek the assistance of an administrator for minor problems. When this happens, it is difficult for the administrator or counselor to support the teacher and take actions that result in desired changes. In addition, poor record keeping can lead to difficulties down the road if the problem is serious and other actions are required.

The proper approach is to make an appointment with the appropriate school official. Present the data to the person and explain what has been done to date. Ask the person for specific suggestions on what needs to be done. It is common at this point for the person to offer some specific suggestions. Take those suggestions and document their impact. If there is improvement, this should be noted and a report given back to the administrator. If there is no improvement, the documentation helps establish a framework for next steps.

If the problem appears to be serious, some schools convene a team of individuals to review the problem. This might consist of the teacher, a counselor, the school administrator, and perhaps a school psychologist. Again, it is important that the teacher have good data and documentation for the committee to review. The committee members may then recommend additional steps. Sometimes a counselor or psychologist asks to visit the classroom and observe the student. This is not always successful because the presence of someone new in the classroom changes student behavior. Additional psychological testing might be done and the committee might then schedule a conference with the parent. They may recommend a different placement or a referral to other agencies that are equipped to deal with these problems. Involving others is an important step in finding a solution if the problem is serious. If serious action such as suspension or expulsion is needed, it is an absolute necessity.

REVIEW OF MAIN IDEAS

1. There are always students in classrooms who have learned to meet their needs and wants through inappropriate behavior. They do not respond to low-profile responses and may actually misbehave even more when attempts are made to stop their behavior. This requires teacher persistence and firmness.

2. A range of alternatives is useful for teachers to develop prior to entering the classroom. Having a range of alternatives that are consistent with the needs and values of the teacher can be extremely valuable when responding to incidents of misbehavior in complex classrooms.

3. Some students are very adept at shifting responsibility for their actions to others. Teachers can help keep the responsibility on students by asking them to define what they are doing and the consequences for doing that. They need to avoid asking "Why?"

4. Both verbal and nonverbal messages are important when responding to persistent misbehavior. Teachers need to develop an "I mean it" demeanor by using clarity and firmness.

5. Limit setting is another approach that emphasizes an "I mean it" demeanor. It involves stopping the class, moving to the misbehaving students, camping out until they get back on task, providing them with a behavioral prompt, and then slowly moving away.

6. Preferred activities are those educational activities that students enjoy. The loss of preferred activity time can be a logical consequence for students who continually waste time or who do not stay on task.

7. When possible, it is useful to shift choices to the student. The cost-benefit analysis spells out the "cost" of a behavior to the students and then allows the students to decide if the benefit they are deriving from their actions is worth the cost.

8. Time-out is frequently used in classrooms. It is most appropriate when a teacher is unable to stop the entire class in order to deal with misbehavior. The student is sent to a time-out area and then a conference follows when there is time to do so.

9. Many problems can be solved by rearranging the environment. This might be done to facilitate proximity control, separate students who cannot exercise self-control, or remove students from an area where there are distractions.

10. Behavioral problem solving can be used with individuals or with the whole class. It includes defining the problem, brainstorming solutions, evaluating possible solutions, making a choice, and evaluating the process.

11. Teaching students to modify their own behavior can be very effective if students learn that there are more constructive ways of fulfilling their needs. It involves helping students identify their feelings and their needs and helping them learn how to search for alternatives to unproductive behavior.

12. Parent conferences are needed when attempts to change student behavior have not worked. The focus of parent conferences should be on cooperation in order to help the student. Teachers and parents need to be working together rather than being adversaries. Considerable planning and thought needs to go into successful parent conferences.

13. Detention is an approach of last resort. It often creates anger and hostility. Some schools have changed detention to an opportunity to teach the students how to control their behavior and how to avoid problems.

APPLICATION AND ENRICHMENT

1. Observe in classrooms and begin developing a list of responses that teachers use when serious or persistent misbehavior occurs. Note the effectiveness of responses. Begin developing a personal range of alternatives.

2. Model using clarity and firmness with colleagues or with a video. Note both the clarity of the verbal message and the firmness displayed in the nonverbal message.

3. Role-play with others the practice of limit setting. Have an individual misbehave and then use moving in, dealing with back talk, camping out, and moving out.

4. Identify those activities during the school day that seem to be preferred by students. If there appear to be none, brainstorm some activities that students might consider preferred activities. State how these might be used as reinforcement for good behavior and as logical consequences for inappropriate behavior.

5. Plan a mock parent conference. Consider how the parents would be contacted, the information that needs to be gathered, and how the parents would be placed at ease and won over as collaborators rather than adversaries.

REFERENCES

Coloroso, B. (1994). *Kids are worth it! Giving your child the gift of inner discipline.* New York: William Morrow.

Elias, M., & Schwab, Y. (2006). From compliance to responsibility: Social and emotional learning and classroom management. In C. M. Evertson & C. S. Weinstein (Eds.), *Handbook of classroom management: Research, practice, and contemporary issues* (pp. 309–341). Mahwah, NJ: Lawrence Erlbaum.

Glasser, W. (1965). *Reality therapy: A new approach to psychiatry.* New York: Harper & Row.

Glasser, W. (1977). 10 steps to good discipline. *Today's Education, 66*(4), 60–63.

Hardin, C. (2006). *Effective classroom management: Models and strategies for today's classroom.* Columbus, OH: Merrill Prentice Hall.

Jones, F. (1987). *Positive classroom discipline.* New York: McGraw-Hill.

Jones, F. (2001). *Tools for teaching.* Santa Cruz, CA: Fredric H. Jones.

Kounin, J. (1970). *Discipline and group management in classrooms.* New York: Holt, Rinehart & Winston.

McLaughlin, T. (1976). Self-control in the classroom. *Review of Educational Research 46*(4), 631–663.

Powell, R., McLaughlin, H., Savage, T., & Zehm, S. (2001). *Classroom management: Perspectives on the social curriculum.* Columbus, OH: Merrill Prentice Hall.

Chapter 9

VIOLENCE AND SERIOUS MISBEHAVIOR

CLASSROOM SCENARIO

One of the authors was in her third year of teaching a sophomore English class. Two students in the class had been having trouble all year. She separated them, placing Don in the front and Sean in the back of the classroom. This worked for a short time. However, one day in the middle of class, Sean stood up, picked up his desk, shouted "F—you, Don. I'm going to hit you with this desk." Marsha demanded that Sean put down the desk, asked another student to call the assistant principal, and asked Don to step out into the hall, all in a matter of a few seconds. She walked toward Sean wondering whether she could safely take the desk away from him. Fortunately, he put the desk down just as the assistant principal arrived to escort him to the office. This situation is a good example of how quickly serious situations can occur in the classroom and how teachers often must react quickly to avert danger not only to the students involved but also to those around them. Often these situations occur so quickly that teachers have little time to think.

CHAPTER OBJECTIVES

After completing this chapter you should be able to:

- Describe the extent of violence in the schools
- State indicators of school violence
- Define three levels of violence prevention programs
- Explain actions to be taken when violence against students and teachers occurs
- Define the reasons for truancy and school attendance
- Describe programs to prevent truancy and school attendance problems
- State causes of academic dishonesty
- Define steps that can be taken to prevent academic dishonesty
- Explain causes of vandalism
- State what teachers can contribute to the prevention of vandalism
- Explain issues relating to substance abuse
- State the role of the teacher when responding to instances of drug and alcohol abuse

An image of education perpetuated by the media, legislators, and uninformed members of the general public is that of out-of-control schools racked by rampant school violence (Dedman, 2007). Indeed, the extensive coverage of violence at Columbine High School in 1999, where 14 students and 1 teacher were killed and 23 others wounded, and the Amish school in Nickel Mines, Pennsylvania, in 2006, where 10 schoolgirls were shot, shocked the nation and raised questions about the amount of violence in the schools. After all, these acts took place in communities where violence is not generally expected. Because sensational stories generate more attention than positive ones, media coverage of education could easily lead to the impression that schools are violent places filled with weapons and drugs.

However, this is a false impression. The most serious forms of violence (robbery, aggravated assault, homicide, rape, sexual assault) rarely occur in schools (Centers for Disease Control and Prevention, 2007). In the 2005–2006 school year, there were an estimated 54.8 million students enrolled in prekindergarten through Grade 12. Among the youth aged 5–18, there were 17 school-associated deaths from July 1, 2005, to June 30, 2006. This included 14 homicides and 3 suicides (National Center for Educational Statistics, 2007). Although homicide and suicide are the fourth and fifth leading causes of death among students aged 5–14 and the second and third leading causes of death among those between the ages of 15 and 24, less than 1% of the homicides and suicides occurred in schools (Centers for

Disease Control and Prevention, 2007). Contrary to popular conception, the rate of violence in schools has dramatically decreased since 1994. The rate of violent crime in schools was about 13 per 1,000 students in 1994 and about 6 per 1,000 students in 2003. This represents a drop of over 50% (U.S. Deptartment of Justice, Bureau of Educational Statistics, 2005). The number of students reported carrying a weapon to school has also dropped about 50% since 1993. Less than 1% of all homicides for school-aged children happen on school grounds or on the way to and from school (TeensHealth, 2008). It is actually safer for children to be in school than to be in a car!

To be sure, there are schools where violence and fear are prevalent. However, these schools are the exception rather than the rule. One study reported that 7 out of 10 high school teachers felt they had substantial or complete control over their students. Only 1% believed they had no control (Hyman, 1997).

We do have the expectation that our schools are safe havens and our children protected from attack. Effective schools should be safe environments where teachers can teach and students can learn without fear for their safety. Therefore, any violence on school grounds is too much. We do need to place attention on protecting all students and all teachers. However, keeping the amount of violence in perspective is important when seeking solutions. Overreactions can also do harm to the learning environment. In addition, we need to protect the rights and the aspirations of the vast majority of the students, who do not engage in violence and who want a good education (Constitutional Rights Foundation, 2007).

Although worries of violence should not be a dominant concern of teachers, one of the important ethical and legal responsibilities of teachers is to protect the students from harm. Therefore, it is a professional and legal obligation for teachers to be ready to respond if violent or potentially violent behavior occurs in the school.

This chapter provides suggestions for dealing with school violence and with other serious problems that cause teachers great concern. These include truancy, theft, vandalism, cheating, and substance abuse.

SCHOOL VIOLENCE

There are no easy solutions to school violence, and violence in the schools is not easy to understand. There are no simple profiles of students who resort to violence. The perpetrators vary considerably, and there is no single reason why they resort to violence. Some experts point out that tendencies toward violence are imbedded in the culture, the economy, and the community. Therefore, as the schools reflect society, violence should not be a surprise. For example, more than in past generations, children are likely to (a) grow up with parents who abuse drugs, get arrested, or disappear; (b) face poverty; and (c) encounter violence in the media and in video games. By the time the average student reaches seventh grade, that student is likely to have witnessed about 8,000 murders and 100,000 acts of violence on television. Although there is still some disagreement regarding the impact of media on the behavior of those watching them, one large study concluded that violent television, films, video games, and music unequivocally increase the likelihood of aggressive and violent behavior (Constitutional Rights Foundation, 2007). Given the facts about violence in society, and the exposure of children to acts of violence, it is surprising that there is such a small amount of violence in the schools.

There is no simple profile of students who may become violent, but there are some indicators that point to an increased risk that a student will be involved in violent behavior. Teachers should be sensitive to the following indicators when one of more of them is present in a student:

- Past history of violent and aggressive behavior
- Victim of abuse and neglect
- History of bullying
- The witnessing of violence in the home
- A combination of stressful family factors including marital breakup, poverty, and severe deprivation
- Recent experiences of loss, shame, humiliation, or rejection
- Failure to adjust to a new school environment
- Gang membership
- Possession of a weapon at school
- Mental illness such as depression, psychosis, or bipolar disorder
- Social withdrawal (adapted from American Academy of Child and Adolescent Psychiatry, 2001)

In 1998, a study commissioned by the Office of Juvenile Justice and Delinquency Prevention concluded that serious and violent juvenile offenders usually are males who display early minor behavior problems that eventually lead to more serious problems. The study identified three pathways that are commonly followed. The *authority conflict pathway* usually begins before the age of 12. Individuals who follow this pathway display stubborn behavior, sensation seeking, defiance, and disobedience. It escalates into authority avoidance, such as truancy, and then violence. The *overt pathway* begins later with acts such as bullying and physical fighting. The *covert pathway* also starts later than the authority conflict pathway and often begins with relatively minor covert behavior such as shoplifting and lying. It escalates into vandalism, burglary, and violence (Office of Juvenile Justice and Delinquency Prevention, 1998).

Table 9.1   Risk Factors Relevant to the Development of Disruptive and Serious Delinquent Behavior

Student Factors	Family Factors	Community Factors
Risk Factors Emerging in Elementary Years		
Aggressive behavior	Harsh discipline	Television violence
Lying	Erratic discipline	
Risk taking	Neglect	
Sensation seeking		
Lack of empathy		
Risk Factors Emerging in Middle Years		
General delinquency	Poor parental supervision	Low-SES neighborhood
Depression		Delinquent peers
Sex and substance abuse		Peer rejection
Poor academic achievement		
Truancy		
Positive attitude toward violence		
Risk Factors Emerging in Later Years		
Drug dealing	History of school dropouts	
Gang membership		
Gun ownership		

SOURCE: Adapted from the Office of Juvenile Justice and Delinquency Prevention (1998).

Results of this study imply violence prevention at an early age is important. School personnel must identify those students who demonstrate one or more of the at-risk factors as well as those who seem to be on one of the pathways. Then they can plan intervention strategies to prevent these students from escalating into violence and delinquency. Table 9.1 summarizes some of the risk factors related to disruptive and serious delinquent behavior.

The most effective responses to violence have been multiple-component programs focusing on prevention as well as response. Most efforts have been directed to the school site. Others have focused on the community by targeting gangs, increased police presence, and violence prevention activities. Some programs have used simultaneous interventions at home and at school. California even directed attention to teacher preparation programs by requiring that all teacher preparation programs include violence prevention.

Responses to violence at the school level have typically been of three types: providing security, administering punishment, and focusing on prevention (Hardin, 2008). Security programs are those designed to increase security at the school site. They include locked campuses, metal detectors at entrances, security guards, identification badges, dress codes, and locker searches. The effectiveness of these approaches is open to question. Although there are claims that these measures reduce some violence and provide an increased sense of safety for teachers and students, others point out that they are expensive to implement and are likely to create an atmosphere of fear. However, given that metal detectors and security guards are now visible in a wide range of public places, it is likely that they have become so commonplace that they no longer elicit much fear.

Punishment programs have emerged in the climate of fear that has followed some of the well-publicized incidents of school violence. These programs address the issue of school violence and the administration of severe punishments. Their intent is to send the message that violence and disruptive behavior will not be tolerated and those involved will suffer severe consequences. Many of the punishment programs fit under the broad label of *zero tolerance,* a term that usually means that no incidents of violence will be tolerated and swift punishment, usually suspension or expulsion, will follow. The rationale behind zero tolerance is that "getting tough" and imposing serious punishments deter misbehavior. In addition, it is argued that removal of some students will increase school safety for others. Some state legislatures have mandated zero tolerance for weapon possession, drug and alcohol possession, fighting, threats, and swearing.

One problem that can arise with zero tolerance is applying it with little common sense. For example, primary-level students have been suspended for playing with paper guns or bringing a butter knife to school to cut an apple! Otherwise good students have been suspended or denied important privileges for what might be termed minor offenses. In fact, the majority of students suspended under zero tolerance appear to be suspended for nonviolent actions. One study reported that about 5% of all suspensions were for possession of weapons and drugs. The other 95% fell into the broad categories of "disruptive behavior" and "other." Disruptive behavior includes abusive language, disobedience, disrespect, cutting class, and tardiness (Skiba & Rausch, 2006). These applications of zero tolerance are likely to make zero tolerance appear to be nonsensical and unfair and therefore make it less effective. The basic principle still applies that a rule or a law is ineffective if it does not have the support of those governed by it.

Furthermore, there is evidence that these "get tough" policies are not very effective in reducing violence. Students who are suspended are more likely to demonstrate an increase in discipline problems when they return, and suspension is a moderate-to-strong predictor of dropping out (Skiba & Rausch, 2006). If zero tolerance is to be effective, it must be applied fairly and must target only the most serious behaviors.

The least-used approach, but one that appears to be gaining in popularity, focuses on violence prevention. Prevention programs can be categorized into three levels. Those levels are primary prevention, secondary prevention, and tertiary prevention (Skiba & Rausch, 2006).

Primary prevention focuses on the development of prosocial attitudes and behaviors. This level of prevention includes conflict resolution, esteem building, bullying prevention, social skill learning, and improved classroom discipline. These approaches are usually addressed schoolwide and include all students, not just those who have engaged in violence.

Secondary prevention approaches focus on early screening and the identification of students who might be at risk for violent behavior. The prevention approach focuses on specific students and how to assist them in learning skills such as anger management and approaches designed to reduce alienation by helping them connect with students and the school.

Tertiary prevention approaches focus on those students who have engaged in aggression or violence. These approaches focus on effective responses to aggression and violence. Because students who engage in aggressive and violent behavior may have issues that go beyond the classroom, they may require the specialized assistance of others, such as school counselors.

Violence Against Students

Aggression and violence against other students is the most common category of violence. Classroom actions that prevent violence against other students are based on developing a positive climate of caring and respect and on increasing student engagement.

Students who engage in acts of violence frequently suffer from alienation and stress. Gang affiliation is often a characteristic of those who engage in violence. Many students seek gang affiliation because they want some place where they belong and where they can feel powerful. Gang affiliation then supports their striking out. Therefore, making the classroom a place where students are connected and engaged helps reduce their sense of alienation. If schools give students a place to belong where they feel respected, violence is less likely to occur and the need for gang affiliation is undercut. Teaching approaches such as cooperative learning, peer tutoring, and classroom meetings can help students connect with each other and provide them with a sense of belonging.

When violence or aggression does occur, there must be a firm but fair response. Students report that clear disciplinary codes are important. This implies that, while schools need to create a positive school atmosphere and make attempts to listen to students, they also need to respond decisively when acts of violence do occur.

Stop Aggression Before It Escalates

Many fights and acts of aggression occur when horseplay and teasing get out of hand. Students with low self-esteem and those with power needs may become easily offended by pranks or comments. They feel disrespected and that they must defend their "turf." So, it is easy for horseplay and teasing to escalate into out-of-control behavior and a physical confrontation. Therefore, teachers need to act to stop horseplay, pranks, and teasing before they get out of hand. One type of prevention is to emphasize respect for others, so teasing and jokes that disrespect others are not tolerated. This means that prevention needs to start with the establishment of classroom rules and be implemented by modeling respect for others.

If horseplay does erupt, and it is highly probable that it will, a first step of intervention might be to use humor or a response that calms the situation. If, however, it has moved beyond the horseplay and teasing stage, and anger is present but there has not yet been any physical aggression, Goldstein, Palumbo, Strieping, and Voutsinas (1995) recommend the following steps:

1. *Eliminate the audience.* One of the stimuli for violence is to "save face." The presence of an audience can stimulate aggression as an attempt to save face in front of others. The onlookers need to be given firm verbal directives that get them focused on something else.

2. *Use calm talk to bring down the level of anxiety and communicate a sense of teacher control.* When the teacher remains calm, it has a calming effect and provides the students with confidence in the ability of the teacher to handle it. This is not the time to display anger, begin blaming or threatening students, or communicate hostility. These actions only increase the anger and can trigger physical action. Providing advice such as "Take 10 deep breaths," "Step back," or "Calm down" can help defuse the situation.

3. *If the situation remains tense, a firm and assertive voice and the "broken record" technique is useful.* This technique involves repeating a student's name or a command over and over until he or she complies. Then the student should be given a clear directive. You might say something like this: "John—, John—, John, go to the desk. John, walk to the desk." Another example might be, "Stop, stop, I said stop, both of you, stop. Now, walk to the bench and sit down."

4. *Give individuals time to cool down, and then conduct a conference with each of them individually.* Listen to each student and allow him or her to make his or her points. They need to believe that the teacher cares enough to listen to their side of the story. Use good, active listening skills such as paraphrasing to clarify their concerns and point of view. This is not a time to judge students or get into a debate about fault. They should understand that regardless of the causes, there are consequences for fighting and violence, and neither is acceptable. After you hear both sides and students have had a chance to cool down, bring them back together to engage in conflict resolution or interpersonal problem solving.

Responding to Fighting

If a confrontation has escalated to the level of a fight, there are other actions that are necessary. In a physical confrontation, an important consideration is to protect yourself and others from harm. Stopping violence does not require that a teacher be placed in jeopardy. There is a responsibility to attempt to stop acts of violence. However, that does not require being placed in jeopardy. A natural tendency of teachers is to rush in and begin grabbing or separating the students. This can result in personal injury or even legal charges of excessive force. Personal injury can occur even with the youngest of students. One of our colleagues attempted to separate a couple of first-grade students and injured her back so severely that she had to stop teaching.

Excessive use of force is a common grounds for lawsuits against teachers. Remember that the widespread presence of videophones almost guarantees that any fight will be recorded and likely to show up on YouTube. Any inappropriate or unprofessional action by a teacher will surely be recorded. Therefore, professionalism, not impulse, needs to guide teacher actions. Consider the following ideas as you intervene during a serious, violent fight:

1. *Quickly assess the situation.* Determine how many students are involved, the level of their anger, their size, whether it is a gang situation, and whether there are any weapons or objects that could be used as weapons. Is there an audience? What is the role of the audience? Is there any blood? Remember that there is always the threat of HIV. If blood is present, back off until help arrives. The next step is to call for help. Some schools have a specific planned sequence for calling for help. A phone call to the office can quickly summon assistance. It might be wise to have the office number on the speed dial of your cell phone. If that is not possible, a dependable student should be sent for help. Most classrooms today have phones with direct connections to the office. If you cannot call, have a student do so for you.

2. *Move in.* Try to disperse the audience. In particular, give firm verbal commands. If you recognize the students, use their names and communicate the consequences of not following directions. Make sure, too, that while issuing verbal commands, you display nonverbal behaviors that communicate firmness and clarity. The students need to know that the teacher means business; this is not the time to be timid and indecisive. Even petite females have been able to break up physical confrontations by using an assertive, take-charge manner. Students need to perceive that someone is in control; it is important that that person is the teacher. Remember that most students involved in a fight are afraid of being hurt. They may act brave for the benefit of others, but they are usually scared. Many of them are looking for an excuse to quit. If a teacher shows up and takes control, this is often enough for both parties to stop without feeling as if they lost face in front of friends.

3. *When moving in, it is important to stay alert and keep hands up for protection.* Most school personnel recommend that about a 45-degree angle from the rear of one of the participants is the path to take when approaching the students. This angle serves a couple of purposes. It helps the teacher to avoid getting hit if a student ducks, and it makes the students aware that someone is moving in. The approach should be performed slowly, and out of the striking range of punches until they stop. If there are no signs of stopping, your verbal commands should continue until help arrives. If the altercation stops, moving the students away from each other and getting a position between them can keep them from resuming the altercation. Specific actions depend on the characteristics of the teacher and students. One colleague with an imposing physical presence would casually step between the students and place a hand on the chest of each one. Students were usually intimidated and would not resist. However, this is not wise if the students are large and the teacher is small.

4. *Once the physical assault has stopped, the task is not over.* You need to manage the situation in order to prevent a recurrence. Good judgment and decision making is required. For example, the students should not be sent to the office together so that they can continue to provoke each other. They need to be isolated, allowed a cooling-off period, and then dealt with. This is where help is also useful. Each adult can take a student to a different location and use a calm, matter-of-fact voice to settle them down.

5. *At this point, document the incident.* This might require talking with other adults and students who witnessed the altercation. This is important in order to avoid later disagreements or assertions of excessive use of force. However, make

sure that as much information as possible is gathered and premature conclusions are avoided (adapted from Goldstein et al., 1995).

Because of the seriousness of violence against students, school administrators need to be informed and involved in the decision about the consequences. Once they arrive on the scene, they can take charge of the situation and conduct conferences with the students and decide on the consequences. There are frequently schoolwide consequences for aggression and fighting, so administrators need to be involved in making those decisions. This is what happened with Sean in the scenario at the beginning of the chapter. The assistant principal scheduled him in detention after a conference with Marsha, Sean, and Sean's mother.

Fighting: Actions to Avoid

There are some things to avoid when dealing with disruptive or violent students. First, don't overreact to the attitude of the students. Keep focused on their actions. If they are complying with requests but demonstrating a bad attitude, don't escalate the situation by focusing on the attitude. Sometimes less is better when confronting a hostile student.

If the student engages in a verbal attack, do not take it personally. It is difficult not to take it personally and not to react to a bad attitude, because none of us wants to be attacked verbally or have our competence or integrity called into question. It takes professional poise to ignore the comments and to de-escalate the anger. Personal insults are usually designed to provoke an angry response. An angry response by the teacher only reinforces the behavior and serves to justify the anger and hostility.

Respect the personal space of the students. Getting "in their face" invades their personal space and makes the individuals feel trapped. This will lead to the predictable response of striking back. Allow the student some space and some time to gain control.

The acronym DEFUSE can be used to remember what to do in tense situations:

D: Depersonalize and don't lose your cool. The actions and words of the students should not be taken personally.

E: Encourage the students to vent, and empathize with them. Let the students talk. Express understanding for their emotions. Try to get them to talk in a respectful voice.

F: Find out the facts. Don't be quick to judge or assign blame.

U: Understand feelings. Keep in mind that in threatening situations, emotions hijack the brain and block rational thought. Recognize that the students may be guided by the fight-or-flight response and may say or do things they do not mean.

S: Suspend ego. Ego can be a dangerous word for teachers in these situations. Letting ego take over is likely to make the situation worse and may lead to actions that the teacher will later regret.

E: End on a positive note. Find something positive or encouraging to say at the end of the confrontation (adapted from The Melissa Institute for Violence Prevention and Treatment, 2007).

What Would You Do?

Read the following incident and suggest how you might respond.

Hector was a middle grade student who was larger and stronger than most of the other students in the classroom. However, he also had serious academic deficiencies. His family moved frequently and he got little support from home. In addition, he was easily frustrated and had a bad temper. The other students steered clear of him, and he had threatened his previous teacher. He did have some positive points. He would work hard if he felt like the task was worthwhile, and he would respond to genuine praise.

Today, when Hector entered the room, it was obvious that he was in a bad mood. He sat at his desk with his eyes downcast. The assignment given to the class was a challenging one, and Hector heaved a big sigh. When one of the other students made a comment, he exploded. He uttered several words of profanity, picked up his book, and threw it across the classroom. He began yelling at the teacher and denouncing the school as a worthless waste of time.

- What do you diagnose as the cause of this incident?

- Could it have been avoided?

- Now that the incident has occurred, what is the next step?

- What would be your primary concern in choosing a response?

Violence Against Teachers

Teachers who worry about their own safety are not in a position to deliver the best possible instruction or to interact with students in positive and constructive ways. It is important, however, for teachers to recognize that violence against them is a possibility so that they do not act naively and invite attack.

Identifying Causes of Violence Against Teachers

A common element that seems to run through reports of violence is that those who commit acts of violence are individuals who suffer alienation from adults and from school. This leads to one explanation of violence against teachers as an outcome of power struggles between students and teachers. Students that become frustrated in their attempts to cope with teacher power ultimately seek revenge on the teacher. The student might feel as if he or she is backed into a corner and the only way to maintain the respect of peers is to strike out at the teacher.

Another reason given for violence against teachers is that teachers, as representatives of authority, are accessible targets for students' anger and frustration. Many students have hostility toward adult society in general. They find it difficult and dangerous, though, to vent that hostility toward other symbols of authority, such as the police or their own parents, so they vent on a teacher instead. These are deeply troubled students who are bent on revenge. They are reinforced by seeing others hurt and suffer, just as they feel they are hurt and suffering. In this situation, the teacher might not be the cause of the anger, just a convenient target.

Approaches to Acts of Violence Against Teachers

A beginning step in preventing violence against teachers is to recognize the cause. If it is the result of a power struggle between the teacher and the student, the teacher needs to take steps to eliminate the power struggle. Again, this might require that the teacher suspend his or her ego and search for a win-win solution. A win-win solution is one where both teacher and the student get their needs met. In this case, the student wants to feel respected and important, and the teacher wants to maintain a constructive learning environment. The teacher, as the professional in the situation, has the responsibility for initiating a search for a solution that does not require a "winner" and a "loser." Remember, teachers can rarely win power struggles with students. Students can make this their primary purpose, whereas teachers have to focus on other things. It is to the teacher's advantage to find ways of helping students meet their needs in socially acceptable ways.

If students have trouble with adult society in general, they need the opportunity to express their anger and need assistance in learning how to cope with it. They need to be given a sense of hope and to feel that there is someone who cares. Those who develop a sense of hopelessness and a feeling that no one cares, and who think that they have no place to turn for help, have nothing to lose by striking out at others. If teachers are able to communicate that they do care about the individual and that they respect the dignity of the student, they usually cease to be convenient targets.

Students who are so hurt by society in general and adults in particular that they are seeking revenge on any convenient target usually need specialized help. As one administrator stated, "It took them years to get this way and they are not going to change easily or quickly." It takes a lot of time and patience to work with this type of student, and professional counseling may be needed. However, if a teacher is successful in winning over a revengeful student, the changes can be very rewarding.

Teachers can also help prevent acts of violence by using common sense in their daily activities. For example, teachers need to make sure that they don't present themselves as easy targets for students who are seeking revenge. Precautions (such as not being alone in the classroom with doors unlocked late in the evening or not entering a volatile situation alone when students are likely to react with aggression) are necessary for personal safety.

When acts of violence do occur, it is serious, and there may be legal issues that cannot be ignored. Consequences must be swift and consistent with the seriousness of the offense. Notify school administrators immediately. There may well be mandatory actions that are required any time there is an act of violence against teachers. To not follow mandated procedures for reporting acts of violence against teachers is unprofessional and could have negative consequences.

In summary, there are a variety of causes for violence against teachers. Teachers need to be alert to the fact they may make themselves a convenient target so they need to be alert and use common sense. Perhaps the most effective approach is to identify those students who feel alienated and disconnected from other students, adults, and the school and to try to help them reconnect and believe that the school is a place that will help them rather than just another source of failure and frustration.

TRUANCY AND ATTENDANCE PROBLEMS

School attendance and truancy are pervasive problems. In one study, school administrators identified absenteeism and tardiness to be the two most serious problems in their school (National Center for School Engagement, 2007). Legal definitions of truancy vary from state to state, but it is generally defined as a subset of absenteeism referring to unexcused absences from school. Because of the variety of definitions of what constitutes an unexcused absence, there are no firm data on the extent of the problem. However, a study conducted in the Denver Public Schools is informative. This study found that about 20% of the Denver Public School students missed at least 10 days a year without a valid excuse.

One of the reasons that truancy and school attendance have begun receiving considerable attention is that lack of attendance is usually an early warning sign of delinquency, substance abuse, school failure, and dropping out. In addition, the

Table 9.2   Truancy as a Risk Factor for Other Behaviors

- Truancy has been clearly identified as an early warning sign of students headed for delinquent activity and school failure.
- Lack of commitment to school is related to substance abuse, delinquency, and teen pregnancy.
- Truants have low self-esteem and greater feelings of rejection from parents.
- Studies of serious juvenile offenders found that truancy was one of three facts most of them had in common.
- A survey of 28 communities between 1980 and 2000 revealed that truancy is a particularly good predictor of middle school drug use.
- After emphasizing truancy and picking up truants on the streets, one community had vehicle burglaries decrease 22%, residential burglaries decrease 19%, and criminal mischief decrease 19%.

SOURCE: Adapted from the National Center for School Engagement (2007).

No Child Left Behind Act (NCLB) requires that school districts collect and submit attendance data in order to receive federal money. However, NCLB may be contributing to the truancy problem. NCLB mandated that by 2014, 100% of the students pass proficiency tests and graduate from high school. Most of the NCLB emphasis, however, has been on the proficiency tests and not the graduation rate, so many school administrators have found that the school will look better if low-performing students drop out (National Center for School Engagement, 2007). Consequently, the number of students who are "discharged," or dropped from school rolls, has increased in some school districts. Table 9.2 provides links between truancy and other risky behaviors.

Causes of Truancy and Attendance Problems

The causes for truancy and school attendance problems can be grouped into family factors, school factors, and personal factors (National Center for School Engagement, 2007). Family factors include homelessness, poverty, family conflict, ineffective parental control, and families having a negative relationship with the school. School factors include feeling unwelcome at school, not fitting in, boredom, falling behind in schoolwork, views that school is irrelevant, and inappropriate placement so that success is impossible and attendance is pointless. Personal factors include low self-esteem, academic failure, feeling rejected by parents, poor relationships with other students, and gang involvement.

There is little that the teacher can do to address family factors. The one factor that can be addressed by the teacher is that of negative family relationships with the school. This negative relationship is often the result of numerous negative contacts between the family and the school. Usually the parents get contacted by the school only when there is a problem. However, teachers can play a role in improving contacts between the parents and the school. They can do this by trying to establish positive contacts with the family during the school year. Parents want schools that care about their children. Making positive contacts with the family helps develop the perception that the school is interested in their children and does care.

School factors are a major contributor to school attendance problems. One study found that just one factor, school performance, predicted 17% of variation in attitudes toward dropping out (National Center for School Engagement, 2007). This means that making sure that students are appropriately placed and achieving success has a major impact on attitudes and attendance. Fear of failure is a powerful influence. Just imagine being required to attend a job or a school where you believed you had no chance of success. After a short time, frustration, shame, and bitterness would take root. This is the way some students feel about school. They face each day with the prospect of more humiliation and failure. For some students, their frustration takes the form of aggression; for others, it takes the form of avoidance. Even the fear of being caught and punished for truancy is minor compared to the humiliation that accompanies persistent failure.

Boredom and apathy are other major causes of attendance problems. Apathetic students see neither the importance nor the relevance of school. They do not enjoy school and do not believe that the school is interested in them or their success. They see the school as a cold and uncaring bureaucracy. The curriculum is viewed as irrelevant, and teachers are seen as symbols of adult power that are out to catch them being bad rather than helping them succeed. In addition, some teachers are simply "burned out" and unenthusiastically just go about doing a job. If the teacher doesn't care, why should the students care?

Schools and classrooms like this are not pleasant places. Attendance problems are a form of passive resistance. Administrators and teachers need to remember that more school rules and stiffer penalties are not the answer to this problem. These "get tough" policies will only lead to further alienation. We all need to make the effort to develop schools and classrooms as places where students feel that they are accepted and their needs are met. Glasser (1986) contends that most schools concentrate on teaching and directing students without taking into account whether this is satisfying their needs. An important step in addressing the truancy and attendance problem is to make schools and classrooms places where the students will want to come because they believe they are satisfying their needs. In fact, it is a sad commentary that the school is one of the few places in society that can meet the needs of many students. School associations and achievements can make them feel important and respected, thus satisfying their need for achievement and their need to belong and to have fun. If this is addressed in the school, many of the attendance problems would disappear.

Teachers can also address personal factors. Student who engage in truancy often have low self-esteem. Self-esteem can be enhanced by helping the student meet the need for achievement. Everyone has a need to feel that he or she is growing and learning. If the students believe they are learning and achieving, they are motivated to continue. Therefore, providing the students with legitimate success experiences through good diagnosis and placement, emphasizing success rather than failure, and decreasing competition between students can help students satisfy their achievement needs. A general principle that is helpful is to try to provide at least one success experience for each student every day. This is easy for elementary teachers but can be quite a challenge for secondary teachers, who often have 35 students in each class. They must plan meaningful lessons and use cooperative activities, such as cooperative learning, that are designed to promote group and individual success.

Because many students with attendance problems feel unwelcome in school and that they do not belong, efforts need to be made to help students connect with each other. This might be accomplished through activities such as cooperative learning so that students have an opportunity to work with a variety of other students. Activities and clubs related to a variety of topics and interests can also help students find a place where they can fit in and help them see school as relevant.

An important step in dealing with attendance problems is to talk with students who are chronically absent or tardy. Allowing them to explain their situation can often lead to solutions that satisfy the needs of the students as well as the needs of the teacher. Sometimes the solution is a relatively easy one. For example, one high school teacher, after several confrontations with a tardy student, finally asked the student about the problem. The student had a locker in a distant corner of the school, and by the time he went to his locker to get the material required for the class and returned, he was late. Circumstances prevented him from taking the material to the previous class. Allowing the student to drop off the material on the way to the earlier class allowed the student to come directly to the class and solved the problem.

Finally, truancy is a community problem. Truants often engage in illegal activities such as shoplifting, burglary, and vandalism. Therefore, the entire community can benefit by helping reduce truancy. For example, after the police in one community began enforcing truancy laws and picking up school-aged youth on the streets during the school day, crime diminished substantially in the neighborhood (National Center for School Engagement, 2007).

One of the advantages of community involvement is that other agencies implement actions that are beyond the authority of the school. For example, the juvenile court system can place sanctions and implement consequences for parents and guardians of chronically truant students. When teachers encounter those students who have serious problems with school attendance and truancy, consulting with the administration may lead to the involvement of other community agencies. However, remember that pressure from the police or the courts will have minimal impact if the school does not do its part in becoming an engaging environment that is concerned about the needs of all students.

ACADEMIC DISHONESTY

Academic dishonesty is a universal concern. Not only is the issue an ethical one, but also academic dishonesty denigrates the importance of school tasks and interferes with valid assessments of student progress. Handling the problem of cheating can be especially difficult because it is so widespread in society. Teachers find it difficult to extol the virtues of honesty when the practices of businesspeople and public officials regularly skirt the law. In recent years, the easy access of technological devices has dramatically increased the potential for cheating. Because of the difficulty in keeping up with new forms of academic dishonesty, prevention is the best response.

The prevalence of technology has provided new avenues for student dishonesty.

© Photodisc

Identifying Causes of Academic Dishonesty

Perhaps the best response to the problem of academic dishonesty is to attack the motivation. One of the basic motives for cheating is fear of failure. This is especially the case with high-stakes tests and assignments, those that have important consequences for the student. These tests have taken increased importance in determining whether or not a student will move to the next grade, graduate, or be admitted to higher education. With so much riding on the outcome, it is not surprising that students find creative ways of cheating.

Another motive for cheating is that students do not perceive the relevance of school tasks. Many students see education as a series of unnecessary and irrelevant hurdles to be cleared rather than something that is important for their lives. The result is that they do not see cheating as unethical and harmful. It is just a way of coping with meaningless tasks. Because school tasks are perceived as being of little value, any means of passing is justified.

Cheating would drop dramatically if students really believed that an honest display of their knowledge and skill would benefit rather than harm them. Unfortunately, most students see school tests and assignments as a part of the ritual rather than an indication of knowledge and ability that can be important to them.

Approaches to Solving Academic Dishonesty

Some teachers become so obsessed with cheating that they engage in a game of "cops and robbers." The teacher is the cop who is always trying to catch the crooks, or in this case the cheaters. These teachers are suspicious and distrustful. This presents a challenge for students to try to fool the teacher. This sort of game, or contest, then distorts the purpose of education. Students can be very creative in their efforts to cheat, and students who want to cheat will find a way. That is why it is best to attack the motivations for cheating.

An important aspect of prevention is to make sure that tests and assignments are relevant and fair. Tests that contain trick questions or that are not perceived by students to be accurate measures of important objectives communicate that there is more concern with spreading students out on a grading curve than actually assessing their learning. For example, one university history professor that used irrelevant and trick questions on tests promoted increased cheating rather than increased study.

If any one test or assignment is given too much emphasis, increased cheating is bound to occur. If the grade for an entire term or unit is reduced to how well students do on one test or one paper, then students will seek to find a way of coping. When the stakes are high and success is dependent on one or two major tasks, cheating becomes a means of self-preservation. More frequent testing and more frequent assignments reduce pressure and thus will reduce the amount of cheating.

When students are caught cheating, private correction rather than public correction is an appropriate response. Public accusations and ridicule only invite denial, defensiveness, and retaliation. The most effective approach (conducted in private and without anger) is to present the student with the evidence, ask for an explanation, and discuss possible consequences. These private conferences are important in diagnosing and eliminating the causes of cheating.

VANDALISM

Vandalism is an intentional act that has the purpose of damaging or destroying the property of another. It is widespread across schools and is not limited to schools in low socioeconomic neighborhoods. In the school setting, it involves graffiti, general property destruction, and break-ins.

School break-ins are usually of three types. *Nuisance break-ins* are those where the act of breaking in is seemingly the purpose. Individuals involved in these types of break-ins are often those who are caught up with the actions of a peer group or who are breaking in just to create some excitement. A good example is the senior prank that many high school seniors believe is necessary at the end of the school year. This is almost a tradition at some schools. One year, when author Marsha was teaching high school, the seniors broke into the school office at the end of the year and stuffed it with crumpled newspapers. They had planned this from the beginning of the year, saved newspapers for months, and spent quite a bit of time crumpling them. Although this was certainly not a malicious break-in, there were expenses involved in repairing locks to the school office. Some of the students felt guilty when they saw the custodians removing the paper and offered to help! (If only they had spent this much time studying!)

Malicious break-ins are those that are committed by individuals who seek to destroy property. This type of vandalism is often committed by individuals who are alienated and seeking revenge. It often occurs in school settings when the student seeks revenge on a teacher who has mistreated him or her. One student in Marsha's school was mistreated by one of his science teachers. He broke into the science lab, stole lab samples, and broke expensive equipment, all because he perceived he had been mistreated.

A third type of break-in is what is called a *professional break-in* because the intent is to steal property. The presence of relatively expensive equipment, such as computers, has fueled this type of break-in (Dedel, 2005). Just recently, an elementary school in our area lost 30 computers that had just been donated to the school. The vandals were caught trying to sell them on eBay.

School vandalism often is little more than somewhat trivial incidents. However, when the costs of these somewhat trivial incidents are combined, the cost to the schools is quite large. In addition to the monetary costs, there are social costs. These costs relate to the negative impact that vandalism has on the morale and the attitudes of the students and the community.

Identifying Causes of Vandalism

Individuals participating in nuisance and malicious vandalism are almost always young males acting in groups. It is most common among middle school youth and becomes less common in high school (Dedel, 2005). Some research (e.g., Horowitz, 2003) contends that vandalism is a product of a modern society that is characterized by alienation and meaninglessness.

The characteristics of those who participate in vandalism are very similar to those of students who commit other serious acts. Vandals are generally individuals who have done poorly academically, feel marginalized, are alienated from school, do not have a sense of belonging, have been suspended or expelled from school, and have a poor understanding of the impact of their actions on others (Dedel, 2005). One of the factors that supports vandalism is that the acts generally do not receive condemnation from other students and other students do not have negative feelings toward those who commit acts of vandalism. Another contributing factor is that many of those participating in vandalism do not have a sense of ownership. They believe the property belongs to no one (Dedel, 2005).

Both objective and subjective factors influence school vandalism. Objective factors include school size (larger schools have more vandalism), age of the student population, teacher turnover rate, and parental support for the schools' disciplinary policies. Subjective factors involve attitudes of the teachers toward students, the uses of teacher power, and the clarity of school rules. In other words, there is a connection (Horowitz, 2003).

Approaches to Solving Vandalism Problems

The problem of vandalism is usually one that needs to be treated at a school and community level. A key variable relating to vandalism is school climate. Schools with high rates of vandalism are those characterized as impersonal, unresponsive, and nonparticipatory, and where the administrative style was oppressive or hands-off. Researchers have especially identified the teacher–student interaction as a causal variable. This has a direct relationship to the responsibilities of teachers.

Specifically, schools with low vandalism rates were found to be places where the students value teachers' opinions, where teachers are not hostile or authoritarian toward the students, where grades are not used as a disciplinary tool, where rules are consistently and fairly applied and enforced, and where teachers have a cooperative, informal, and fair working relationship (Dedel, 2005).

As with other serious misbehaviors identified in this chapter, efforts to reduce student alienation and helping them feel like they belong are important aspects of a prevention program. Addressing the students' academic needs and preventing school failure, along with increasing the contacts among students through activities such as classroom meetings and cooperative learning, are important classroom actions that can prevent vandalism.

The classroom approach can focus on a couple of variables specific to vandalism. First, an emphasis should be placed on developing ownership. Students need to realize that they and the community are paying the costs of vandalism. The money spent to repair acts of vandalism, as well as the insurance costs, needs to be viewed as reducing the funds available for other activities that benefit the students.

In addition, all students need to understand both the monetary and the social costs of vandalism. Participating in acts of vandalism needs to be condemned by the peer group as socially unacceptable. Instituting peer sanctions for vandalism could be one of the most powerful tools for preventing vandalism.

Finally, punishment has not been found to be a successful deterrent to vandalism. In fact, harsh punishment might only provoke additional vandalism (Horowitz, 2003). The implementation of natural and logical consequences for individuals who commit acts of vandalism is probably more effective than punishment. Students can clean up the mess, repair the damage, and make restitution. Adding a personal cost to acts of vandalism can help reduce the motivation.

SUBSTANCE ABUSE

In 1994, Congress passed the National Educational Goals Act. One of the major goals of this act was that by the year 2000, the schools would be alcohol and drug free. This obviously did not happen, and some have defined this as a failure of the schools. However, since the schools exist in a social context, it would be unrealistic to believe that the schools alone could eliminate substance abuse and that they should be held accountable for doing so. Schools can be expected to be alcohol and drug free when society is alcohol and drug free.

However, there is good news. Since 1996, the peak year for reported drug use during the past year by 8th graders, the use of drugs has declined by 44%. For

10th graders and 12th graders, the peak year for drug abuse was 1997. Since that time, the reported use of illicit drugs during the past year has declined by 27% for 10th graders and 15% among 12th graders (National Institute on Drug Abuse, 2008). This can hardly be labeled as a complete failure. However, there are still challenges to face.

One of the biggest challenges is to change public perception. Many adults view experimentation with tobacco, alcohol, and illegal drugs as something that young people can be expected to do and something they will get over. However, a high percentage of students who experiment with these substances continue to use them throughout their high school years.

Another challenge that has received increased attention in recent years has been abuse of prescription drugs. There has been virtually no drop in the nonmedical uses of prescription drugs. Data on this use of prescription drugs are now being gathered; about 15% of high school seniors reported the nonmedical use of at least one prescription drug over the past year (National Institute on Drug Abuse, 2008).

Identifying Causes of Substance Abuse

The causes for substance abuse are numerous. Some individuals begin abusing drugs as a result of peer influence to be a part of the "in" group. Others take drugs as a coping mechanism for difficult life situations. Still others get involved as a symbol of rebellion. Those who tend to be more mature and who are prematurely attempting to be adult are also likely to engage in alcohol and drug abuse.

Many of the students who are involved in drug and alcohol abuse are those who have low self-esteem, a lack of confidence, and a perceived incompetence in dealing with reality (Hyman, 1997). School factors can contribute to drug and alcohol abuse by furthering feelings of inadequacy and insignificance. School failure is strongly associated with substance abuse.

Approaches to Solving Problems of Substance Abuse

One of the most commonly used approaches to substance abuse is *zero tolerance.* Although zero tolerance has been effective in addressing the most important factors in substance abuse, the availability of drugs and the perceived risks of using them, the severity of zero tolerance also encourages parents and students to remain silent about drug abuse. In addition, school programs focusing on "just saying no" and providing information about the risks of substance abuse have been of limited value. The reasons for the lack of impact of these programs is that they do not address factors such as depression, low self-esteem, anxiety, learning disabilities, lack of parental engagement, and parental substance abuse. Effective programs of substance abuse need to have the active engagement of the entire community,

Some schools have implemented severe measures to prevent crime.

© Photodisc

including parents, students, administrators, community agencies, and government (National Center on Addiction and Substance Abuse, 2008).

In addition, remember that at the adolescent stage of development, most students have the perception that bad things may happen to others but will never happen to them. Therefore, information about the risks of addiction has little impact because they believe they are different and they can handle it.

Like other issues addressed in this chapter, prevention programs should focus on academic success, social skills such as enhancing peer relationships, self-control, and drug refusal skills. Once again, schools need to help students feel significant, provide them with success, and create an open climate so that they feel free to discuss feelings of fear and anxiety. Because of the importance of peers, group activities designed to help students deal with peer pressure should be a component of substance abuse programs.

Substance abuse involves both physical addiction and psychological dependency. It is important to keep these two dimensions in mind because it is very difficult for schools to treat physical addiction. School psychologists or drug counselors may be needed to help coordinate this aspect of treatment with local agencies that treat substance abuse problems. This also requires the involvement of the family.

In summary, prevention should be the goal of school programs. When students abuse substances, it is seldom a problem that an individual teacher can solve alone. To attempt to do so may be harmful to the student. The student needs professional help and counseling as soon as possible.

REVIEW OF MAIN IDEAS

1. Although there is a widespread public perception that schools are violent places, the evidence indicates otherwise. In fact, schools are one of the safest places to be, and incidents of serious acts of violence have actually been decreasing.

2. There are no easy solutions to acts of school violence. There is no simple profile of individuals who commit acts of violence. Zero-tolerance programs and those with strong punishment components have not been very effective and have sometimes been abused by educators who do not use common sense.

3. Teachers need to learn how to defuse situations that might lead to violence. There are steps they can take when acts of violence do occur.

4. Truancy and sporadic school attendance is an area of great concern and is identified by school administrators as one of their most serious problems. The causes of truancy and attendance problems can be grouped into the categories of school, family, and personal. Teachers are best equipped to focus on the school factors. Removing the threats of school attendance and making schools places where students' needs are being met is an effective step in prevention.

5. Academic dishonesty is a serious concern. The availability of new forms of technology has opened the doors for new forms of academic dishonesty. Creative students can always find ways of cheating, so the best approach to academic dishonesty is prevention.

6. Vandalism is often a series of relatively minor incidents. However, taken as a whole, they add to a significant loss for schools. Again, vandalism is often rooted in alienation and a negative educational climate. While approaches to vandalism

need to engage the whole school and the whole community, teachers can do their part by helping reduce student alienation and by creating a safe and productive learning environment.

7. Substance abuse continues to be a major concern. Even though substance abuse has declined in the last decade, many challenges remain. One of the most difficult challenges is to change the general perception that it is okay for students to experiment with substances and that they will get over it. A more recent challenge has been to help students understand the risks involved with the non-medical use of prescription drugs.

APPLICATION AND ENRICHMENT

1. Reflect on the various serious problems addressed in this chapter. Which are of the most concern for you? Why do they concern you? Identify a plan of action that you could take to obtain the necessary background and skill to help you become more comfortable with this type of problem.

2. Interview teachers at several different grade levels. Identify which of the serious problems discussed in this chapter are of most concern to them. How do they and how does their school respond to these serious problems?

3. Choose one of the serious problems discussed in this chapter and do some additional research on this issue. There are many Internet sites that focus on each of these issues. Become an "expert" on this topic and identify various agencies that are helping educators address this issue.

REFERENCES

American Academy of Child and Adolescent Psychiatry. (2001). *Understanding violent behavior in children and adolescents (no. 55): Facts for families.* Washington, DC: Author.
Centers for Disease Control and Prevention. (2007). The effectiveness of universal school-based programs for the prevention of violent and aggressive behavior. *Morbidity and Mortality Weekly Report, 56,* RR-7.

Constitutional Rights Foundation. (2007). *Talking points: Causes of school violence.* Retrieved November 12, 2007, from http://www.crf-usa.org/violence/intro.html

Dedel, K. (2005). *School vandalism and break-ins.* Center for Problem-Oriented Policing. Retrieved May 20, 2008, from http://www.popcenter.org/problems/vandalism/

Dedman, B. (2007, Oct. 10). *Ten myths about school shootings.* Retrieved May 2, 2008, from http://www.msnbc.msn.com/id/15111438/print/1/dispaly mode/1098/

Department of Justice, Bureau of Educational Statistics. (2005). *National crime victimization survey: Table 2.2. Indicators of school crime and safety.* Washington, DC: Author.

Glasser, W. (1986). *Control theory for the classroom.* New York: Harper & Row.

Goldstein, A. P., Palumbo, J., Strieping. S., & Voutsinas, A. M. (1995). *Break it up: A teacher's guide to managing student aggression.* Champaign, IL: Research Press.

Gonzales, R., & Mullins, T. (2004). Addressing truancy in youth court programs. In T. Mullins, (Ed.), *Selected topics on youth courts: A monograph.* Washington, DC: U.S. Department of Justice: Office of Juvenile Justice and Delinquency Prevention.

Hardin, C. (2008). *Effective classroom management: Models and strategies for today's classroom* (2nd ed.). Upper Saddle River, NJ: Merrill Prentice Hall.

Horowitz, T. (2003). *School vandalism: Individuals and social context.* Retrieved May 28, 2008, from http://findarticles.com/p/articles/mi-m2248/is_149_38/ai_103381765/

Hyman, I. A. (1997). *School discipline and school violence: The teacher variance approach.* Boston: Allyn & Bacon.

Melissa Institute for Violence Prevention and Treatment. (2007). *The way not to handle disruptive students.* Retrieved November 12, 2007, from http://www.keepschoolssafe.org/the-way-not-to-handle-disruptive-students/

National Center for Educational Statistics. (2008). *Indicators of school crime and safety: 2007.* Retrieved May 15, 2008, from http://nces.ed.gov/programs/crimeindicators/crimeindicators2007/

National Center for School Engagement. (2007). *Pieces of the truancy jigsaw: A literature review.* Denver, CO: Author.

National Center on Addiction and Substance Abuse. (2008). *Malignant neglect: Substance abuse and America's schools.* Retrieved May 23, 2008, from http://alcholism.about.com/library/blcasa011105.htm

National Institute on Drug Abuse. (2008). *NIDA infofacts: High school and youth trends.* Retrieved May 23, 2008, from http://www.nida.nih.gov/infofacts/hsyouthtrends.html

Office of Juvenile Justice and Delinquency Prevention. (1998). *Serious and violent juvenile offenders.* Washington, DC: U.S. Department of Justice.

Skiba, R., & Rausch, M. (2006). Zero tolerance, suspension, and expulsion: Questions of equity. In C. Evertson & C. Weinstein (Eds.), *Handbook of classroom management: Research, practice and contemporary issues* (pp. 1063–1085). Mahwah, NJ: Lawrence Erlbaum.

Chapter 10

BULLIES AND BULLYING

CLASSROOM SCENARIO

Stephanie moved with her parents across the country to a new community. When she went to fifth grade in her new school, she knew no other students. Stephanie was quite shy and missed her old friends. When she entered the room, several girls giggled and pointed. She felt embarrassed but was not quite sure what was wrong.

As the morning wore on, she was aware of others whispering and pointing. She began to realize that the way she was dressed was quite different from the other students.

Then, when the teacher asked a question, she quickly raised her hand and was called upon. "Excellent answer, Stephanie!" exclaimed the teacher. She heard a whispered "teacher's pet!"

At recess, she went to the playground with the rest of the students. Once on the playground, someone flicked the back of her hair with his or her hand. Someone else remarked, "Where did you get that dress? Goodwill?" Others started laughing. Stephanie quickly ran to the corner of the playground. She started to cry quietly.

CHAPTER OBJECTIVES

After completing this chapter, you should be able to:

- Define bullying and state the importance of addressing bullying in schools
- Explain the impact of bullying on the school environment, including victims, onlookers, and bullies

- Explain cyberbullying and the general motives individuals give for engaging in cyberbullying
- Define the general characteristics of bullies
- Explain the basic characteristics of effective antibullying programs
- State how to confront incidents of direct bullying
- State what teachers can do to address cyberbullying
- Define the general characteristics of victims
- Describe the basic components of programs to assist victims

B ullying has long been present in American education. The history of education reveals that in earlier times, older students often committed acts of violence against other students and against teachers. For example, in 1837, rebellious students disrupted over 300 schools in Massachusetts. Students in rural schools often threw bullets into potbellied stoves as a joke! Older students often "put out," or assaulted, teachers whom they disliked (Altenbaugh, 2003).

Bullying was generally considered a normal part of growing up and was not an item of concern. However, educators have recently realized that bullying has devastating effects on learning. Programs related to preventing and responding to bullying can now be found in many schools. The National Education Association added emphasis to the campaign against bullying by identifying bullying as a major concern in schools across the nation (National Education Association, 2003b).

Efforts to address the problem of bullying have been fueled by troubling data. Estimates are that approximately 160,000 students a day stay home from school because they are afraid of being victimized (Sanchez et al., 2001). Somewhere between 15% and 25% of all students report that they are bullied frequently. Over half of the students report being victimized to the extent that they developed stress symptoms (Hyman et al., 2006). Victims of bullying often fear going to school, using the bathroom, or riding on the school bus (National Education Association, 2003a). In addition, they are more likely than other students to be depressed, be lonely, have low self-esteem, and contemplate suicide (Olewus, 2003).

Bullying also has a negative impact on the observers and on the bullies. For victims and observers, this threatening and hostile environment interferes with learning. To make matters worse, this is an environment where they are all forced to return every day! It is only natural that individuals seek to escape hostile environments. Others find themselves unable to learn under these conditions.

In addition, bullying can be an antecedent to increased violence (Hardin, 2008). However, many teachers do not grasp this connection between bullying and school violence (Metropolitan Life Survey of the American Teacher, 1999). The sense of hopelessness felt by repeated victims of bullying can lead to their use of extreme and desperate measures. For example, a common thread that runs through school shootings is that the shooters have been the victims of bullies (Blassone, 2007). Two thirds of school shooters felt bullied, harassed, or victimized. They were motivated by a desire to get even (Melissa Institute for Violence Prevention and Treatment, 2007a). This is a situation where hopeless victims retaliate and become the victimizers.

Bullying can also have some negative effects on the bullies. Bullying may establish patterns of behavior that lead to serious problems. Bullies do not establish effective prosocial behaviors and come to rely on power and intimidation as a way of meeting their needs and wants. These inappropriate behavior patterns often lead to trouble later in life. For example, students who bully are more likely to engage in acts of vandalism and fighting, and they are more likely to drop out of school than those who do not (Olewus, 2003). Students who bully are four times more likely to engage in delinquent behavior and become involved in substance abuse than those who do not. Children identified by their peers at age 6 as bullies are six times more likely to commit a crime by age 24 and five times more likely than nonbullies to end up with a serious criminal record (Melissa Institute for Violence Prevention and Treatment, 2007a). Although girls generally bully less frequently than boys, they are just as likely as boys to develop long-term adjustment problems (Melissa Institute for Violence Prevention and Treatment, 2007a).

Although there is a growing awareness of the problem of bullying, teachers seem to be largely unaware of the extent of bullying. One study revealed that 70% of the teachers believed that they responded to almost every incident of bullying. However, only 25% of the students agreed with their assessment. Many students believe they will get little or no help from teachers and adults when they are bullied. They indicate a hesitancy to report bullying because they believe it will be ignored or trivialized and they fear retaliation (Hyman et al., 2006). Furthermore, a significant number of teachers (25%) see nothing wrong with bullying or put-downs and choose to ignore these incidents or intervene with only about 4% of the bullying incidents (U.S. Department of Health and Human Services, 2008a).

In summary, bullying is a serious issue. Numerous incidents of bullying may signal that a school is in trouble. It has a negative effect on everyone in the school, not just the victims. It is not a normal part of growing up, and the simplistic advice to "stand up for yourself" is neither effective nor wise. Bullying usually targets the most vulnerable in school as the victims and creates scars that last for a lifetime. Teachers have an ethical obligation to protect all students and to create conditions that are safe for everyone. Not to do so is to neglect one of the most important professional duties of teachers. Teachers must develop an increased sensitivity to bullying and need to learn how to prevent bullying and how to respond consistently to incidents of bullying. The educational, social, and emotional costs of bullying are simply too high to be ignored.

DEFINING BULLYING

One reason educators fail consistently to respond to bullying is an inadequate understanding of bullying and the different forms it may take. In broad terms, bullying can be defined as repetitive, aggressive behavior intended to cause harm or discomfort. It involves a power differential between the bully and the victim and usually is directed toward victims who cannot or will not defend themselves. Bullies often get a sense of power and status that they cannot obtain as easily through prosocial activities.

In general, there are two types of bullying: direct and indirect. *Direct bullying* is face-to-face bullying. Indirect bullying is bullying that takes place behind someone's back. Direct bullying includes physical bullying such as shoving, pushing, hitting, and kicking. However, it might also take the form of verbal actions such as teasing, taunting, name-calling, insulting, humiliating, and making sexist or racist comments. Nonverbal behaviors, such as gestures, facial expressions, and staring, can also be a part of direct bullying.

Indirect bullying is often called *social* or *relational* bullying. It involves gossiping, spreading rumors, undermining friendships, excluding, and shunning individuals. This type of bullying is often called intentional exclusion and can start as early as preschool when kids say things such as "If you don't let me play with that toy, I won't invite you to my birthday party" (Italie, 2008). Another form of indirect bullying that has been especially devastating is cyberbullying, now quite pervasive in kids as young as 10.

Teachers are more likely to respond to incidents of direct bullying that involve physical threats or harassment. However, verbal bullying is the most common type and is less likely to elicit a teacher response (Hazler & Miller, 2001). Physical bullying tends to increase during the elementary years, peaks around the middle school years, and declines in high school. Males are more likely to be involved in physical bullying whereas females are more likely to be involved in verbal or psychological bullying (Melissa Institute for Violence Prevention and Treatment, 2007a). In her unforgettable memoir, *Please Stop Laughing at Me,* Jodee Blanco chronicles her own bullying experiences throughout her school years. She says that as early as fifth grade she began to see subtle changes in her peers and in the social environment. Students were forming cliques, and if you did not belong to

Social exclusion is a form of bullying.

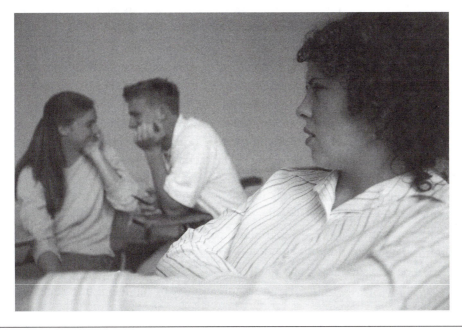

© Artville

one, you were an outcast. She noticed that it was more acceptable to make fun of others than to be kind. This was fast becoming the way to make friends. She noticed other changes, too. "Instead of being admired for participating in class the way we were in earlier grades, those of us who raised our hands frequently were laughed at and labeled teacher's pets" (Blanco, 2003, p. 38). Recognizing these bullying tactics early on can be the key to success in dealing with student issues before they worsen.

In recent years, many students have been given increased accessibility to electronic devices such as cell phones and computers. For example, 8 out of 10 teens reported using the Internet "yesterday." About 59% of 13- to 15-year-olds and 74% of 16- to 17-year-olds report that they have a cell phone. Of those teens with a cell phone, 60% use text messaging and 25% report sending text messages while in school (National Crime Prevention Council, 2007). This increased availability has made these devices potential tools for bullying and has led to the serious problem of *cyberbullying.*

Cyberbullying is quite common among teens, and 43% of teens report experiencing some form of cyberbullying in the past year (National Crime Prevention Council, 2007). Even younger students are familiar with cyberbullying, as 16% of students in Grades 6–8 report being cyberbullied at least once in the past couple of months. Cyberbullying is more common among females than males. Girls in Grades 6–8 were twice as likely to be engaged in cyberbullying, either as victims or perpetrators, than were boys (U.S. Department of Health and Human Services, 2008c).

Students cite several reasons individuals engage in cyberbullying. The reason cited most often is that the perpetrator thinks it is funny. Others say that the cyberbully simply does not like the person he or she is bullying. A third reason students cite is that the cyberbully views the victim as a "loser." Nearly half of the students surveyed indicated that they thought cyberbullying occurs because the cyberbullies do not think they will get caught or experience any tangible consequences (National Crime Prevention Council, 2007).

Cyberbullying occurs through e-mails, instant messages, blogs, chat rooms, and Web pages. It involves sending threatening or harassing e-mails or instant messages, creating Web sites that belittle or demean others, taking and posting inappropriate or unflattering photographs, sending private or sensitive information about someone to others, stealing passwords and using them to send inappropriate messages, and sending threatening or harassing messages using cell phones.

Cyberbullying can be especially devastating to young teens, who are searching for identity and for whom appearance and acceptance from peers is of critical importance. One dramatic example of cyberbullying that received national attention was a situation where a mother actually helped her daughter engage in cyberbullying a neighbor girl. The victim was so upset over the content of the messages that she committed suicide. Students need to learn that cyberbullying is not innocent fun. People can be seriously harmed and reputations ruined.

CHARACTERISTICS OF BULLIES

The majority of students do not engage in bullying. Research indicates that between 10% and 15% of students are occasionally involved in bullying. About 5% to 10% of the students are engaged in frequent bullying, defined as engaging in bullying twice a week or more. There is no one profile that fits all bullies.

Because many teachers focus on physical bullying, they have an inadequate understanding of the characteristics of bullies. Indeed, many bullies are those who fit the stereotype of students with poor social skills who have a strong need to dominate others and to get their own way. These students often have a low tolerance for frustration and are generally defiant toward adults. Male bullies are almost always physically stronger than other males of the same age. They come from homes where aggression is modeled and where there is a lack of parental supervision. Bullies have developed "striking out" as an appropriate method for handling problems.

However, this is not the whole story. Some bullies are popular, have high self-esteem, and are leaders in their peer group (Melissa Institute for Violence Prevention and Treatment, 2007a). These students value their ability to manipulate people and feel being powerful is important. In essence, they have high power needs as well as a need to be dominant (Hyman et al., 2006). They tend to engage in aggressive behavior when their ego and status are threatened. Some of us have encountered these types of bullies in the workplace!

This type of bully more frequently engages in indirect or relational bullying. Because much of their bullying is indirect, their bullying activities are often over-looked by teachers. Females are more likely to engage in relational or indirect bullying than males. They use indirect methods of aggression such as gossiping and social exclusion. However, 24% of the female students also report being involved in a fight in the previous year (Melissa Institute for Violence Prevention and Treatment, 2007a).

Females usually do not define gossiping, exclusion, or other relational behaviors as forms of bullying. Therefore, females usually report lower rates of bullying. This indicates a need for teachers to bring indirect and relational bullying out into the open so that there is a better recognition of bullying and an understanding of the consequences.

Bullies demonstrate insensitivity to the feelings of others. They have little empathy for victims and only consider their needs for power and status. Many bullies appear to be effective social interpreters who are able to identify the most vulnerable victims (Hyman et al., 2006). The victims of bullies are often younger, weaker, more passive individuals. They are usually the more unpopular and tend to be socially isolated. By picking on these students, bullies are more likely to have support from others and face a decreased risk of retaliation.

Bullying usually takes place in the context of a group. The presence of an audience is important in order for bullies to demonstrate their dominance and power. Therefore, the group is an important component in bullying. The fact that bullying increases when students make transitions to middle school and to high school highlights the social status dimension of bullying. Bullies making these transitions need to demonstrate their dominance and status in front of a new audience. This is the perfect time to implement training programs to help kids and teachers identify the different forms of bullying. If we can train students during these transition periods, we can stop some of the bullying before it starts. Table 10.1 list some general characteristics of bullies.

Table 10.1 General Characteristics of Bullies

- Lack of empathy toward others
- Low tolerance of frustration
- Defiant toward adults
- Aggression modeled in the home
- Higher-than-normal aggressive behavior
- High power needs, a need to dominate others, be in control
- Aggressive toward those who are smaller and weaker, not as self-defense
- Tease others in a hurtful way

PREVENTION AND RESPONSE

Systematic efforts directed at bullying are relatively recent. European schools have been leading in the development of antibullying programs. The first antibullying program was developed in Norway in 1983, prompted by three suicide deaths of victims. This initial program proved to be very effective, as there was a reduction in bullying of around 50%. Not only were the incidents of bullying reduced, there was also a decrease in vandalism, theft, and truancy (Melissa Institute for Violence Prevention and Treatment, 2007b). Recent research indicates that properly implemented programs of bullying prevention are effective. Good programs reduce bullying from 30% to 70% (Hyman et al., 2006). Bullock (2002) contends that effective programs must be implemented at both the school level and the classroom level.

School-Level Programs

Schoolwide programs are important because much bullying behavior takes place outside the classroom. The schoolwide plan needs to focus on developing a social climate that makes bullying socially unacceptable. All school personnel need to be trained to respond and must have a genuine interest in stopping bullying. The notion that bullying is normal and that students need to learn to solve the problem themselves must be replaced with the perspective that no person deserves to be bullied.

Schoolwide programs should begin with a policy statement against bullying, a clear plan for addressing it, and clear definitions that students can understand. Parents need to be made aware of the bullying policy, and students need to know that there will be consequences for bullying. All school personnel and parents need to understand the seriousness of bullying. In addition, effective bullying programs need to establish schoolwide support for victims (Bullock, 2002).

Schoolwide antibullying programs require consistent and sustained effort. Immediate change should not be expected. A cultural change is what is required, and it takes time to change cultural patterns. Experts estimate that it takes at least 2 years of intervention to significantly reduce the incidents of bullying (Melissa Institute for Violence Prevention and Treatment, 2007b).

Within the context of a schoolwide response, the support of the administration is critical (Melissa Institute for Violence Prevention and Treatment, 2007b). When antibullying programs are ineffective, it is frequently because of the lack of administrative support. Hardin (2008) suggests that school administrators may not be as involved as they need to be because other problems make bullying seem rather insignificant. However, like teachers, they need to understand that bullying is often a precursor to additional violence and is usually the sign of a troubled school.

Classroom-Level Programs

Classroom programs should be multifaceted. One important facet of effective classroom programs is one that is a recurring theme of this book: Classrooms need to emphasize respect and convey a sense of warmth and concern. Respect for others is an important ingredient in any antibullying program.

Another facet of a classroom program is the modeling of prosocial skills such as empathy, respect, and anger management. This is based on research indicating that many bullies come from homes where aggression is modeled and where more prosocial behaviors are not modeled. Students need to see and experience alternatives to aggression. This is especially important in the early elementary years, when teachers are viewed as significant adults and their actions have a significant impact on the students. However, the power of positive models at the secondary level should not be discounted.

Another classroom dimension that needs to be included in bullying prevention is the curriculum, especially a curriculum that includes social skills training. Approaches such as role-playing, creative writing, classroom meetings, and literature selections can focus on issues of empathy, anger control, and impulse management. Including these elements in the curriculum can help establish attitudes and a social climate where bullying becomes unacceptable.

Peer relationships are the core of bullying prevention. As has been indicated, bullying almost always takes place in a group context. Therefore, the role of the audience is critical. Bystanders need to know that they may be providing reinforcement for the bully. Bullies want power and acceptance. They need to be taught how to respond in socially acceptable ways to both the bully and to the victims when they witness bullying incidents. In fact, studies indicate that peer intervention is more effective in deterring bullying than victim aggression and retaliation (Hyman et al., 2006). When the bully senses that bullying is not gaining them power and respect, they are more likely to stop. The bystanders need to communicate very clearly that bullying is unacceptable and it is not being supported by the dominant group. As well, the rights of the victim to be free from bullying need to be clearly supported (Hyman et al., 2006).

Table 10.2   Checklist for Bullying Prevention Programs

_____ Classroom climate promotes respect for all class members.

_____ Classroom rules and procedures encourage involvement and student engagement.

_____ Regular classroom meetings discuss respect for others.

_____ Programs are established to take away peer support for bullying.

_____ Antibullying material is built into the curriculum.

_____ Role-playing, creative writing, and cooperative learning activities focus on empathy development and building relationships.

_____ Antibullying and cyberbullying information is disseminated to parents.

_____ School rules define bullying as unacceptable and identify consequences.

_____ Programs are established to welcome new students and provide engagement for marginalized students.

_____ One-on-one programs are designed for meeting with bullies and victims of bullies.

_____ Training is provided to victims for assertiveness training, friendship building, and social skills training.

_____ Community members engage in developing and supporting antibullying programs.

_____ Teachers are taught how to intervene in bullying episodes.

SOURCE: Adapted from The Melissa Institute for Violence Prevention and Treatment (2007b).

When working with the whole class, it is important for them to understand different types of bullying. Many students only define bullying as involving direct and physical acts. They do not understand that indirect, relational, or cyberbullying are forms of bullying. Those who might find physical aggression against weaker students abhorrent may still be providing indirect support for indirect or relational bullying. Gossiping, spreading rumors, exclusion, and cyberbullying are still bullying and therefore unacceptable. The checklist in Table 10.2 can help you assess the bullying-prevention programs planned for your district.

Confronting Incidents of Direct Bullying

There is no one correct response to incidents of direct and physical bullying, and many teachers are uncertain how to respond. Not responding only serves to reinforce the bully and promotes additional incidents. When confronting direct or physical bullying, the following actions can be useful:

- Immediately stop incidents of bullying, even teasing and taunting.
- Define the bullying and state the rules against bullying. Follow advice previously given and do not open the door for excuses. Do not ask the bully "Why?" Using as calm a voice as possible, clearly state what was observed or heard and declare that it is bullying and is against the school rules.

- Provide support for the victim and respond in ways that allow the victim to save face. For example, it may not be appropriate to try to comfort the student on the spot, as it might only lead to further embarrassment. Questioning the bully and the victim in front of others can lead to additional embarrassment and play into the motives of the bully by providing an audience.
- Do not demand an apology on the spot. Insincere apologies are not effective and may only anger the bully and create other incidents of bullying when the teacher is not present.
- If there is an audience, inform the audience that you observed their inaction or their support for bullying. Encourage them to take a more proactive role in letting the bully know that this type of behavior is unacceptable. Support those students who attempted to stop the bullying. However, do not support attempts at physical intervention because physical interventions only lead to increased violence. Give suggestions for acceptable alternatives.
- Notify the bully that he or she will be observed and any additional incidents will lead to further consequences.
- If consequences are required, the consequences should be logical and connected to the offense. For example, if the incident took place on the playground, the bully might not be allowed on the playground for some specified amount of time. If it took place during an athletic event, the student might be prohibited from participating in the event in the future.
- Follow up. If a follow-up is needed, meet with the students separately. Meeting with the bully and the victim together can be intimidating and traumatizing for the victim. When meeting with the bully, discuss with him or her the seriousness of bullying. If appropriate, help the bully find ways of making amends that would be meaningful to the victim.
- Consider follow-up support for the victims. They may need to vent their feelings and frustrations. They need to learn that the classroom and school will be a safe place. Since many victims have low self-esteem, seek ways of helping them improve their self-esteem. Remember, however, that you are not a therapist. If it is clear that the needs of the victim are serious, you should recommend counseling. Follow-up for the bully might also be needed. The bully may need to learn how to cope with his or her anger and how to take responsibility for his or her actions. Provide the bully with alternative ways of using power and gaining status (adapted from U.S. Department of Health and Human Services, 2008b).

Confronting Cyberbullying

Cyberbullying is indirect bullying that usually takes place outside the school. Many of those engaged in cyberbullying do so because they believe they will not get caught. Because of this, it is difficult for schools to respond to cyberbullying.

In fact, many teens do not think that cyberbullying is an issue that should be addressed at school (National Crime Prevention Council, 2007). However, school does have a role to play, and there are steps that can be taken in response to cyberbullying.

Because some cyberbullying does occur at school, the first steps should be to address cyberbullying at the school site. About 45% of preteens and 30% of teens report receiving cyberbullying messages at school (U.S. Department of Health and Human Services, 2008a). Action is needed to eliminate this aspect of the problem.

Steps taken at the school setting should include discussing the dangers of cyberbullying. As indicated previously, a large percentage of students believe others engage in cyberbullying because they think it is funny. This provides a perfect opportunity to discuss the serious consequences that can result from cyberbullying. Just as we recommended earlier regarding direct bullying, we recommend creating a climate that makes cyberbullying unacceptable. Students who may not be directly engaged in cyberbullying need to realize that they have a role to play by not accepting cyberbullying and by not passing on messages or photographs that are hurtful to others.

School policies and rules of conduct dealing with bullying must include cyberbullying. These policies and rules of conduct should be shared with parents and the community and should alert parents to the dangers of cyberbullying. The policies can become models that might be used in the home or in other community organizations. The rules of conduct should include a reporting protocol that encourages students to report any incidents of cyberbullying they encounter. Encourage students not to delete the messages; instead, they should save them for evidence if the cyberbullying does not stop.

School officials must also install appropriate filtering and tracking software on the computers. Although this will not stop all cyberbullying, it will help eliminate some of it. When cyberbullying occurs using the school or the district system, teachers and administrators are obligated to respond. The district may be able to assist in identifying the cyberbully.

Teachers should be alert to incidents of direct or physical bullying that may be related to the cyberbullying. Often, cyberbullies are individuals who know the victims. Fewer than 25% of the incidents of cyberbullying are committed by someone the student does not know (National Crime Prevention Council, 2007).

If cyberbullies are identified, confront them with their actions and immediately implement the school policies and rules of conduct. It might be useful to contact the parents. If this is done, it should be done in a nonthreatening manner and the examples of the cyberbullying presented to them. Some parents may not think cyberbullying is harmful, so they need to understand the potential consequences.

In fact, school officials might consider providing parent training programs. In all cases of cyberbullying, the parents of the victims need to be notified. Again, take care to let the parents know that the school does not tolerate this form of bullying and that steps are being taken to eliminate it.

In addition, school leaders can teach students some steps that they can take when they encounter incidents of cyberbullying. Encourage them to report any incidents of cyberbullying to their parents. Then they should see if they are able to block future messages. Although cyberbullies may be able to find ways around blocks, they still must put forth additional effort and this might be sufficient to discourage some of them.

Another individual action that can be taken is not to respond to incidents of cyberbullying. Although a common response to cyberbullying is anger, seeking retaliation through a response only reinforces the cyberbully and will likely result in more incidents. Students who are aware of cyberbullying messages are encouraged not to pass them on. Approximately 62% of teens believe that refusing to pass along cyberbullying messages is an effective deterrent (National Crime Prevention Council, 2007).

Students also need to understand that if cyberbullying messages, whether at school or at home, contain threats of violence, extortion, harassment, stalking, or pornography, these messages are illegal and the police should be notified. The police may then assist in the tracking and take action against the cyberbully. In addition, students need to know that cyberbullying may involve the use of language that violates the terms and conditions of the service provider or cell phone companies. Filing a complaint with these companies may result in the provider taking action (U.S. Department of Health and Human Services, 2008a). Also, civil law permits victims to sue bullies for damages. Thus, there can be real, monetary damages. In summary, there can be serious legal consequences for cyberbullies. Once students understand these consequences, they may not view cyberbullies as funny, and they may stop and think before sending hurtful or even illegal messages to others.

Cyberbullying has become a huge problem. To address cyberbullying requires actions at the school and the individual level. Perhaps the most effective deterrent is making cyberbullying socially unacceptable. Like many other issues, cyberbullying requires the cooperation of the entire community.

ASSISTING VICTIMS OF BULLYING

An important part of an antibullying program in schools is providing assistance to the victims. Remember that bullying involves an imbalance of power. Victims are not usually in a position to defend themselves. For this reason, programs such as conflict resolution and mediation are not appropriate responses to the problem of bullying. Bullying is more a form of victimization than that of a conflict. Conflict resolution and peer mediation requires more of a balance of power that enables individuals to work it out. Mediation carries the message that both parties are partly right and partly wrong. Victims are not partially wrong. No one deserves to be abused or bullied, so we must send the message that bullying is wrong and it must stop.

Victims of bullying are often students who have few friends and tend to be more cautious, sensitive, or withdrawn. Some victims of bullying have learning disabilities, have physical characteristics that vary from the age norm, or differ in their sexual orientation. For example, late-developing males that are smaller and weaker and do not fit the "macho" stereotype are often victims. Early-maturing females who are larger might be the targets of relational bullying (Melissa Institute for Violence Prevention and Treatment, 2007a).

However, there are some students who can be classified as provocative victims. These tend to be students who are hot-tempered or aggressive. They are likely to have emotional and behavioral problems and are often rejected by teachers and peers (Melissa Institute for Violence Prevention and Treatment, 2007a). These students often feel marginalized and do not understand how to develop friendships or relate to others. However, teachers must be cautious in how they approach these students. Many victims believe that bullying is their fault. They often direct their anger toward themselves rather than at others. Focusing on their actions just confirms their belief that they are at fault (U.S. Department of Health and Human Services, 2008d). Other victims are afraid to report incidents of bullying because they view telling as a sign of immaturity or that they are tattletales. Table 10.3 lists characteristics of victims. These might help you recognize the victims early enough to prevent some of the problems.

Table 10.3   General Characteristics of Victims

- Tend to be withdrawn, cautious, sensitive
- Lack assertiveness
- Have underdeveloped social skills
- Have low self-esteem
- Males tend to be smaller and weaker than peers
- Females tend to be less physically attractive than peers
- Are shy, have few friends
- Relate better to adults than to peers
- Differ from the norm in some way: learning disability, ethnicity, physical deformity, sexual orientation
- Have overprotective parents

Programs for working with victims should build on our knowledge of the characteristics of victims. Perhaps the starting point is building relationships between the victims and other students and adults. This might be accomplished by creating programs that allow students in the classroom to interact with potential victims. For example, we can create special programs for students who might feel marginalized, especially those who are new to the classroom. Buddies might be assigned to help them learn about the school and to begin developing new friendships. Cooperative learning groups that emphasize the need for students with different skills and abilities can also allow the shy, withdrawn, or cautious students to demonstrate their abilities.

When bullying does occur, teachers need to be cautious not to provide too much public support for the victims. Since victims are often concerned about peer group perceptions, they may become embarrassed about the attention. Remember that the dignity of the victim needs to be protected. It is much better to meet individually with the victim and emphasize confidentiality. Many victims might be cautious about discussing the problem with the teacher because they are afraid of retaliation and they are not sure they can trust adults to change things.

In discussions with the victims, it is important to allow them to talk. They may need to vent their anger or express their feelings. They need to be assured that they have support from the teacher. Encourage them to talk and express what they need in order to feel safe. Gather as much information as possible about the bullying episode and reinforce that they are not to blame. The meeting with the victim should elicit data that could be used in determining next steps. It may be that victims need help in learning how to develop friendships or how to state their needs and wants.

Don't force a meeting between the bully and the victim. These meetings are likely to do more harm than good. Remember that bullying is a situation of unequal power. Bullies are not likely to be influenced by the comments of the victim. In addition, it is often uncomfortable for the victim to once again have to face the bully. Meetings with the bully should keep the source of information confidential. They can be informed that information about their bullying was gathered from a variety of sources.

Bullying has become a major concern in schools across America and the world. Many bullying prevention programs have been implemented and tried. The following are some of the basic lessons that have been learned:

- Bullying prevention programs are effective. However, a concerted effort by the entire school is the most effective approach.
- The leadership of the school administrator is key to the success of a program. The commitment of the administrator sends the message that bullying will not be tolerated.

- A successful program creates a climate where peers support victims and send the message that bullying is not acceptable behavior.
- Bullying prevention programs that are most effective are those directed at younger (elementary age) students.
- Teachers with good management skills, high student engagement, and positive discipline approaches have fewer problems with bullying.
- There is no simple solution. Effective programs involve training in social skills and empathy development, nurturing prosocial behavior, modeling respect, and incorporating the curriculum. In addition, the program is ongoing (adapted from The Melissa Institute for Violence Prevention and Treatment, 2007b).

Resources for Teachers

The following are some Internet sites that can be useful to teachers:

Bullying UK: http://www.bullying.co.uk

Keep Schools Safe: http://www.keepschoolssafe.org

Kids Health: http://www.kidshealth.org/teen/school_jobs/bullying/school_violence.html

National Youth Violence Prevention Resource Center: http://www.safeyouth.org

Stop Bullying Now: http://www.stopbullyingnow.hrsa.gov

TeachSafeSchools: http://www.teachsafeschools.org

REVIEW OF MAIN IDEAS

1. Bullying has emerged as one of the serious concerns facing education across the nation. This concern has been fueled by data that show the devastating effect of bullying on students and on the educational environment.

2. Teachers seem to be largely unaware of the extent of bullying in school. Although they think they respond to most incidents of bullying, students report that they do not. Many students do not expect teacher support when they are bullied. Part of the problem is that many teachers have a narrow understanding of bullying, and they tend to respond only to physical bullying although verbal bullying is the most prevalent type.

3. Bullying can be classified into direct bullying and indirect bullying. It can involve physical actions, verbal behavior, and nonverbal behavior. Relational bullying is the type of bullying that is directed at harming the relationships between individuals. Using technology to bully others, or cyberbullying, has become a serious form of bullying.

4. Bullies are generally individuals who have a strong need for power and dominance. They are usually insensitive to the feelings of others. Onlookers often support bullies by giving them attention and status. Males are more likely to engage in direct and physical bullying whereas females are more likely to engage in indirect and relational bullying.

5. Prevention programs are effective deterrents of bullying. Effective prevention programs need to be developed at both the school level and the classroom level. The support of the administration and all school employees is critical at the school level. Multifaceted approaches should include developing a climate of respect, developing curriculum programs that focus on bullying, teaching specific skills to respond to bullying, and providing support for victims.

6. Classroom programs need to focus on creating a climate of mutual respect. Modeling of prosocial behavior by teachers is an essential element.

7. Classroom programs should be multifaceted and include a curriculum focused on developing empathy, activities and strategies that develop positive peer relationships, a focus on the role of the onlookers, and activities addressing stopping bullies and providing support for victims.

8. Direct bullying should be stopped immediately when it is observed. The teacher response should identify the act as bullying, focus on it as against school rules, help the victim save face, and focus on the role of the audience.

9. Teachers are limited in their responses to cyberbullying. The first step should be to address any cyberbullying that takes place at school. Students should then be informed regarding the impact of cyberbullying, provided information about how to respond, and clearly told the possible consequences.

10. Provide support programs for victims. These programs should be confidential so that the victims are not embarrassed. Because victims often blame themselves, these programs should focus on bullying as inappropriate behavior that no one deserves. Other actions might help students build their self-esteem as well as establish new friendships.

APPLICATION AND ENRICHMENT

1. Research school policies regarding bullying. Compare different school policies and identify core elements.

2. Discuss with practicing teachers their definitions of bullying, their attitudes toward bullying, and their responses. Compare their responses with those discussed in the chapter.

3. Begin developing an antibullying program for the classroom. Brainstorm with others how to establish a positive classroom climate, and potential curriculum elements and ideas for assisting bullies and victims.

4. Develop a program focused on cyberbullying that could be implemented in the classroom.

REFERENCES

Altenbaugh, R. (2003). *The American people and their education: A social history.* Upper Saddle River, NJ: Merrill Prentice Hall.

Blanco, J. (2003). *Please stop laughing at me . . . One woman's inspirational story.* Avon, MA: Adams Media.

Blassone, M. (2007, November 13). Working to stop bullying at school. *Modesto Bee*, pp. A1, A12.

Bullock, J. (2002). Bullying among children. *Childhood Education, 78,* 130–134.

Hardin, C. (2008). *Effective classroom management: Models and strategies for today's classroom* (2nd ed.). Upper Saddle River, NJ: Pearson Education.

Hazler, R., & Miller, D. (2001). Adult recognition of school bullying situation. *Educational Research, 43*(2), 133–146.

Hyman, I., Kay, B., Taboria, A., Weber, M., Mahon, M., & Cohen, I. (2006). Bullying: Theory, research and intervention. In C. M. Evertson & C. S. Weinstein (Eds.), *Handbook of classroom management: Research, practice and contemporary issues* (pp. 855–884). Mahwah, NJ: Lawrence Erlbaum.

Italie, L. (2008, June 24). Hard-core bullies sometimes start as "Barbie brats." *Modesto Bee,* p. A6.

Melissa Institute for Violence Prevention and Treatment. (2007a). *About bullying.* Retrieved November 12, 2007, from http://www.teachsafeschools.org/bully_menu1.html

Melissa Institute for Violence Prevention and Treatment. (2007b). *Reducing bullying: Meeting the challenge.* Retrieved November 12, 2007, from http://www.teachsafeschools.org/bullying-prevention.html

Metropolitan Life Survey of the American Teacher. (1999). *Violence in America's public schools: Five years later.* New York: Louis Harris.

National Crime Prevention Council. (2007). *Teens and cyberbullying.* Retrieved March 2, 2008, from http://www.surfsafety.net/Cyberbullying

National Education Association. (2003a). *National bullying awareness campaign.* Retrieved January 20, 2008, from www.nea.org/schoolsafety/bullying.html

National Education Association. (2003b). *School safety facts.* Retrieved May 2008 from www.nea.org/schoolsafety/ssfacts.html

Olewus, D. (2003). *Bullying at school: What we know and what we can do.* Cambridge, MA: Blackwell.

Sanchez, E., Robertson, T., Lewis, C., Rosenbluth, B., Bohman, T., & Casey, D. (2001). *Preventing bullying and sexual harassment in elementary schools: The expect respect model.* In R. A. Geffner, M. Loring, & C. Young (Eds.), *Bullying behavior: Current issues, research and intervention* (pp. 157–181). New York: Haworth Press.

U.S. Department of Health and Human Services: Health Resources and Services Administration. (2008a). *Cyberbullying.* Retrieved March 29, 2008, from http://www.stopbullyingnow.hrsa.gov/adult/indexAdult.asp?Area=cyberbullying

U.S. Department of Health and Human Services: Health Resources and Services Administration. (2008b). *How to intervene to stop bullying: Tips for on-the-spot intervention at school.* Retrieved January 19, 2008, from http://www.stopbullyingnow.hrsa.gov

U.S. Department of Health and Human Services: Health Resources and Services Administration. (2008c). *What we know about bullying.* Retrieved January 19, 2008, from http://www.stopbullyingnow.hrsa.gov

U.S. Department of Health and Human Services: Health Resources and Services Administration. (2008d). *Working with young people who are bullied: Tips for mental health professionals.* Retrieved March 29, 2008, from http://www.stopbullyingnow.hrsa.gov

Chapter 11

CONFLICT RESOLUTION

CLASSROOM SCENARIO

Joan believed that building a caring and supportive community was important in preventing problems in her sixth-grade classroom. She modeled respect for the students, involved them in decision making, used cooperative learning activities, and tried to accommodate their needs and interests. Therefore, she was troubled when she observed students putting each other down and excluding other students from participating in some activities. At first, she tried talking with individual students to see if she could assess the reasons for the tension. Finally, she was able to identify that the source of the problem was the playground activities during recess. She made it a point to go to the playground and observe the interactions between students. After a couple of days of observation, she noted that several of the students in her class were very competitive. The same couple of students always got to choose the teams. They emphasized picking the best players first and were unhappy if some of the members of their team were not as skilled as they wanted. There were lots of arguments during the activity, and some of the students got quite upset if their team didn't win.

At this point, Joan decided it was time for a classroom meeting focusing on the tension and anger that were occurring as a result of the classroom activities. She pulled the class together in a circle, and she placed her chair as one of the members of the circle. She started by noting that she had noticed that some students were not treating other students as respectfully as they should. She asked the students if they could explain why this was happening. At first, there was a reluctance to speak. She finally mentioned what she had observed on the playground and asked if that could be related to the problem. Finally, students started discussing how they felt to be left out. Others mentioned how upset they became when they lost a game. This acknowledgment of the situation by the students opened the door for negotiation.

The next step was to focus on their attitudes to determine if they were interested in change. She asked the students if they were happy with the situation. She asked if they wanted to change and improve their relationships with others and the fun they could have during recess. When there seemed to be overwhelming support for making changes, it was time to determine a course of action.

She started by summarizing what the students had identified as the problem. She noted that competition between the teams and the way the teams were chosen appeared to be the problem. She then stated, "Now that we have identified the problem and just about everyone has said they would like to change the situation, what are some concrete things we can do?"

CHAPTER OBJECTIVES

After completing this chapter, you should be able to:

- Identify two basic types of conflict that occur in the classroom
- Defend the inclusion of conflict resolution programs in the school curriculum
- Define the five components that influence the success of conflict resolution approaches
- State the characteristics of passive approaches to conflict resolution
- Explain assertive responses to conflict resolution
- Provide examples of facilitative responses to conflict resolution
- List the steps of problem-solving negotiations
- Identify responses appropriate for responding to controversy
- Describe the differences between negotiation, mediation, and arbitration

Conflict is a natural part of life, and most of us experience some type of conflict on a daily basis. Therefore, learning how to resolve conflict is an important life skill. Unfortunately, many people are deficient when it comes to resolving conflicts in a satisfactory manner. In fact, the media are filled with situations where individuals deal with conflict through yelling, screaming, name-calling, and violence. Poor conflict resolution skills are almost celebrated! It should not be surprising that students know of no other way for dealing with conflict than through aggression and violence. However, the basis for our whole form of government requires the productive and peaceful resolution of conflict. A major reason individuals are dismissed from their place of employment is because they cannot get along with others. A central ingredient in creating a successful classroom environment is helping students learn how to resolve conflicts.

Two types of conflict typically emerge in the classroom. The first type, *conflict of interest*, occurs when the efforts of one individual to reach a goal or meet a need interfere with the ability of another person to meet a need or achieve a goal (Johnson & Johnson, 2006). This can take place between students, or it can take place between teachers and students. Teachers and students inherently have different goals. For example, a teacher has a primary goal of instructing students and facilitating academic growth. However, students are interested in having fun and establishing peer relationships. In order to develop a successful classroom, this conflict between goals needs to be addressed.

Students often have conflicts of interest with each other as they strive for attention, power, and acceptance. This is especially the case in classrooms where competition is emphasized. When students must compete with others for attention, status, and power, conflicts are inevitable because there must be some winners and some losers.

A second type of conflict that we see appear in classrooms is *controversy*. Controversy exists when the ideas, values, theories, and opinions of one individual are different from those of others (Johnson & Johnson, 2006). The tremendous diversity of students found in contemporary classrooms guarantees that students will come into direct contact with others who are not like them. This creates an environment where controversy is inevitable.

Teachers contribute to conflict through inflexible and unreasonable rules, unrealistic expectations, favoritism for some students, and an overemphasis on competition (Hardin, 2008). Therefore, both teachers and students need to understand the sources of conflict as well as productive and prosocial ways of resolving conflict. Teachers and students who possess the knowledge and skills of conflict resolution, mediation, and negotiation will be able to resolve and prevent conflicts in productive ways that will help them throughout life. Conflicts of interest and controversies are not going to go away. To develop a productive society, individuals must learn to understand and deal with them rather than ignore them.

Until recently, conflict resolution in the classroom has been largely ignored. This is true even though there is evidence that many teachers spend a considerable amount of time and energy dealing with time-consuming and destructive conflicts. Research indicates that attending to constructive conflict resolution can increase classroom productivity (Johnson & Johnson, 2006). This evidence, along with fear of violence in the classroom, has led to the development of several approaches to conflict resolution (Johnson & Johnson, 2006).

Conflict resolution does take time and requires skill and a special effort. In the contemporary educational climate that places primary emphasis on test scores and accountability, some teachers and administrators hesitate to include conflict resolution in the curriculum because they think it will take time away from academic instruction. This seems to be a misplaced priority. What is the value of knowledge acquisition if individuals cannot get along with each other? In addition, a safe environment where students feel free from fear is important in creating the conditions for learning.

Because classroom management and discipline is an area of conflict within a classroom, it is logical to include conflict resolution as a part of the total management and discipline plan (Johnson & Johnson, 1995). Implementing conflict resolution as a part of a total plan has several advantages. First, teaching students how to resolve conflicts can make teaching easier and can actually result in a more efficient classroom because less time is needed to respond to conflicts. Students will know how to resolve many problems on their own and eliminate the need for teacher intervention. Second, conflict resolution can help decrease serious misbehaviors such as violence, vandalism, and truancy. Third, mediation and negotiation are important skills that all members of a democracy should possess in order to fulfill their civic responsibilities. Fourth, conflict resolution teaches listening, communication, and critical thinking skills that are basic to the goals of all of education. Fifth, learning conflict resolution provides a student with important life skills (Bodine, Crawford, & Schrumpf, 1994). In summary, there are so many benefits to conflict resolution that it seems obvious that it should be an important part of any school and classroom.

UNDERSTANDING CONFLICT

There are several definitions of conflict. It has been described as a struggle over values, status, power, and resources or as the result of differences between and among individuals. Conflict also arises when incompatible activities occur. This occurs when one activity prevents or interferes with other activities. These conflicts can be intrapersonal (conflicts within an individual), interpersonal (conflicts between individuals), intragroup (conflicts within a group), and intergroup (conflicts between groups) (Borisoff & Victor, 1998).

Lee, Pulvino, and Perrone (1998) suggest that conflict is a part of the human condition because of many naturally occurring conditions. They note that common sources of conflict are gender, ethnicity, age, physical size, status, and socioeconomic differences. Because conflict is a natural part of life, elimination of conflict is not an option. Rather, conflict needs to be understood and managed so that individual interests and differences are acknowledged and a harmonious balance is maintained (Lee et al., 1998). Johnson and Johnson (1995) reinforce this perspective when they state that it is how conflicts are managed, not their presence, that is important. They observed that schools can either be *conflict negative* or *conflict positive*. Conflict-negative schools are schools where conflict is viewed as destructive and of no value. The goal of conflict-negative schools is to deny, avoid, or attempt to eliminate any evidence of conflict. Conflict-positive schools are those that recognize that conflict is natural, inevitable, and potentially valuable. They manage and use conflicts to create exciting and positive learning environments.

In summary, because conflict is a natural part of life, learning how to respond constructively is one of the most important and relevant skills that needs to be taught. We need to accept conflict and create conflict-positive classrooms and schools. Creating conflict-positive classrooms and schools, although requiring some time, has many productive outcomes that can actually facilitate the accomplishment of important educational objectives. Table 11.1 summarizes some of the findings from research on the importance of conflict resolution (Johnson & Johnson, 2006).

RESPONSES TO CONFLICT

Borisoff and Victor (1998) identify five components (or five "A's") that influence the success of conflict resolution approaches: assessment, acknowledgment, attitude, action, and analysis. Understanding these five components can assist in the development of successful conflict resolution programs.

Assessment is the initial component. It is appropriate because responses need to address the specific needs of the individuals involved in the conflict. Often, the assessment of an appropriate response to a specific situation requires a quick, informal assessment. It is most effective when the teacher has some knowledge

Table 11.1 Reasons for Teaching Students Conflict Resolution

- It teaches students an important skill that can be used throughout life.
- Peaceful conflict resolution is central to the development of democratic society.
- Students develop socially and have a greater sense of efficacy.
- It helps students develop self-control.
- Students involved in conflict resolution become more engaged in school.
- Costs related to faculty and staff time devoted to resolving conflict, costs of vandalism, and costs related to violence are reduced.
- More positive interpersonal and intergroup relationships are developed.
- Students involved in conflict resolution demonstrate more prosocial and less antisocial behavior.

of the individuals involved and the probable causes. Conflict resolution is most effective when there is knowledge of the attitudes and traits of the participants (Borisoff & Victor, 1998).

Acknowledgment requires getting participants to admit that there is a conflict and that the needs of others are important. As noted earlier, because of ethnocentrism, individuals often fail to recognize that another person with different perspectives, needs, and beliefs is involved. Acknowledgment requires participants to step back and view a situation from a different perspective. If individuals remain self-centered and refuse to acknowledge that others also have rights, conflict resolution is not likely to be productive (Borisoff & Victor, 1998). For example, this is the situation in bullying, where perpetrators lack empathy for their victims.

Attitude refers to a willingness to engage in conflict resolution. Individuals must have a desire to resolve the conflict and be willing to cooperate. Unfortunately, there are those who are not interested in resolving conflicts. They may be obtaining attention through prolonging the conflict, feeling a sense of power by engaging in the conflict, or be motivated to get revenge. For an intervention to be successful, there must be a motivation to want to solve the conflict. If the proper attitude is not present, it is better to stop the conflict to keep it from escalating and then come back at a later date when there has been an opportunity to change attitudes.

Developing a climate of engagement and trust is important in creating an attitude conducive to conflict resolution. Individuals who perceive the classroom environment as hostile and threatening, and as one where they do not feel accepted, are not likely to have an attitude that leads to productive conflict resolution.

Action when developing a program starts with data from the assessment, an acknowledgment of different perspectives, and attitudes taken into account. Action that is taken without reference to the assessment and the attitudes of the participants is not likely to be successful.

Analysis is the last component of conflict management approaches. Analysis requires a focus on the important findings from the previous steps. A few questions can be useful in analyzing a potential response to a conflict. Does the response address the needs of the participants? Does it take into account the attitudes of the participants? Are the proposed actions realistic and reasonable (Borisoff & Victor, 1998)?

Addressing these five A's helps teachers in deciding how to respond to conflict in the school setting. Specific conflict resolution approaches can be classified as one of three basic types: passive, assertive, and facilitative (Lee et al., 1998).

Students need to learn conflict resolution skills.

© Banana Stock

Passive Approaches

Passive approaches take a neutral stance and do not attempt to force a resolution. The main goal of a passive approach is to try to maintain the relationship between individuals and to keep the situation from escalating. Passive responses are often useful for conflicts that take the form of a controversy. They do not demand change; they allow others to express their points of view or disagreements without escalating the conflict. Examples of passive approaches are doing nothing, smoothing, and withdrawing.

Doing Nothing

"Doing nothing" is really not an accurate description of this approach. It is basically a wait-and-see approach where overt action is delayed. To some extent, this approach recognizes that not all conflicts need to be resolved. For example, it is often healthy to have different political perspectives and controversies. Constructive conflict can be important in bringing about positive change. It would be foolish, and detrimental to democratic society, to demand there be no disagreement or controversy.

There are times when the doing-nothing approach might be useful in a conflict of interest. When engaged in a conflict of interest, if it appears that the other person is demonstrating self-control, and he or she has a constructive attitude, then the appropriate action might be to do nothing. This might be defined as "agreeing to disagree" without demanding that the other person change.

If the teacher is a mediator in a conflict, taking a neutral stance can allow some time to consider options and provide the students time to reach a resolution or to reach a point where they welcome mediation. Many of us have observed situations where hasty action by a third party has only made the situation worse. If, however, an analysis indicates that the neutral stance is not working and the conflict is escalating, then a more active response is needed.

If the teacher is one of the parties in the conflict, there are several things that are needed in order to implement the doing-nothing approach. The teacher needs to observe and listen carefully and to control emotions in an attempt to be objective. The teacher should try to avoid getting ego involved and not be concerned with winning or saving face. Maintaining a neutral or low-key response can calm the situation and reduce tension and is more likely to earn student respect than displays of teacher authority and power. These are important prerequisites to resolving a conflict.

Smoothing

Smoothing is another passive approach that is best used when the goal is maintaining a relationship. Again, smoothing is useful in the controversy type of conflict. Smoothing also has a primary goal of maintaining a positive relationship between the individuals. Some conflicts, even though one individual feels he or she is right, are not worth the cost in terms of a broken relationship.

The purpose of smoothing is to avoid a confrontation by refusing to be defensive or to engage in a confrontation. This can be very difficult because individuals often let their ego get in the way. They place priority on being right rather than being friends. It takes two or more people to engage in a conflict; if one refuses to be drawn in, the potential for conflict is removed.

Humor is a good smoothing technique. Laughter helps reduce tension, and it is hard to have a confrontation when laughing. However, humor should not be at the expense of others. Sarcasm or shaming others is destructive to relationships and usually increases rather than lessens the conflict.

Active listening is another good smoothing technique. Active listening involves providing feedback to others so that they feel their ideas and feelings are being respected. The basic technique of active listening is that of paraphrasing. When engaged in talking with another, the listener paraphrases what he or she thinks the person talking has said. This should not have any sort of evaluative component but should merely say to the speaker, "This is what I heard you say." This allows the speaker to clear up any misunderstandings and to rethink what he or she means. Active listening allows the other to express his or her needs or feelings without challenge. Active listening requires avoidance of inflammatory statements or criticism.

Johnson and Johnson (1995) point out that smoothing is one of the most common approaches used by competent managers and executives. When maintaining a relationship is important, smooth.

Withdrawing

All of us are familiar with conflict situations in which the anger and the emotions seem to run so high that reason and logic are lost. This is a situation where withdrawal might be the most appropriate approach. Withdrawing is appropriate for both conflicts of interest and controversies. Most of us can remember with regret a situation in which a relationship might have been preserved or a long-term solution found if a confrontation had been terminated before it spiraled out of control and things were said or actions taken that could not be reversed. It would have been better to withdraw, let emotions cool, and give reason an opportunity to reassert itself. Again, this is a situation where our ego becomes an enemy. We feel challenged and our power is questioned. Ego involvement can turn a difficult situation into an impossible one. When ego is involved, withdrawing is then viewed as a sign of weakness and winning is the most important goal. However, it sometimes takes more courage and wisdom to withdraw from a situation than to continue to escalate an already out-of-control one. Withdrawing requires an attitude where resolution rather than power is given priority.

When withdrawing, individuals need to learn how to look for a way out and take it. This might be as simple as saying, "I understand your point of view," and walking away. This says to the other that he or she has made his or her point but it does not imply acceptance or agreement. It is time to stop debating and simply get away from the confrontation. Withdrawing allows individuals to cool down and reflect with the clear intention of resolving the situation at a later time.

Assertive Responses

Assertive approaches require direct action. Assertive approaches are best used when it is more important to stop a conflict than to preserve a relationship. Assertive responses are almost always required when there is a conflict of interest that is escalating toward confrontation and violence. There are simply some conflict situations where the conflict must be resolved even if it means that the feelings of another will be hurt. In this situation, passive approaches are inappropriate. The confrontation cannot be allowed to continue. On the negative side, assertive approaches do have the potential for evoking more anger and hostility. Therefore, when teachers are intervening in a conflict situation with an assertive response, they need to take care to allow a cooling-off period to defuse some of the anger. Some follow-up would be required to address the anger and hostility so that the conflict is not just moved somewhere else. Examples of assertive techniques are confronting and standing firm.

Confronting

The confronting approach is useful when there are unresolved and sometimes unspoken tensions that are preventing resolution of the conflict. There are times when conflicts persist because the disputants do not acknowledge the central issue (Lee et al., 1998). Confronting often requires a third party to help the disputants resolve the conflict. However, confronting can also work when those in conflict have an attitude of trust. Then one of the disputants can take charge by defining his or her interpretation of the conflict and its impact. If those involved in the conflict do not trust each other, they may react to the confrontation with defensiveness and hostility.

The purpose of confronting is to clarify the reasons for the conflict and to get unstated issues out in the open. Confronting carries something of a negative connotation. However, effective confrontation involves mutual respect and honest communication. Confronting should not involve personal attacks, judgments, or blaming. It should clearly state the issue that needs to be resolved.

One of the first steps in the confronting process involves establishing a common goal, such as the restoration of harmony or friendship. For example, one of the participants might state, "I want to make sure we continue to be friends. I think we are having a conflict because . . ." If the other member of the conflict does not accept the common goal or the stated reasons for the conflict, the confrontation may well turn into a power struggle rather than a resolution of differences.

Once one of the participants in the conflict, or the teacher as a third party, has started the confrontation, each participant then needs to communicate his or her wants and perspectives on the conflict. Sometimes a role reversal is useful in helping each participant identify the nature of the conflict.

Active listening is a useful tool in helping individuals clarify the problem and their feelings. Active listening facilitates clear communication and makes each individual listen to the other. Once there is clarity of perspectives, solutions are often easily identified. The best solutions are those that are win-win solutions that accomplish the mutually agreed upon goal and meet the needs and wants of both individuals.

Standing Firm

Standing firm is an approach used by one of the participants in the conflict. Often, there is no other option but for one of the participants in a conflict to take a firm stand. This occurs when individuals are physically or psychologically attacked and stand up for their rights and needs. The goal of standing firm, however, is not to win but to establish a balance in the situation and reduce the potential of additional conflicts. Standing firm does not imply fighting back.

Lee et al. (1998) note several components of standing firm. They suggest that it is important when standing firm to remain focused on the problem, not on feelings. Allowing feelings to take over may result in anger and fear, states that can lead to escalation. It requires an acknowledgment that a problem exists. The actions and comments should be specific and focus on the present problems, not on past history or personalities. Standing firm involves physically standing ground, making eye contact, and squarely facing the other person. This communicates a sense of seriousness to the other person that may give him or her cause to stop for a minute and rethink his or her actions. When some participants in a conflict realize that the other person is going to stand up for rights, they often rethink their actions.

Facilitative Responses

Facilitative responses require more time and effort. They are actions that are intended to help the participants in a conflict learn how to resolve their problems and maintain their self-control and respect. They are useful in maintaining a relationship between the parties (Johnson & Johnson, 1995). Examples of facilitative approaches are compromising and problem solving.

Compromising

Recently, compromise has developed a negative image. Politicians, commentators, and editorialists have characterized those who compromise as weak and without clear values. It is unfortunate that this characterization has received such widespread support. In fact, compromise is a time-honored approach to conflict resolution. Compromising need not be a sellout of deeply held values or the refuge of those who lack strength. Compromise respects the dignity of all individuals and seeks to find a solution that respects the values of others and one that is mutually rewarding. Compromising focuses on getting disputants in a conflict to identify priorities.

Conflicts often involve a number of dimensions and issues. The act of compromise is one of identifying places for agreement and then building on agreements rather than emphasizing the disagreements. Finding places where those in conflict are willing to agree can help defuse an immediate conflict and establish a foundation for resolution of more serious issues. It is simply not the case that in every situation someone must win and someone must lose or someone must give up on his or her values and beliefs. Compromising helps find solutions where everyone can achieve some success.

There are times when individuals in conflict have become so entrenched in the conflict that they cannot find a compromise. Finding a mutually agreeable compromise may require a mediator. The mediator needs to understand the issue enough so that he or she can suggest a compromise that will satisfy those in conflict. Teachers often find themselves as mediators in student conflicts. In order for a compromise to work, all those involved must feel that it is fair and that they are achieving something. Compromises will not be successful if one party believes he or she has lost or that the compromise was one-sided. The advantage of compromise is that it can often be relatively quick. For example, a teacher might quickly assess the situation, identify the needs of those involved, and propose a compromise that preserves the dignity and respects the rights of the disputants. There are times when a compromise solves the problem. However, there are times when the compromise is only a temporary solution. If the compromise is a temporary solution, it may stop the conflict long enough to implement problem solving.

Problem-Solving Negotiations

Problem solving is a useful approach when addressing conflict-of-interest situations. It is the process that helps the disputants remove the conflict by solving the underlying problem. Problem solving will work only when there is adequate time to implement the process and when there is an open and trusting environment. Table 11.2 summarizes these responses to conflict.

Several models of conflict resolution that focus on conflict-of-interest situations have been developed. The following is a combination of some of these approaches:

- Defining the problem
- Switching perspectives
- Brainstorming possible solutions
- Selecting a solution acceptable to both parties
- Formalizing a plan
- Implementing the plan
- Evaluating the plan

Table 11.2   Responses to Conflict

Type of Response	When to Use
Passive Responses	
Doing nothing	The disagreement is not destructive, and maintaining a relationship is most important.
Smoothing	When the conflict is one involving controversy.
Withdrawing	When the reduction of tension is most important.
Assertive Responses	
Confronting	Useful for dealing with conflicts of interest.
Standing firm	The confrontation cannot be allowed to continue.
	There is a danger of escalation.
	Some of the issues are unspoken and need to be made public.
	The rights and needs of an individual are most important.
Facilitative Responses	
Compromising	The goal is maintaining a relationship.
Problem-solving negotiations	There is not a lot of time, and both parties are willing to give up something.
	Participants in the dispute are willing to become engaged.

Defining the Problem. This state of the process requires arriving at a clear definition of the problem. However, to arrive at this definition, all participants must describe what they want and why that is important to them. They should also identify their feelings. They may need assistance and clarification in order to get to their feelings. Sometimes individuals may appear to be angry when their feelings are actually those of frustration or fear.

It is common for individuals to get involved in a conflict of interest over the use of time and resources and not understand why it is important to the other person. When individuals identify their reasons for what they want, this might help them clarify their feelings and reveal some hidden dimensions of the conflict that are important in arriving at a solution. Once the wants and the reasons have been identified by both parties, then a clear and simple definition of the problem can be developed.

Switching Perspectives. When switching perspectives, each side must describe the problem, the needs, and the motivations of the other side. Switching perspectives is an important step in trying to get those involved in the conflict to understand the issues that are involved. This understanding is crucial in finding a productive solution.

Brainstorming Possible Solutions. At this point, the possible solutions are not evaluated. The goal is to get as many solutions as possible out in the open. Take care not to move too quickly from brainstorming. Taking adequate time often results in creative solutions.

Seeking a Solution Acceptable to Both Parties. Each solution should have a mutual benefit for those involved in the conflict. If the proposed solutions do not meet the needs of those involved or are unacceptable, then they are rejected. When one or more proposed solutions are identified, they need to be carefully analyzed to make sure that they do address the central issues. Does the proposal address the basic problem? Does it take into account the needs and the reasons of both sides? Is the proposed action realistic and reasonable?

Formalizing a Plan. Once a possible solution is identified, a plan needs to be developed. There might be times when an informal plan can be developed and implemented. However, it is usually more beneficial to clearly define the responsibilities and the actions of everyone involved so that there are no additional misunderstandings. It is usually a good procedure to write the plan down, go over it carefully with those involved, and have them sign that they agree with the plan.

Implementing the Plan. It may be helpful to provide reminders to those involved regarding their actions and responsibilities. If a problem arises during the implementation, a conference needs to be conducted to review what happened and to determine if the plan needs to be changed. It is rare that a perfect plan is developed, and revising a plan is common.

Evaluating the Plan. Each plan needs to be evaluated. It is useful to have numerous formative evaluations to determine if the program is working. Formative evaluation requires frequent discussions and data gathering. For example, a teacher might ask those involved on a daily basis, "Is the plan working? Is there anything that needs to be changed? How are you feeling about the plan?" This frequent evaluation can help catch problems before they occur and provide constant feedback to those involved that the plan and the actions are being monitored. Just the act of conducting formative evaluations can provide reinforcement for individuals to stick with the plan. If one or more of the individuals feel that the plan is not resolving the conflict, then another brainstorming session is held to develop another plan.

An important dimension of problem solving for teachers is not to give up. Some students have a history of conflict, and they may have the attitude that they do not care if they resolve conflicts. They may participate in developing a plan and then not put forth effort to make it work. When that occurs, the student needs to be involved in making a new plan. Plans for this type of student should be relatively short term and simple. The goal is for the student to learn that he or she can be responsible and can follow a plan. The student needs to know that the teacher will not stop until a plan can be made that the student will follow. It may require several plans and revisions for some students until they get the message that the teacher will not give up.

It is also important that students receive encouragement and reinforcement when they do follow the plan. Remember that some of the students involved in conflict feel alienated from the school and have found that they can get more attention through defiance and confrontation than they can through cooperation. Providing reinforcement to those who can successfully follow the plan provides them with attention and reinforcement for positive behavior.

Responding to Controversy

Controversy exists when ideas, opinions, theories, values, or conclusions are incompatible (Johnson & Johnson, 2006). Interpersonal controversy or conflict occurs when different individuals hold different ideas, opinions, or values. Intrapersonal conflict or controversy exists when an individual has an internal conflict of ideas, opinions, or values. Intrapersonal controversy or conflict can lead to personal confusion, anxiety, and uncertainty. Interpersonal controversy, if not addressed appropriately, can escalate to hostility and even violence. History is filled with examples of violence that was the result of differences of opinions, theories, or values. This is usually labeled intolerance or prejudice.

Individuals need to learn how to cope with both interpersonal and intrapersonal controversy. In the intrapersonal dimension, learning how to deal with conflicting ideas and values helps individuals live more purposeful lives and make better choices. It is a part of growing and learning. In the interpersonal dimension, learning how to address controversy and differences of opinion is central to citizenship. It is essential that everyone learn that change is constant and diversity is a fact of life. Therefore, controversy is a given. No one can expect to live their life in isolation where they never encounter different ideas or different opinions.

Rather than avoiding controversy, recognize that controversy can be constructive. It helps us clarify our thinking and our beliefs. Because controversy is so much a part of the human experience, there is a natural bridge between conflict resolution and the academic curriculum. Controversy provides an excellent opportunity for teachers to engage students in affective dimensions of learning, that dimension of learning that deals with attitudes and values. Controversy also allows an excellent opportunity to engage in what is generally termed *critical thinking*. Critical thinking means not merely having an opinion but also being able to defend the opinion by giving reasons.

The beginning step in dealing with controversy is creating a climate where alternative opinions and perspectives are encouraged. In order to deal with controversy, individuals must be willing to receive conflicting opinions and ideas. Creating this type of an environment involves at least two dimensions. The first dimension is that of *respect*. The classroom must be one where students have enough respect for others in the classroom to allow them to express their ideas without fear of ridicule. The teacher must take the leadership in building a classroom based on respect and in making sure that expression of divergent opinions and ideas are encouraged. Keep in mind that creativity is often the product of the expression of divergent ideas and opinions. If individuals are trapped in viewing the world in one way, their thinking is trapped and they are not truly free.

A second dimension to creating a climate where alternative perspectives are encouraged is through *modeling*. The teacher must model openness and the search for alternative ideas and perspectives. Teachers need to remember that classrooms are very public places and students are constantly watching their actions. If teachers welcome diversity and view controversy as an opportunity to learn, students will be more open to alternative views and opinions.

Johnson and Johnson (2006) have created a program they label *constructive controversy*. It is based on the assumptions that when individuals are confronted with different ideas and conclusions, they become less certain about the correctness of their own opinions and ideas. This uncertainty motivates an active search in hopes of resolving the uncertainty. The outcome of this search, and trying to accommodate the perspectives of others, leads to new solutions and conclusions. Based on these assumptions, a program to deal with controversy would have the following elements:

1. Groups or individuals are confronted with a controversy. They draw an initial conclusion and define their opinion, or beliefs.

2. These groups or individuals are then confronted with one or more opposing points of view or conclusions.

3. Presentations are made on each position. Each group attempts to be as persuasive as possible in advocating their position.

4. Each group then is required to reverse their perspective and argue the opposing point of view. They are free to add new information or new dimensions that were not included in the initial presentation.

5. Everyone is brought together, and they attempt to develop a synthesis of the arguments relating to the controversy (adapted from Johnson & Johnson, 2006).

The outcome of this process is not to change the opinions and the values of all the students or to win an argument. In some instances, it is not desirable that individuals feel they must give up deeply held values. The goal is to develop a climate of openness and respect for alternative views and for evidence. This process can make them think more deeply about their positions and can help them develop a respect for alternative perspectives. This process helps them engage in more civil discussion of alternative opinions and values.

In summary, there are two general types of conflict: conflicts of interest and controversies. There are different approaches that can be used for each of these types of conflict. When deciding on an approach, it is important to consider the type of conflict, assess the nature of the conflict, define the goals to be attained, consider the attitude of the students involved, and reflect on the amount of time that is available. Teachers and students need to know different approaches to conflict resolution and practice using them so that they will have options when confronting conflict.

What Would You Do?

Read the following incident and suggest how you would respond.

A parent called and requested a conference. This was somewhat surprising because the student was academically able and almost never caused any difficulties. When the parent arrived, it was clear that the parent was unhappy. After a few preliminary comments, the parent came right to the point.

"I am concerned about my son being in your classroom. I do not think that what you are teaching in this classroom is what we want for our child. We have high aspirations for him and want him in an environment that emphasizes academic excellence. However, in your classroom, you are wasting time teaching vague social skills such as 'interpersonal problem solving and conflict resolution.' That is our job as parents. We'll tell him how to get along with others. We don't want time being wasted on a lot of 'soft' content. It is your job to teach the academic content that will prepare our son for higher education."

- How might you apply conflict resolution to this situation?

- What might be a common interest around which you could begin to find a solution?

- What must a teacher in this situation avoid?

SOLVING CONFLICTS WITH NEGOTIATION, MEDIATION, AND ARBITRATION

Negotiation, mediation, and arbitration are three fundamental processes that can be used when individuals are having conflicts of interest. Negotiation is a process in which two individuals sit down and work out a resolution together. Mediation involves a third party who assists individuals in finding a solution when they seem to be unable to do so. Arbitration also involves a third party and is usually instituted when negotiation and mediation fail (Johnson & Johnson, 1995).

Negotiation

Negotiation is an activity that individuals use in a variety of situations throughout life. It is an unassisted problem-solving process in which two or more people sit down voluntarily to discuss differences and to reach a joint decision. It is a step-by-step process that uses communication and thinking skills to guide individuals toward a mutually acceptable resolution (Girard & Koch, 1996). Using negotiation skillfully is time-consuming and requires a positive attitude and skill.

Many individuals do not know how to negotiate differences and conflicts. Bodine et al. (1994) identify six steps in the negotiation process:

1. Agree to negotiate.

2. Gather points of view.

3. Find common interests.

4. Create win-win options.

5. Evaluate options.

6. Develop an agreement.

Agree to negotiate. Negotiations cannot succeed unless those who are involved in the conflict are agreeable to negotiations. Negotiation works best if there is some interdependence between those involved so that they need each other in order to achieve success. There must be some shared interest in negotiating. This shared interest might be as simple as a desire to maintain a relationship or a mutual desire to forego the consequences of continued conflict. Individuals must be accepting of negotiation. If one of the parties in a dispute has such firm convictions that there is no room for movement, negotiation simply will not work. The basic ground rules for the negotiation are established during the agreement to negotiate. Basic ground rules usually involve taking turns talking and not using name-calling or put-downs.

Gather points of view. The next step is to gather information about the different points of view or perspectives. To reach a satisfactory agreement, each person must clearly understand the common and the opposed interests in a conflict. In order for negotiation to be successful, each person needs to understand the perspective of the other. No two people will see an issue the same way, and in conflict situations, individuals tend to see only what they want to see (Johnson & Johnson, 1995). Gathering points of view starts by having one person tell his or her point of view. The other person uses active listening to clarify points. The first person is not challenged nor are his or her statements disputed. When the first person is finished, the other person summarizes what the first person said and then shares his or her point of view. The first person then uses active listening to clarify and summarize the other's point of view. When this step is complete, each person has the opportunity to share additional information or clarify what he or she said. Questions may be asked if they lead to additional clarification or understanding (Bodine et al., 1994).

Find common interests. This is a key step in the negotiation process. In addition to sharing his or her perspectives on the conflict, each person needs to be willing to state what he or she wants or needs. At this point, both individuals need to honestly describe their wants, needs, and feelings. They should alternate in doing this as was done in Step 2. At this stage, it is appropriate for each participant in the conflict to share how actions of the other are creating a conflict of interest (Johnson & Johnson, 1995).

The focus at this stage should be on needs and wants and not on positions. It is easy to get the two confused, and some people become so locked into a particular position that they overlook constructive options. The purpose is to try to identify some common or compatible interests because they provide the basis for finding a resolution (Bodine et al., 1994). At the conclusion of this step, the disputants should be able to state the interests they have in common.

Create win-win options. The purpose of this step is to brainstorm options that take into account the common interests of the parties so that both will have needs and wants met. The process involves stating any idea that comes to mind. The ideas should not be immediately evaluated or discussed. They should try to come up with as many options as possible. Bodine et al. (1994) suggest that together the disputants invent at least three options. They emphasize the importance of them working together so that the more assertive person does not dominate. This must be viewed as a joint responsibility that will benefit both of them.

Evaluate options. Once several options have been identified, then the individuals work together as problem solvers to evaluate each of the options. The options should be evaluated on the basis of how they provide benefits for each party. They may elaborate on an option or combine parts of the options that were invented. Each of the options should be viewed from different perspectives and reformulated if needed. When evaluating the options, they should be judged against reality. What are the strengths and weaknesses? What does each person gain and lose? How does the option maximize benefits for both parties (Johnson & Johnson, 1995)?

Create an agreement. At this step, individuals meet together to create a mutually acceptable agreement that will help them resolve the conflict. The agreement should meet certain criteria. The agreement should state who, what, when, where, and how for both individuals. It must meet the needs of both parties and must be viewed as fair by everyone involved. The agreement should strengthen the individuals' ability to resolve future conflicts. It is important for individuals to understand what not to do that might trigger a conflict as well as what to do to resolve those that do occur (Johnson & Johnson, 1994).

Some attempts to reach a mutual agreement will fail. When this occurs, everyone goes back to Step 1 to clarify perspectives and wants. Persistence usually pays off. Johnson and Johnson (1995) suggest that students who have trouble arriving at a successful agreement might be sent to a problem-solving area where they stay until they work out an agreement. They are not allowed to touch, only talk, and they are to inform the teacher when an agreement has been reached. If students cannot generate an acceptable agreement or refuse to negotiate, then mediation might be implemented.

Mediation

Mediation is an extension of the negotiation process. It follows the same basic steps of the negotiation process but involves a mediator or a neutral third party who helps them resolve the conflict. Mediators do not tell others what to do or decide who is right or wrong. Mediators are facilitators who help individuals implement the process (Johnson & Johnson, 1995).

Mediation is appropriate when individuals involved in a conflict do not understand the negotiation process or when they are unsuccessful in resolving a conflict. The role of mediator can be filled by a teacher or by other students, as peer mediators. Some schools have conducted workshops for students and have trained a number of students in the school to become peer mediators. These students are then available to serve as peer mediators whenever other students request them. Schools using peer mediation report resolution rates of up to 95% (Girard & Koch, 1996).

The role of a mediator requires that he or she follow certain steps. The first step is to end any hostilities. The mediator needs to remember the difference between mediation and enforcement (Johnson & Johnson, 1995). The mediator should not attempt physically to intervene if there is a fight. If there is an increase in anger and hostility, the peer mediator might suggest a down period before engaging in mediation.

The first step of mediation, like the first step of negotiation, is for individuals to agree to mediation. Mediation should take place in a private area away from distractions and the ears of others. The mediator should be placed between the disputants. At the beginning, the mediator needs to make sure that the disputants agree to follow any ground rules that have been established for mediation. The ground rules are often the same as those used in the negotiation process. Both individuals agree to take turns talking, agree to avoid name-calling and put-downs, and agree to cooperate (Bodine et al., 1994). If they do not agree to these conditions, the mediation session is over.

The mediator should then review the steps of the mediation process and explain that the role of the mediator is not to take sides or to tell the disputants what to do. The individuals involved need to be asked if they have any questions and if they understand the process.

One variation for beginning the mediation process, as well as gathering different perspectives of each individual, is to ask each individual to fill out a conflict form (Johnson & Johnson, 1995). On these forms, the students identify the person with whom they are having a conflict, the nature of the conflict, and what they want. Students who cannot write well can dictate their responses to the mediator. These forms can then be read or shared with the other person involved in the conflict.

During a mediation session, the mediator may ask clarifying and open-ended questions in order to promote communication and understanding. One technique that is sometimes useful is for the mediator to have the disputants reverse perspectives and take the role of the other person. This is often useful when addressing stubborn disagreements (Johnson & Johnson, 1995). The role of the mediator is to help the participants move through the steps of sharing points of view, identifying common interests, inventing win-win solutions, evaluating solutions, and reaching an agreement.

At the end of a mediation session, it is useful for each student, as well as the mediator, to sign any agreement that they reach. The participants are told that all they should do is to inform their friends that the disagreement is ended. The mediator then keeps the agreement. If the agreement is not fulfilled, the mediator can ask the individuals to reconvene in order to reach a new agreement. If peer mediation is unsuccessful, the problem should be referred to the teacher.

Arbitration

The teacher has the final responsibility to resolve conflicts. If negotiation and mediation did not work, arbitration is the next step. If this does not work, the conflict may be referred to the school administrator.

Arbitration is a process in which a third party makes a final decision regarding the resolution of the conflict. It is not unlike what many teachers do on a daily basis. They are constantly serving as informal arbitrators for classroom conflicts. However, arbitration is more effective if it is formalized, used sparingly, and implemented only for the most difficult problems. Some changes might need to be made to alter the traditional teacher role so that the arbitration process will be more acceptable to students.

A potential shortcoming of arbitration is that responsibility to negotiate and solve the problem is shifted from those involved to someone else. The disputants are not taking responsibility for their actions, and the resolution is less likely to be accepted than those that have been worked out together.

When formal arbitration is used in the classroom, the following steps are used:

1. Each individual involved in the dispute defines the problem. If possible, they should define the problem in writing.

2. Each person is allowed to tell his or her side to the arbitrator without interruption from the other. If there is evidence to substantiate the story, it is presented.

3. Each person is given the opportunity to respond to the other person's story. However, this is done in an orderly fashion with each taking a turn.

4. Each person then tells the arbitrator what he or she wants and would like to see happen.

5. The arbitrator makes a decision. A wise arbitrator will try to find a win-win solution so that both individuals get their needs met.

In classrooms where teachers serve as mediators, they can combine mediation and arbitration. Students then know that if they do not reach a mediated decision, the teacher will impose one through arbitration. Johnson and Johnson (1995) point out that this increases the success of mediation because the students would prefer having a voice in the solution rather than allowing the teacher to impose one.

REVIEW OF MAIN IDEAS

1. Conflict is a normal part of life that cannot be avoided. Learning how to respond to conflict is an important component of learning and of becoming a productive member of society.

2. Two basic types of conflict occur in the classroom: conflicts of interest and controversy. Each of these types requires a different response.

3. There are five components that influence the success of conflict resolution approaches. Those components are assessment, acknowledgment, attitude, action, and analysis.

4. Passive approaches to conflict are useful when the objective is to maintain a relationship between the individuals involved in the conflict. Passive approaches help keep a conflict from escalating to something more serious.

5. Assertive approaches to conflict involve action. They are best used when a conflict needs to be stopped. An assertive approach has the potential of damaging a relationship between individuals.

6. Facilitative approaches to conflict are those that are designed to help individuals learn how to handle and resolve conflict.

7. Problem-solving negotiations require time to work out a solution. This process involves working out a solution that helps meet the needs of those involved in the conflict.

8. Responding to controversy requires a climate of openness, where differences are respected and welcomed.

9. Constructive controversy is an approach that helps individuals think more deeply about their opinions and ideas and helps them develop a respect for the ideas and opinions of others.

10. Negotiation is an approach where individuals involved in a conflict come together and work out their differences without assistance.

11. Mediation involves a third party that assists the participants in implementing the negotiation process.

12. Arbitration involves a third party, often a teacher. This person listens to both sides, gathers data, and then makes a decision about a solution.

APPLICATION AND ENRICHMENT

1. Reflect on conflicts you have had in the recent past. Identify one situation in which the outcomes were positive and one situation in which the outcomes were negative. What do you think accounted for the differences in outcomes? What could you have done that might have changed the outcomes of the negative one?

2. Identify a situation that involved a controversy. How could the steps of constructive controversy be applied to this situation? Practice using the steps of constructive controversy with friends who may have different opinions and ideas.

3. Observe in classrooms and be alert for conflict. Classify the conflicts as conflicts of interest or controversies. Develop a curriculum approach that you could use for teaching conflict resolution.

4. Create a plan for teaching members of your class to be peer mediators. What would you include in your plan? How would you implement it in the classroom?

REFERENCES

Bodine, R. J., Crawford, D. K., & Schrumpf, F. (1994). *Creating the peaceable school: A comprehensive plan for conflict resolution.* Champaign, IL: Research Press.

Borisoff, D., & Victor, D. A. (1998). *Conflict management: A communication skills approach* (2nd ed.). Boston: Allyn & Bacon.

Girard, K., & Koch, S. J. (1996). *Conflict resolution in the schools: A manual for educators.* San Francisco: Jossey-Bass.

Hardin, C. (2008). *Effective classroom management: Models and strategies for today's classroom* (2nd ed.). Upper Saddle River, NJ: Merrill Prentice Hall.

Johnson, D. W., & Johnson, R. T. (1995). *Reducing school violence through conflict resolution.* Alexandria, VA: Association for Supervision and Curriculum Development.

Johnson, D. W., & Johnson, R. T. (2006). *Conflict resolution, peer mediation, and peacemaking.* In C. M. Evertson & C. S. Weinstein (Eds.), *Handbook of classroom management: Research, practice, and contemporary issues* (pp. 803–832). Mahwah, NJ: Lawrence Erlbaum.

Lee, J. L., Pulvino, C. J., & Perrone, P. A. (1998). *Restoring harmony: A guide for managing conflicts in schools.* Upper Saddle River, NJ: Merrill.

Chapter 12

LEGAL DIMENSIONS OF CLASSROOM MANAGEMENT AND DISCIPLINE

CLASSROOM SCENARIO

The junior high school girl had been a problem in the school. Her constant quarrelling and aggressive behavior had been so disruptive that she was eventually transferred to another junior high school. However, this did not change her behavior. In the 3 months she was in the new school, she assaulted other students on three different occasions and continued to quarrel and demonstrate aggressive behavior toward other students and teachers.

The regular teacher was absent one day, and a substitute teacher was teaching the class. During the course of the day, the girl assaulted another girl in the classroom. The parents of the assaulted student sued the regular teacher and the school for negligence, claiming that appropriate care had not been taken to prevent the assault (*Ferraro v. Board of Education of New York*, 1961).

Chapter Objectives

After completing this chapter, you should be able to:

- State the importance of knowing basic principles of school law
- Define the purposes of the Teacher Liability Protection Act
- Explain changes in the in loco parentis doctrine and how it impacts discipline
- Define the basic rights of teachers
- Define teacher negligence
- Explain the impact of *Tinker v. Des Moines* on student rights
- State what is required in applying due process rights to students
- Define students' rights to be free of unreasonable search and seizure
- Explain considerations when disciplining students with disabilities

Ignorance can be costly. Few teachers would disagree with that statement. However, there is an area of ignorance that can be very costly to teachers: ignorance about the law. Most teachers have little exposure to school law. The knowledge that many teachers have about their legal rights and responsibilities is usually distorted and incomplete. Several surveys of teachers in different states have found that most teachers do not have a coherent understanding of the law, do not possess an adequate knowledge of their legal responsibilities, have misconceptions about the law, and view the law as a source of anxiety (Higham, Littleton, & Styron, 2001).

Ignorance of school law can be costly to teachers because it can lead to a loss of employment, loss of a teaching credential, criminal charges, or even monetary damages. Perhaps an even greater cost is the poor learning climate that results when teachers are unsure about their responses to incidents of misbehavior.

Not understanding the legal rights and responsibilities of teachers and students leads to two major problems: (a) a lack of knowledge leads some educators to overreact to incidents and unknowingly violate student rights, and (b) lack of knowledge leads to uncertainty and anxiety about possible lawsuits. These anxious teachers then fail to act when they have a legal and professional obligation to do so (Schimmel, 2006). Both of these problems can have serious educational and legal consequences.

Examples of overreacting involve responding to misbehavior with excessive use of force, establishing unreasonable rules and regulations, and responding to classroom incidents in ways that violate protected student rights. In one case, a student was ordered to remove a T-shirt that contained a political perspective that some found "disrespectful." However, the courts held that wearing the shirt was protected by the First Amendment (*Barber v. Dearborn,* 2003).

Examples of the hesitancy to respond involve teachers failing to respond to incidents when they have a professional and legal obligation to do so. In one case, a student was injured when struck in the eye with a pencil. The court ruled that the school had been negligent in providing a safe environment because there had been other incidents of pencil throwing, eraser throwing, and disruptive events that had not been stopped (*Maynard v. Board of Education Massena Central School District,* 1997). Teachers who look the other way or ignore misbehavior are placing themselves in legal jeopardy just as much as if they overreacted to an incident.

Fear of being sued and an uncertainty about legal rights and responsibilities is often noted by students and used to their advantage. One of the authors observed a teacher confronting a student in the school hallway for dangerous and inappropriate behavior. The student retorted, "Don't touch me or I'll sue!" This response so intimidated the teacher that she responded by telling the student to go to class and then walked away! It is not likely that this type of a response would prevent future occurrence of the same dangerous actions.

Knowledge about basic legal principles is important for a couple of reasons. One reason is, like other legal issues, ignorance of the law is not an acceptable defense. Just as individuals are rarely successful in getting out of a traffic citation because they profess ignorance of speed limits, so teachers rarely are excused from actions that violate legal principles because of a lack of understanding of school law. Understanding basic legal principles is a part of being a professional. Second, knowledge of the law can help teachers act with confidence and certainty. Knowledge helps identify acceptable options when problems do occur in the classroom. They do not need to be paralyzed because of a lack of knowledge. One illustration is a situation where teachers are afraid to use any force to protect themselves or others from harm because they fear being sued for monetary damages if there are any injuries (Schimmel, 2006).

The incident at the beginning of the chapter illustrates the danger that can occur when teachers are unaware of their legal responsibilities. In this case, the court found the school negligent and ruled in favor of the parents of the assaulted girl. The court noted that because of her history of aggressive behavior, the teacher and the school should have known that there was a strong probability of harm coming to other students and the teacher has an obligation to protect the other students. Therefore, the substitute teacher should have been informed about the aggressive tendencies of the girl so that steps might have been taken to prevent the assault. For example, when one of the authors taught a class of "behavioral adjustment" students, some of whom had a history of aggressive behavior, the most aggressive students were removed and placed in the classroom of another experienced teacher whenever a substitute was required.

On the other hand, teachers do have legal rights and responsibilities. There is a tendency to think that only students have rights. Teachers do have a right to establish reasonable rules. They have a legal right to establish a safe and orderly classroom environment. They have a right to protect themselves and others from harm. There are legal consequences for individuals who interfere with the rights and responsibilities of teachers to teach and students to learn. Teachers are protected from disrespectful and disruptive criticism from students. However, to properly exercise these rights and responsibilities, teachers must know what they are.

TEACHER LIABILITY PROTECTION ACT OF 2001

Concern about legal issues relating to discipline and their impact on teaching and learning led to the inclusion of a provision in the No Child Left Behind Act of 2001 labeled the Teacher Liability Protection Act (Schimmel, 2006). The purpose of this act is to provide educators with legal protection when they implement reasonable actions to maintain order, to discipline students, or to establish a safe and appropriate educational environment. Specifically, the act states that a teacher is not liable for harm that resulted from an act or an omission if the purpose of the action is to control, discipline, or maintain order and control in the classroom or school. However, this does not protect acts that include willful or criminal misconduct, gross negligence, reckless misconduct, or a conscious or flagrant indifference to the rights or safety of the students (Teacher Liability Protection Act, 2001, p. S1338).

Proponents of the act correctly noted that teachers who cannot maintain order in the classroom cannot teach effectively. Other supporters of the act cited the need to protect educators from "frivolous" lawsuits that could damage their careers (Schimmel, 2006).

This act provides additional support for the need for teachers to be able to control the classroom. It indicates that there is support from leaders for the actions of teachers in establishing discipline and a safe learning environment. However, it must be emphasized that teachers are still required to act responsibly and legally. This act adds to protections that are already available to teachers.

Protections from frivolous and harassing lawsuits already exist. Attorneys can be sanctioned for filing frivolous lawsuits. Under the Federal Rules of Civil Procedure, Rule 11 states that attorneys must certify that the claims they file are warranted by law and that there is evidence to support the case (Fischer, Schimmel, & Steelman, 2007). This means that in all lawsuits, attorneys should make sure that there is a legal basis for the suit. In one case, an attorney was fined $100,000, to be paid to the defendants, for a pattern of frivolous lawsuits against local teachers and administrators. In other cases, the courts have reprimanded parents and attorneys for filing frivolous lawsuits against schools and teachers (Fischer et al., 2007).

The rights and responsibilities of teachers and students continue to be defined by the courts, and the Teacher Liability Protection Act does not replace the need for educators to understand those definitions. Numerous court cases have defined the rights of students, gross negligence, reckless misconduct, and other responsibilities of teachers that must be followed when responding to misbehavior and discipline. Acts that violate these definitions would still make the teachers vulnerable to legal actions.

Teachers have a duty to teach students how to use equipment safely.

© Photodisc

UNDERSTANDING TEACHER RIGHTS AND RESPONSIBILITIES

A source of confusion for many teachers is misunderstandings about their rights and responsibilities. Some of this confusion stems from changes in traditional views of the role of the teacher. Historically, the role of teachers in relationship to students has been defined under the doctrine of *in loco parentis*. In loco parentis basically defines the role of teacher as that of serving "in the place of parents." In other words, teachers were legally viewed as "wise" parents. The assumption behind in loco parentis is that the authority of teachers is derived from the parents.

In loco parentis made teacher decisions about their rights and responsibilities somewhat easier. Their rights were defined as similar to the rights of parents. If a parent might respond to an incident of misbehavior with physical punishment, then it was acceptable for teachers. If parents are concerned about their child possessing something they did not want them to have, there is no concern of a "right to privacy." They are free to conduct any type of search. Therefore, educators, acting in loco parentis, were free to conduct any type of search, even if it invaded the privacy of the students. The basic standard by which a teacher could make a decision was "What would I do if this were my child?"

However, there have been some important modifications of the in loco parentis doctrine. In the past, the schools were usually more a part of the local community. The communities were typically smaller, and teachers usually lived in the community, attended local churches, and knew many of the parents. Teachers were expected to dress in a certain way and act in a certain way. If teachers did not reflect the values of the community, they did not last long. In this environment, it would be easy to conclude that the authority of the teacher did derive from the parents and the parents would trust the teacher to act as a surrogate parent.

However, the contemporary reality is very different. The majority of parents have little, if any, knowledge of the individuals teaching their children. Teachers are hired based on the evaluation of members of the central administration, and parents have virtually no say over who will teach in the schools. Teachers have more rights, and tenure laws have made it more difficult to remove teachers. Teachers often do not live in the community and may commute many miles to work. As a result, teachers and the schools are not as close to the community. In some instances, students might attend schools that are not in the neighborhood where they live. In addition, compulsory attendance laws require parents to send their children to school. These changes have resulted in a loss of communication and trust between the parents and the schools. Parents' perceptions of the school may be formed largely by the information they get from the local media. The result is that parents are less likely to trust the local school and the teachers to act as surrogate parents.

Another modification of in loco parentis is related to compulsory attendance laws. The fact that it has been determined that the education of the youth is a compelling state interest and that parents are required to send their children to school has implications for the rights of parents and students. For example, a landmark Supreme Court decision stated that the concept of parental delegation of authority is not consonant with compulsory attendance laws and that teachers act as delegates of the state, not merely as surrogates of the parents (*New Jersey v. T. L. O.,* 1985). Therefore, the standard that must be used by teachers in making decisions is no longer, "What would I do if this were my child?" The standard now is, "What is the appropriate response of a knowledgeable professional?"

In addition to changes in the standard of care required of teachers related to in loco parentis, a number of important court decisions have modified and changed the rights and responsibilities of teachers. Some of these changes apply to all teachers because they are the result of decisions by the Supreme Court. These important decisions of the Supreme Court, called *landmark decisions*, apply to all teachers across the nation. However, state courts and legislative bodies make decisions and pass legislation that applies to the teachers in that state. These legislative decisions are usually pulled together in the education code for that particular state. There are many common elements in education codes across the state, but there are some differences.

For example, a case that was brought before the Supreme Court in 1977 addressed the issue of corporal punishment. *Corporal punishment* is generally defined as the infliction of bodily pain as a penalty for unacceptable behavior (McEllistrem, Grzywacz, & Roth, 2001). This case claimed that corporal punishment violated the Eighth Amendment, which prohibits cruel and unusual punishment. The Court disagreed (*Ingraham v. Wright*, 1977). Corporal punishment was not ruled as cruel and unusual punishment as defined by the Eighth Amendment. However, because of concerns about child abuse, and well-publicized incidents of excessive use of corporal punishment, many states have passed state statutes prohibiting the use of corporal punishment. Teachers in those states do not have the right to administer corporal punishment and can lose their teaching credentials for doing so.

In order to help teachers understand their rights and become the informed professionals that are expected by the courts, state agencies and professional educational associations often distribute materials that identify specific rights and responsibilities of teachers in that state. Teachers are advised to get a copy of those materials. The following are some rights and responsibilities that generally apply across all states.

Establishing Reasonable Rules

Teachers do have a responsibility to ensure that the classroom is a safe and productive educational environment. In order to do this, teachers have a right to establish reasonable rules and regulations. However, these rules cannot violate constitutionally guaranteed rights. In addition, due process procedures indicate that students cannot be disciplined for violating unwritten rules. Rules must be clear, unambiguous, and not excessively broad. For example, some teachers respond that they only have one rule for the classroom, the "golden rule." However, this would probably be defined as excessively broad as the basis for disciplining a student. Teachers need to be explicit in defining the rules and regulations and in making sure that students understand them. In some places, teachers send the rules and regulations home for the parents to read and sign. This helps guarantee that students and parents understand the rules and the consequences if they are violated.

In general, when enforcing the rules, teachers have the right to exercise reasonable physical control over a student in order to protect student safety and to maintain conditions conducive to learning. Disruption of school and willfully defying authority are usually grounds for suspension from school.

Use of Force in Discipline

The use of corporal punishment has long been a controversial issue. On the one hand, there are those who oppose corporal punishment on the basis of values. They view the infliction of pain on anyone else as simply immoral. Others oppose corporal punishment on the grounds that any use of violence is a form of child abuse and therefore teaches students that force is an acceptable means of resolving conflict.

On the other hand, there are those who view corporal punishment as an appropriate way to get the attention of students and stop serious misbehavior. They contend that teaching students to behave is so important that reasonable use of force is justified. Many people point out that corporal punishment has long been an acceptable form of punishment in American families and most children who experience it do not grow up with any more tendency toward abuse and violence than others.

The current trend in school is away from corporal punishment. In addition to the fact that many states have developed statutes against corporal punishment, there are some legal reasons why teachers should avoid the use of force.

Although the Supreme Court ruled that the use of corporal punishment is not cruel and unusual punishment, it still does not remove the threat of legal action. If the administration of corporal punishment aggravates a previous medical condition, even if the teacher was unaware of the condition, the teacher could be liable for damages. If excessive use of force in discipline results in injury, the teacher could be subject to assault changes and criminal prosecution. In summary, the risks of using force in discipline are great. Regardless of one's views of the appropriateness of corporal punishment, the wise choice would be to avoid it.

Negligence

Understanding teacher negligence is important in defining teacher rights and responsibilities. *Negligence* refers to acts or omissions demonstrating a failure to use reasonable or ordinary care. Note that this definition includes omissions, meaning that teachers can be charged with negligence if they fail to act when they have a responsibility to do so. A pattern of negligence can be deemed "willful misconduct" (McEllistrem et al., 2001).

Specific conditions must exist in order for negligence to apply. First, it requires the presence of a legal standard of care in order to protect students from unreasonable risks of injury. Second, the teacher failed to follow due care. Third, the actions of the teacher were directly related to the injury. Fourth, the student sustained provable damages (Fischer et al., 2007).

Teachers do have a legal responsibility to exercise reasonable care to protect students from harm. Reasonable care is often based on how an informed professional would have responded in a similar situation. This means that teachers are not liable to charges of negligence just because a student is injured. The actions of the teacher must be related to the injury. For example, teachers are not expected to prevent all injuries that might occur. The ability to foresee the probability of an injury is often considered by the courts in making judgments about negligence. They typically consider the following three categories of negligence when making their decisions: malfeasance, misfeasance, and nonfeasance.

Malfeasance is the type of negligence that involves actions that are taken deliberately or knowingly to harm someone. For example, if a teacher uses a form of punishment that results in harm to the student, malfeasance could be charged. Another example might be when a teacher attempts to stop a fight between students. If the teacher goes beyond the force that is needed to stop the fight and deliberately acts to hurt a student, this could also be malfeasance. Excessive use of force in discipline is a common cause of lawsuits against teachers. This could fall into the category of malfeasance.

Misfeasance occurs when a teacher acts unwisely or without taking proper safeguards to keep the students from harm. In this case, the teacher doesn't deliberately harm the student. However, the student is hurt because of the unwise actions of the teacher. One example might be when a teacher removes a misbehaving student from the classroom and places him or her in an unsupervised area (like the hallway). If the student then wanders away and is injured, the teacher could be found liable. The teacher did not intend to injure the student but placed him or her in an area where there was no supervision. The teacher's action, therefore, was a contributor to the harm.

Nonfeasance occurs when teachers do not act when they have a duty to do so. This is the omission part of negligence. An example might be when a teacher fails to stop students from engaging in actions that have a high probability of injury. For example, if students are engaged in throwing things in the classroom, there is a good probability that someone will be injured. A teacher has a duty to attempt to stop the behavior.

In summary, lawmakers and other professional groups recognize that orderly and safe classrooms are important. Teachers, as professionals, have rights as well as responsibilities. Court cases will continue to define both the rights and responsibilities. Although it appeared for a while that the rights of students were receiving attention at the expense of the rights of teachers, there is now more attention being given to the rights of teachers so that they can develop safe and productive learning environments.

UNDERSTANDING STUDENT RIGHTS

Another source of confusion for teachers is an understanding of student rights and responsibilities. Teacher rights and responsibilities are heavily influenced by student rights and responsibilities. Decisions must take into account both perspectives. The rights of teachers and of schools to establish a safe and orderly educational environment must be balanced against the rights of students guaranteed by the Constitution. Although important court decisions regarding student rights have been made over the last 40 years, there are still teachers and administrators who do not understand these rights and continue to violate them (Schimmel, 2006).

One of the key court decisions that has impacted both teacher and student rights is the landmark *Tinker v. Des Moines* case in 1969. In this case, the Supreme Court recognized that schools have the authority to control student conduct. However, there are limits to their actions. The court indicated that neither students nor teachers lose their constitutional rights when they enter school. In other words, students are citizens with rights guaranteed by the Constitution. These rights cannot be ignored simply because they are students. The court decision stated that "state operated schools cannot be enclaves of totalitarianism." Furthermore, schools could not limit student rights merely to avoid the discomfort that might accompany an unpopular viewpoint (Schimmel, 2006). This decision represented a dramatic expansion of student rights and caused considerable consternation among educators.

Briefly, the *Tinker v. Des Moines* case involved students who defied a rule passed by the Des Moines Independent School District designed to prohibit students from wearing black armbands to protest the Vietnam War. They were ultimately suspended, and the case made its way to the Supreme Court. The Supreme Court ruled that the wearing of armbands was a symbolic act of freedom of speech protected by the First Amendment. In order for the school to limit rights protected by the Constitution, it must demonstrate that the exercise of these rights materially and substantially interferes with the right of the school to establish a safe and productive learning environment.

The significance of the *Tinker* decision can be seen when it is contrasted to that of a case that took place in 1915. In this case, a high school student in California gave a speech that was critical of the school district for requiring students to learn in "unsafe" facilities. School officials declared that the speech violated school discipline and was intended to discredit the school board. This, along with the student's refusal to apologize, led to an expulsion. The state court upheld the expulsion (*Wooster v. Sunderland,* 1915).

Another landmark case that influenced the rights of students and impacted the response to incidents of student discipline occurred in 1975. The *Goss v. Lopez* case focused on the issue of suspension and expulsion. In this case, the court ruled that students had the right to due process before they were suspended or expelled from school. Up until this decision, like the Wooster case, schools customarily suspended or expelled students at their own discretion. Education was generally considered a privilege, and students attended school at the pleasure of the local school authorities. School officials felt free to establish any rules they felt necessary and retained the right to enforce them as they saw fit. For example, if they felt the need to establish rules about such issues as student dress, grooming, and even the wearing of makeup by girls, they did so. Courts were reluctant to override the authority of local school officials, so they had almost unlimited discretion in establishing school rules and establishing consequences.

However, in *Goss v. Lopez,* the Supreme Court declared that education is more than a privilege. They declared that students have substantial property and liberty rights guaranteed by the Fourteenth Amendment. *Liberty rights* refer to the right of individuals to be free from arbitrary acts that limit their freedom. This means that decisions by schools must not be arbitrary. School actions must be based on reasonable rules and regulations. *Property rights* are the right to tangible and intangible property. This means that a good education is a form of property. Denying individuals an education removes the possibility of obtaining an intangible asset that can have a measurable impact on their lives.

Therefore, before denying students access to school through suspension and expulsion, school authorities must follow due process procedures. The court did recognize that there are times when immediate suspension might be required in order to protect the health and safety of others. In these situations, due process must be implemented as soon after the suspension as is practicable (McEllistrem et al., 2001).

Due process involves the basic procedures one would expect when accused of any violation that might result in a loss of a right. Students faced with suspension or expulsion must be given notice of the charges against them, provided with an opportunity at a hearing to present their version, be allowed to be represented by an attorney, and be given the right to appeal.

Goss v. Lopez also created considerable concern in schools. Educators who were used to using their own discretion and judgment when making disciplinary decisions were now confronted with the need to defend those decisions in a hearing with attorneys present. Many educators felt that this decision would seriously handicap the ability of the school to maintain discipline and enforce rules. Indeed, there were school administrators who were so afraid of the due process procedures that they did look the other way when serious violations occurred and did allow discipline and control to deteriorate. However, in recent years, school officials have learned how to define reasonable rules and how to enforce them in ways that are consistent with due process.

Search and Seizure

One area related to the in loco parentis doctrine was that of searching students. School officials have contended that in loco parentis gave them authority from parents to conduct any type of search. This was addressed in 1985 in the landmark case *New Jersey v. T. L. O.* The Supreme Court ruled that students are protected by the Fourth Amendment and do have a right to be free from unreasonable search and seizure. However, the court did stop short of requiring a search warrant. They indicated that searches that were not excessively intrusive could be conducted on the basis of "reasonable suspicion" rather than the more rigorous standard of "probable cause" (Fischer et al., 2007).

Reasonable suspicion requires that evidence is sufficiently compelling to convince a prudent and cautious individual that some illegal activity has occurred or someone is in possession of something that is prohibited. What this means is that if there is a reasonable suspicion that someone is in possession of a weapon or an illegal substance, then a search can be conducted. In fact, when there is suspicion that someone might be in possession of something that can be harmful to others, the school has a duty to find and remove the danger.

However, if the search is to be intrusive, officials must give attention to the right of privacy of the student, and more firm evidence must be available. Some educators still do not understand these limitations on their rights. In one case, a female third-grade teacher discovered that some money was missing from her desk. The teacher requested that three students empty their pockets and book bags and turn down the waistbands of their pants. When this did not turn up the money, one student was taken to a supply closet and ordered to pull down her slacks and her underwear so that the teacher could look for the missing money. The court ruled in this case that the search invaded the privacy rights of the student. The court stated that a teacher should know that students have Fourth Amendment rights against unreasonable search and seizure (*Watkins v. Millenium School,* 2003).

When determining the appropriateness of a search, teachers need to consider the following:

- The target of the search
- The quality of the information that has led to the search
- The nature of the place to be searched
- The nature of the search

The target of the search means that if the search is for something like a gun or explosives, a more intrusive search might be warranted. The quality of the information that has prompted the search must also be considered. If the search is conducted on the basis of some rumor, teachers must be more cautious about conducting a search than if there is a report from several reliable witnesses. If the place to be searched is a place where there is a high expectation of privacy, such as a purse or a car, solid evidence is needed. If the search is going to be intrusive, once again, more than generalized suspicion is required.

In summary, students do have privacy rights, and schools have the right to establish a safe school environment. Court cases relating to search and seizure try to balance those rights. School searches can be conducted on the basis of reasonable suspicion. However, the rights of individuals to be free of unreasonable search and seizure must also be respected.

What Would You Do?

Read the following incident and suggest what you think would be the appropriate response.

At a recent faculty meeting, concerns had been expressed about the possibility of controlled substances being on campus. Teachers were asked to be especially vigilant. This morning after third period, you stepped out of the classroom after having dismissed your seventh-grade social studies class. At the end of the hall, you saw a group of boys gathered together. One of them was handing money to another boy. You quickly walked down the hall.

"What are you boys doing?" you inquired.

The boys looked startled and quickly put the money in their pockets.

"Nothing," responded one of the students.

Another student stated, "We're just buying some tickets to the concert Friday night."

- Should you conduct a search?

- Would you be obligated to conduct a search in order to protect the health and safety of students?

(Continued)

(Continued)

- Are there grounds for reasonable suspicion?

- What other choices are open to you?

Freedom of Expression

Freedom of expression is one of the most fundamental and cherished rights guaranteed by the Constitution. Balancing the needs of the school to establish an orderly educational environment with the rights of students for freedom of expression has been the subject of a number of cases. As noted in the *Tinker* case cited in this chapter, the courts struck down arbitrary rules that limit student freedom of expression. Schools cannot limit student freedom of expression simply because it is unpopular, uncomfortable, or contrary to the views of school officials. For example, in a ruling on one attempt of a high school to suspend students for distributing an underground newspaper that included controversial articles, the court noted that, in a democracy, controversy is a matter of constitutional law and is not a sufficient excuse to stifle the opinion of any citizen (*Shanley v. Northeast School District,* 1972, p. 971).

However, student freedom of expression is not unlimited. Student freedom of expression can be limited if the exercise of the right results in a material or substantial interference with the work of the school or with the rights of others. Others have limited symbolic expressions of speech, such as political buttons or certain articles of clothing that have caused fights or disturbances. For example, some schools have banned the wearing of certain colors to school because they represent gang colors and have prompted acts of violence. The First Amendment does not protect student speech that includes threats of violence or serious harm to others. Students who engage in this type of speech are likely to find little sympathy in the courts.

Additional grounds for limited freedom of speech was stated by the courts in a case where a student who gave a nominating speech for a friend used language filled with sexual innuendo. The student had been warned not to do so by teachers. He was suspended and appealed his suspension to the courts. The court upheld the suspension and ruled that the public schools, as an instrument of the state, can establish standards of civil and mature conduct (*Bethel School District No. 403 v. Fraser,* 1986).

Students need to understand that freedoms are accompanied by responsibilities. Unfounded or untrue statements that expose another person to contempt or ridicule, or harm their reputation, could lead to charges of slander or libel in courts. Therefore, students need to learn that unwise use of freedom of expression could have serious consequences.

In summary, teachers must be very cautious about limiting the First Amendment rights of students. Teachers and school officials do not have unlimited rights in limiting student speech (or symbolic speech). Limiting freedom of expression requires evidence that the exercise of the right will lead to material interruption of the educational environment. Teachers and administrators need to be tolerant of uncomfortable statements. They also need to teach students about their rights and the limitations on their rights.

Dress Codes

Dress codes, including school uniforms, is an area where there is still some legal uncertainty. Judges have been divided on their opinions, and regulations relating to personal appearance differ from state to state. The courts have ruled that schools do have the right to establish dress codes. However, not all dress codes are legal, and there are standards that must be followed.

As a general rule, school boards can establish dress codes for reasons of safety, order, and discipline. For example, schools can establish dress codes that prohibit the wearing of dirty clothes as posing a health hazard; scantily clad students as posing a distraction in the educational environment; or articles of clothing that have led to fights, thefts, or taunts. However, dress codes have been struck down that prohibit the wearing of jeans, hats, shirts with logos or political messages, and slacks for females (Fischer et al., 2007).

One of the common arguments against dress codes is that student dress is a part of the right to freedom of expression. However, school officials often argue that certain types of clothing compromise student health and safety or that some types of clothing have the potential to be disruptive to the learning process. Therefore, they argue, dress codes are within the rights of the school. Therefore, many schools have dress codes, and in some instances require school uniforms. The argument in favor of uniforms is that they help prevent discipline problems and create more productive learning environments.

When deciding dress codes, the courts have generally focused on two issues. The first issue is related to whether the choice of dress or appearance is symbolic freedom of expression that is protected by the First Amendment. For example, cases relating to this concern might focus on dress as a means of legitimate protest (like *Tinker*). This means that schools cannot limit articles of clothing simply because it conveys a critical or unpopular point of view. In one case, the courts ruled against a school district that restricted the dress of a boy who wore a T-shirt with a message critical of the president of the United States (Schimmel, 2006). If dress codes are arbitrary and restrict First Amendment rights, they are likely to be overturned. On the other hand, student challenges to dress codes prohibiting the wearing of certain types of jewelry on the basis of symbolic freedom of speech have not been upheld. The reasoning was that the wearing of the jewelry did not send a particular message that would be understood by those who viewed it (Fischer et al., 2007).

The second issue is related to whether the dress involves constitutionally protected liberty rights. Some dress codes have been challenged on the grounds that they restrict dress that communicates ethnic pride or religious affiliations. The basic question is, does the dress code arbitrarily limit student freedom for no legitimate reason? For a dress code to pass the test on these grounds, it must be demonstrated that the dress code is directed to furthering an important state interest, such as preventing conflict. For example, dress codes that have limited the wearing of certain colors have been upheld because it was demonstrated that these were gang symbols that had led to fights and a disruption of the educational environment. In other instances, courts have upheld dress codes that have a direct relationship to the health and safety of students.

In summary, teachers need to be cautious about disciplining students based on their dress and appearance. If dress codes are established, they should be established at the school level with the input and support of the parents. Above all, appearance should not be limited simply because it makes someone uncomfortable.

Harassment

Schools are responsible for maintaining a safe and orderly educational environment. That means that if someone is creating a hostile environment, he or she needs to be stopped. Harassment might include physical harassment, such as bullying, or sexual harassment. This is another area where teachers cannot look the other way. The requirement for teachers to take action may extend beyond the classroom. In this emerging area of concern, the courts have tended to rule that the schools have a responsibility to act to stop harassment if they know or should have known of harassment that is taking place outside the classroom. What this means is that if teachers become aware of student-to-student sexual harassment or bullying that is occurring outside the classroom, they should not dismiss the behavior as something that is none of their business.

Freedom of Conscience

Freedom of conscience is another area where students have rights. One area where there has been some attention to freedom of conscience is related to issues such as saluting the flag. In general, the courts have ruled that students can refuse to salute the flag because of religious or moral convictions. Generally, it has been concluded that failure to salute the flag does not constitute a serious threat to the welfare of the state. Therefore, the state has no compelling interest in making sure that all students participate in this activity.

Some students, or their parents, may also object to some parts of the curriculum. For example, some parents have objected that sex education content violates freedom of religion. Others have objected to dancing in physical education classes or watching movies or playing cards.

The basic rule that the courts have applied to these sorts of decisions is whether or not that part of the curriculum addresses a compelling state interest. For example, it is certainly a compelling interest of the state that all citizens have an education that allows them to make informed decisions. Proponents of sex education argue that the costs to the state of sexually transmitted disease and teenage pregnancy certainly make it a compelling state interest. On the other hand, it would be hard to argue that some activities, such as dancing, do involve a compelling state interest.

Students With Disabilities

Students with disabilities have been given special protection by federal legislation. Many of these students will be spending at least a part of their day in the regular classroom. Many teachers have found inclusion of special needs students to be very rewarding, but there are some special challenges that can arise when disciplining students with disabilities.

A major consideration when disciplining students with disabilities is to consider whether the behavior is related to the disability. If a behavior is a manifestation of the student's disability, it may be beyond his or her their ability to control the behavior, and responses that would be appropriate for other students are not useful. If the behavior is disruptive to the class, it would be appropriate to discuss the situation with the rest of the class and engage their assistance in ignoring some behavior and in helping the student.

The first step a teacher must take is to become familiar with the individualized educational plan (IEP). The IEP will include mandated procedures that must be followed. If serious misbehavior leads to a consideration of suspension or expulsion, this is considered a change of placement and can only be done by following the steps required by law.

Next, teachers need to develop a good working relationship with the parents of students with disabilities. Some of these parents may exhibit frustration because of previous difficulties in working with schools and teachers. This takes some patience on the part of the teacher to win them over and convince them that the teacher is interested in the success of their child. Having good communication with the parents can be very useful in creating a successful classroom where all students benefit from the inclusion of a special needs student.

In addition, it is important to become informed about special services that might exist in the school district and in the community for providing services to these special students. The intent is to create a seamless web of services that includes the community, the parents, and the school in meeting the needs of these students.

REVIEW OF MAIN IDEAS

1. Ignorance of school law can be costly to teachers and can lead to loss of employment, loss of teaching credentials, and even monetary damages.

2. Both teachers and students have rights and responsibilities. Teachers must know these rights and responsibilities in order to respond to problems professionally and with confidence.

3. Historically, teachers have functioned under the in loco parentis doctrine. This means that teachers act in the place of parents and can discipline students as they might their own child. However, modification to the interpretations of the in loco parentis doctrine has required that the teacher respond as an agent of the state and as an educated professional rather than as a surrogate parent.

4. Landmark Supreme Court decisions have established that students do have the rights of a citizen. These rights are not surrendered when they enter school. The court has also determined that students have liberty and property rights. These cannot be abridged unless due process is implemented.

5. The use of force in discipline has long been a controversial topic. Although the Supreme Court has ruled that corporal punishment is not a form of cruel and unusual punishment, many states have outlawed it. In addition, excessive use of force in discipline is a common reason for civil suits against teachers. Teachers are advised not to use force when responding to misbehavior.

6. The courts have moved away from the definition of education as a privilege and have declared that students have liberty rights and property rights involved in getting an education. These rights cannot be abridged without the implementation of due process.

7. Students are protected from unreasonable search and seizure. Although teachers are not required to obtain a search warrant in order to conduct a search, they must protect the students' rights of privacy and must have at least reasonable suspicion.

8. Student freedom of expression can be limited if the speech disrupts the educational environment or if it is not conducted in a civil and mature manner.

9. Students with disabilities have additional rights that must be considered when administering discipline.

APPLICATION AND ENRICHMENT

1. Obtain a copy of the education code for your state. These can usually be obtained through the state education agency. Many states now have them online at department of education Web sites. Look through the code and find material relating to corporal punishment, suspension, expulsion, freedom of speech, and dress codes. Summarize your findings and place them in your professional portfolio so they can be a quick reference.

2. Many professional education organizations produce material relating to legal concerns of teachers. Contact the professional education associations for your state and ask for publications they might have on the legal rights and responsibilities of teachers.

3. Interview local teachers and school administrators regarding discipline policies and procedures the district follows regarding such topics as search and seizure, due process, corporal punishment, disciplining special needs students, and so on. How do these policies relate to the material covered in this chapter? Are there any policies that appear to have questionable legal foundations?

4. Search through professional journals such as the *Phi Delta Kappan* and *Educational Leadership* for articles and columns relating to legal issues. Identify emerging issues or recent court decisions that impact teachers.

REFERENCES

Barber v. Dearborn Public Schools, 286 F. Supp. 2d 847 (E.E. Mich. 2003).

Bethel School Dist. No. 403 v. Fraser, 478 U.S. 675. 106 S. Ct. 3159, 92 L. Ed. 2d 549 (1986).

Ferraro v. Bd. of Educ. of New York, 212 N.Y.S. 2d 615 (NY App. Term, 1961).

Fischer, D., Schimmel, D., & Steelman, L. (2007). *Teachers and the law* (7th ed.). Boston: Allyn & Bacon.

Highman, R., Littleton, M., & Styron, K. (2001). *Educational law preparation for school administrators.* Paper presented at the Educational Law Association Conference, Albuquerque, NM.

Maynard v. Board of Education of Messena Central School District, 663 N.Y. S.2d 717 (A.D. 3d Dep't 1997).

McEllistrem, S., Grzywacz, P., & Roth, J. (Eds.). (2001). *Deskbook encyclopedia of American school law.* Birmingham, AL: Oakstone Legal & Business Publishing.

New Jersey v. T. L. O., 469 U.S. 325 (1985).

Schimmel, D. (2006). Classroom management, discipline, and the law: Clarifying confusions about students' rights and teachers' authority. In C. M. Evertson & C. S. Weinstein (Eds.), *Classroom management: Research, practice, and contemporary issues* (pp. 1005–1018). Mahwah, NJ: Lawrence Erlbaum.

Shanley v. Northeast Independent School District, 462 F.2d (5th Cir. 1972).Teacher Liability Protection Act, 20 U.S.C. Sections 6731–6738 (2001).

Tinker v. Des Moines Independent School District, 393 U.S. 503 (1969).

Watkins v. Millenium School, 290 F. Supp. 2d 890 (E.E. Ohio 2003).

Wooster v. Sunderland, 148 P. 959 (Cal. Ct. App. 1915).

INDEX

ABOUT THE AUTHORS

Tom V. Savage (Santa Clara University) began his educational career as a teacher in the Los Angeles Unified School District. Among other assignments, he spent a couple of years teaching behaviorally disordered students. This experience triggered a career-long conviction that good management and good teaching can change the lives of even the most difficult students. Dr. Savage continued his education at the University of Washington, Seattle, where he received a PhD in social studies education. His higher-education career has included appointments at Western Washington University, Whitworth College, Texas A&M University, California State University, Fullerton, and Santa Clara University. He has served as Department Chair at four of the higher education institutions. He was honored as Faculty Member of the Year for the College of Education at California State University, Fullerton. He has made numerous contributions to professional journals; has conducted numerous workshops; and has presented numerous papers to professional associations, including the American Educational Research Association, the American Association of Colleges of Teacher Education, the National Council for the Social Studies, and the National Council of Teachers of English. In addition to *Successful Classroom Management and Discipline,* he has authored or coauthored several books, including *Teaching Today* (eight editions), *Teaching in the Secondary School* (six editions), and *Effective Teaching in Elementary Social Studies* (six editions). He teaches classes in classroom management, social studies curriculum and methods, instructional observation and leadership, and foundations of education.

Marsha K. Savage (Santa Clara University) was a high school English teacher for 17 years before receiving her PhD in curriculum and instruction from Texas A&M University, where she also served as a lecturer in the Department of Education. She later served as Chair of the Department of Education and Chair of the Division of Professional Services at California Baptist University in Riverside, California. Currently, Dr. Savage is Professor of Education and Coordinator of the Secondary Credential Program at Santa Clara University. She is also a member of the Board of Institutional Reviewers for the California Commission on Teacher Credentialing. Her primary interests include English education, children's and young adult literature, reading across the curriculum, classroom management issues, and accreditation issues. She has coauthored two books and a number of articles in a variety of professional journals. She has also presented numerous papers at professional meetings around the country, including the American Educational Research Association, American Association of Colleges of Teacher Education, National Council of Teachers of English, and the National Council for the Social Studies. Dr. Savage has been honored twice for her expertise in teaching: first as Teacher of the Year in her high school and second as Professor of the Year at California Baptist University. She currently teaches classes in English methods, classroom management, secondary methods, reading in the content areas, and multiethnic literature.

Supporting researchers for more than 40 years